A Strategy of Interdependence

We live in an age of interdependence.

JOHN F. KENNEDY
ADDRESS AT FRANKFURT, GERMANY, 1963.

A Strategy of Interdependence

*A Program for the Control of Conflict
Between the United States and the Soviet Union*

VINCENT P. ROCK

CHARLES SCRIBNER'S SONS   *New York*

To my wife

and

to our sons,
the men of tomorrow

ACKNOWLEDGMENTS

While many have helped to shape this study of the control of conflict between the United States and the Soviet Union, the responsibility for the views expressed is that of the author alone. In a world of group research, the study is essentially the work of an individual. Yet, no man works alone. My obligations are numerous and extensive.

I am deeply grateful to those who have given advice and encouragement in a difficult task. In equal measure, I am appreciative of the comments and suggestions of those with whom, most reluctantly, points of difference remain. In great issues of public policy there can be no absolute answers, only the search for preferred solutions. In the present search, many individuals have been of assistance. I would like to acknowledge the following specifically.

For the opportunity to undertake the study and for the freedom granted in pursuing the research from which this book emerged I am indebted both to the United States Arms Control and Disarmament Agency (ACDA), under the direction of William Foster, and to the Institute for Defense Analyses (IDA), under the leadership of Richard Bissell. The study was initiated in cooperation with the United States Disarmament Administration. It was carried to conclusion as IDA-supported research. I would like to express my special appreciation to James E. King, Jr., Director of the International Studies Division of IDA and Kent K. Parrot of the Policy Staff of ACDA for the guidance and advice they have given without measure.

Ideas and suggestions for improving the study have come from many sources. I am deeply grateful for Klaus Knorr's appraisal of the volume. It was invaluable and timely. The trenchant analysis of Arnold Wolfers both challenged and improved the text. The view of man which underlies the report stems from Hadley Cantril. The historical perspective and high sense of style of Shaw Livermore added a new dimension and enhanced the presentation. The insights provided by John O. Coppock into the economics of interdependence were cardinal. The judgments and suggestions of Sidney F. Giffin were indispensable. Margaret Mead's response was reinforcing. Charles E. Osgood's study of United States initiatives provided an original impetus for the work. Discussions with Bryant Wedge suggested new lines of investigation.

Among others to whom special appreciation is due for their advice and constructive comment are Arthur Brayfield, Jerome Frank, Harold Guetzkow, Stewart Meacham, Thomas Milburn, Omar K. Moore, Robert R. Nathan, Robert C. North, Hugh Odishaw, Ralph Reid, Wilbur Schramm, Muzafer Sherif, Joseph Slater, Richard Snyder, Carl Stover, Lester Van Atta, and Kenneth Walker.

With respect to Soviet behavior and motivations, Raymond Bauer, Harrison Brown, Zbigniew K. Brzezinski, Alexander Dallin, Paul Doty, Hugh Dryden, Merle Fainsod, Roswell Garst, Alex Inkeles, and Roger Revelle were most generous in sharing their knowledge and experience.

The concepts on which the structure of the analysis is built represent an eclectic selection from the important and highly relevant body of theory and studies developed by scholars in recent decades. I am especially indebted to the creative contributions of Kenneth Boulding, Karl Deutsch, John H. Herz, Morton Kaplan, Walter Lippmann, R. M. MacIver, Rollo May, Hans Morgenthau, Gunnar Myrdal, Talcott Parsons, James N. Rosenau, Thomas Schelling, Sidney Verba, and Quincy Wright, as well as to the others mentioned previously.

Among the most stimulating and useful analysts of military affairs on whom I relied are Bernard Brodie, Samuel Huntington, Herman Kahn, William Kintner, Henry Kissinger, and Albert Wohlstetter.

Many in government provided advice and assistance. Among those whose help was especially valuable are Marion Boggs, Howard Furnas, Arnold Frutkin, Richard Hirsh, Robert Johnson, David Mayer, Robert Packard, Bromley Smith, Lazar Volin, and Ralph White.

Among my colleagues of the IDA staff the support of Joseph Barmack was unstinting and the comments of Jesse Orlansky unsparing. John Lawson also provided helpful criticism and Thomas Belden contributed to shaping several of the concepts.

I wish also to acknowledge the valuable papers submitted by Robert Angell, Curtis Barker, Benjamin Caplan, Rosemary Klineberg, J. David Singer, John Thomas, and Stephen Withey, which contributed substantially to the evolutionary process through which the inquiry has moved. For his continual reminders of the obstacles to be overcome in engaging in common action with the Soviet Union or any of its citizens, I am further indebted to John Thomas.

The study could not have been carried to completion without the help of Barbara Lee. Throughout, her loyal and intelligent assistance has been invaluable.

V.P.R.

CONTENTS

FOREWORD

United States foreign policy, since the cold war fastened its grip on the world, has rested on a strategy and a hope. The strategy is one of conflict, or deterrence. The hope is for detente and accommodation. The strategy of deterrence pre-empts immense resources and a large proportion of the intellectual capital of the nation. In contrast, the hope for accommodation has inspired modest investments in a limited number of policy gambits such as scientific and cultural exchanges and disarmament negotiations designed to keep open the way to detente.

Thus in the atmosphere of the cold war the strategy dominates the hope. Indeed, at times, during the periodic crises, the hope has all but disappeared. But this can never really be permitted to happen in a nuclear-armed world. Throughout the years, though more prominently when tensions ease, policy elements have persisted upon which the government might build a renewed effort towards more peaceful relations with the Soviet Union. They persisted if for no other reason than to be brought forward in response to Soviet peace feelers to indicate that United States policy was not crippled by unyielding hostility.

The duality and the imbalance between the strategy of deterrence and the hope for detente have long impressed thoughtful observers of the national scene as unsatisfactory. Two aspects are especially troublesome. The first is the unsystematic, "bag of biscuits," nature of the efforts at detente. These programs are in sharp contrast with the scope and commitment to the massive reliance on military programs for deterrence. In the search for accommodation, a number of "good" causes are thought of as belonging together but in the absence of an integrating strategy of detente the resources devoted to the realization of these causes have not been significant.

The second troublesome aspect of United States policy is its very duality. Many doubt that the nation is well served by two diametrically opposed national policies between which its interest, and its image, shuttles. The doubt arises, not from belief that consistency is a necessity in our essentially pragmatic national life, but from awareness that the democratic process demands continuity to be effective.

It is not an overnight affair to achieve informed popular support for a major national policy. Nor is it possible for the support that has been generated to sanction one policy line, by dint of long and often costly effort, to be casually shunted to sanction another.

Moreover, the dual lines of national policy are supported by different publics, one, naturally, far smaller than the other. Similarly, because Congress and the Federal Government reflect the American people, there has been a parallel separation of support and operations in Washington. Would not the national interest be better served by a single policy that has within it places both for deterrence and accommodation? If the two strategies are worthy, both require at all times careful planning and adequate resources, which they are not likely to receive if they are poles between which policy oscillates.

A Strategy of Interdependence suggests how the duality of United States cold war policy might be bridged. Vincent P. Rock, the author of the book, is a veteran public servant and observer of the Washington scene. Noting the threat to the nation's existence posed by nuclear weapons, he is one of those who have become concerned over the anomaly of the dual policies. This book is his contribution to the search for a way through the unsatisfactory present to a more promising future. In it he has set himself two major tasks. The first, and foremost, task is to provide an intellectual basis for the strategy of detente or accommodation that will bear comparison with the massive literature that buttresses the conflict strategy of the cold war. This is a formidable enough task. But he has gone further and endeavored to design in his "strategy of interdependence" a comprehensive single national policy. Thus, he has sought to resolve the duality to which he and others take exception.

He has brought impressive resources of experience, understanding, and application to his work. The measure of his success is for each reader to decide for himself. If questions remain, is this not to be expected when such fundamental issues are at stake? He has undertaken a task that needed doing, and by daring to suggest that a better integration of national policy is possible he has performed a pioneering service.

JAMES E. KING, JR.
Director, International Studies Division
Institute for Defense Analyses

INTRODUCTION

THE UNITED STATES is in need of a new strategy which will enhance the nation's security, maintain its freedoms, and open the door to a future in which the vital energies of its people may be directed to constructive purposes. The Soviet Union is in no less need of a new strategy which will ensure its security, permit the swift completion of the task of modernizing the society, and enable its vast and growing number of educated people to play their legitimate roles in the world as free men.

The most urgent need of both is for a strategy by which they may avoid a nuclear holocaust and ensure survival. The most profound challenge to both is to find a strategy which will lead both to use their capabilities to shape the world of tomorrow in constructive ways that each will view as legitimate.

Since World War II both sides have been engaged in building devastating nuclear arsenals to achieve security—security from each other. The effect has been to put the security of each in the hands of the other. While neither may attack with impunity, neither can avoid destruction if for some irrational or inadvertent reason the other should attack. The result is now known as the precarious balance of terror. Even to maintain the balance each side must invest huge resources and a large proportion of its best talent in constantly improving the technological foundation of terror.

The search for security from each other has generated insecurity. Insecurity arises from potential man or machine failures in the vast nuclear weapons systems which are required by the strategies of terror. The possibility of inadvertent triggering of nuclear war as a consequence of machine failure or human impulse has given rise to a substantial effort to protect or ensure against them. While extensive and intelligent effort on both sides can reduce the risk, "no system is foolproof."

Meanwhile, each side attempts to strengthen the cohesion of its own camp. The results have been unexpected. Within the Communist camp a centrifugal movement has developed. In the non-Communist world, both within and without the vast system of alliances, a sense of restlessness has continued to grow. Hundreds of millions of people and scores of national groupings have pursued their search for identity and for respect in the modern world. Among them, the two great powers compete for world-wide influence. While the competition of the two powers may have certain positive effects (e.g., economic assistance to third areas), it is far more disruptive than it would need to be if their anxiety were reduced and their antagonism mitigated.

The disruption of development creates additional risks of war. In the longer run the risk cannot be adequately met by a greater capacity for waging limited wars. The reason is that, in the absence of a more constructive strategy, as one side increases its capacity the other side will feel bound to respond. Order which rests largely on a balance of force will remain precarious.

Fortunately, the United States and the Soviet Union have both recognized the dangers inherent in unrestrained conflict. They have taken modest steps to control and occasionally reduce the tensions arising from the conflict. Diplomatic channels have normally been kept open. Disarmament discussions continue *ad infinitum*. Cultural exchanges at a minimal level have been initiated and continued through periods of calm and crisis alike. But these activities, while helpful in avoiding inadvertent war, have made only a marginal contribution, since they have not represented a mainstream of strategy for either power.

In a strategic sense for some years now both the United States and the Soviet Union, each in its own way, have relied on the panacea of nuclear power for their security. Efforts to avoid inadvertent war, competition in third areas, and gestures in the direction of the control of tensions, useful as they may have been in a given instance, are adjuncts to the nuclear fulcrum on which policy rests.

Gradually, it has become apparent that the nuclear panacea—like any other panacea—cannot provide the basis for an adequate strategy for the future. Yet, it must be added, the large and fundamentally unproductive expenditures to maintain the nuclear posture cannot be eliminated until a more viable and promising strategy is found and put to the test.

Tensions are bound up in the relations of man to man in a changing world. Among the most significant changes occurring are those in the international environment. Change gives rise to conflict. Thus the question of this inquiry is posted: Can conflict in the changing international system be controlled?

In the international system the most important factors are the purposes and instrumentalities of the states. The principal actors today are the United States and the Soviet Union not only because of their size and the destructive force they hold in their hands but because they are engaged in a world-wide competition that affects all others.

Conflicts of purpose give rise to tension. Yet tension seems to be necessary to produce the creative frustration out of which emerge new purposes required for survival and progress in a changing world. Thus control of conflict in the international system may be viewed as an ongoing process by which, on the one hand, incompatible purposes are eliminated, modified, or reduced in relative importance and, on the other hand, new purposes emerge which serve the interests of the entire system, but most especially those of the parties at issue. In short, conflict has to be controlled to permit progress, but tensions cannot be eliminated if progress is to continue. Successful control of conflict depends upon the creation of an environment in which control is in the interest of the main adversaries.

Finding solutions to present specific conflicts of purpose—in Berlin and elsewhere—is the task of diplomacy through negotiation and compromise. On these current issues, while special studies may sometimes be useful, investigation will usually show that, within the accepted definition of the problem, what can be done is being done. Thus, the emphasis in this inquiry is on the creation of new purposes and an international environment in which they may be pursued. The suggestions for action to control conflict are tentative. A substantial program of research, development, testing, and operation will be required to elaborate and perfect each element of the strategy.

In the nuclear age, however, the approach which is termed "a strategy of interdependence" gives an improved promise for survival of the nation and its basic values. This stems in part from the proposed balanced use of all the means available to control conflict, rather than overwhelming reliance on a single instrument—military force.

The strategy requires that not only the United States government but individual Americans take the initiative. Americans must act because they are free and because their action is necessary if they are to remain free. The government must act because the United States is at present the only nation with the power, resources, and commitment to freedom necessary for the initiation of the strategy. Admittedly, there are grave impediments to the acceptance and support of the strategy, but it has great promise for the years to come.

The theoretical basis for the strategy is relatively simple. It views international society as a single, imperfect, but rapidly developing community. It is a system in which control over force is diffused in the hands of the nation-state. Control of conflict in this system requires an offsetting, cross-national diffusion of power and self-evident interests. Two areas are of paramount importance: first, positive constructive endeavors and enterprises; second, arrangements for restraint on the use of force. Positive action is needed to reshape the goals of men and nations. Restraint on the use of force is essential to provide time.

Men gain their purposes from the conditions in which they find themselves. The strategy seeks to create conditions which will increase the probability that conflict can be controlled. There is no single cause of conflict and no single solution to its control. Our endeavors must therefore be comprehensive. In a period of rapid change the investment must be substantial.

Unity of mankind may yet prove to be the most fundamental natural law. Beneath the troubled surface of the clamor of ideologies, the clash of arms and the confusion of cultures, deep in the mind of man, is found again and again the aspiration for unity. An ancient philosophical and religious concept, unity has gained new meaning and significance in the twentieth century. States and political movements have made world unity the objective of their action. Such aspirations are not new. What is new is that in the twentieth century the advance of science and technology—of communications and weaponry and many other fields of human endeavor—has made the goal appear a material possibility and indeed a necessity. Increasing numbers of men have found it credible to focus their mind's eye on the objective of unity and to commit themselves to work for its achievement.

But, it may be truly said, there is a more urgent task before us. A way must be found to ensure our survival against nuclear catastrophe. When class conflict divides us; when containment separates us; when the precarious balance of terror threatens us, in which direction should we turn to find a true strategy of survival? It may be that a true strategy must give paramount importance to the preparations for the time of unity.

The inquiry which follows is an attempt to search out a strategy of survival through a new series of approaches to the control of conflict. The study represents a preliminary exploration of an immense terrain. The hope is that the map it provides may have a modest value in stimulating a further search.

Since the primary focus of the study is on the Soviet-American confrontation, there are certain related but distinct questions which it does not attempt to deal with at length. Specifically, other advanced countries, especially those in Europe, have an important role to play in the developing international system. However, from the point of view of this study, the contribution of Europe—East and West—to international interdependence is viewed as a distinct problem worthy of being dealt with in its own right. Similarly, while the accommodation of Soviet-American competition in developing areas is discussed, a full-scale treatment of the role of these areas in the evolving world system is not attempted. Certainly, both Europe and the developing areas have a significant part to play in the achievement of a just and stable world order.

I *Interdependence—An Approach*

"Some say that it is useless to speak of peace or world law or world disarmament—and that it will be useless until the leaders of the Soviet Union adopt a more enlightened attitude. I hope they do. I believe we can help them do it.

"But I also believe that we must re-examine our own attitudes—as individuals and as a nation—for our attitude is as essential as theirs."

JOHN F. KENNEDY
Commencement Address
American University, June 10, 1963

SURVIVAL is an interest shared by the United States and the Soviet Union. Since the survival of each is in the hands of the other, neither is sure what is necessary for it to survive. Interaction between the two exists in the fields of weapons, science, communications, culture, economics, and politics. Actions of one may affect the well-being and threaten the survival of the other. Both recognize the threat to survival posed by general nuclear war. Both wish to avoid such a war. But the two nations have many goals and aspirations in addition to survival. When these other values loom large, widely different views emerge on what must be done and what cannot be done if war is to be avoided. Thus the fundamental question: What is necessary in order to survive?

Common Purpose and Force

Survival requires the control of conflict. But progress involves conflicts in values. Men have frequently been unwilling to purchase survival at the cost of all change. Within the nation-state, conflict is controlled and progress is permitted when force is concentrated but power is diffused.

A primary problem in all states is to control conflict while permitting an optimum satisfaction of the changing values and purposes of the individual. In this process a balance must be struck between the needs of the individual and the needs of society.[1] Two methods have been found useful. Since neither is infallible, they are frequently used to reinforce one another. The first is to devise common purposes of continuing value. The second is the employment of force.

Many different techniques are used to encourage the members of a society to attach value to common purposes. By education men are taught to value certain goals and certain procedures for achieving them. The public information media and the pronouncements of leaders serve to reinforce these values. Most important, men acquire a role or a place in an organization in which they may work with others for the achievement of common goals. Their efforts are rewarded with satisfying careers and material benefits. They come to see their interests entwined with the institutions with which they are linked, whether business, agriculture, science,

[1] For the Communist formulation of the balance to be struck between the needs of the society and the development of the individual, see Jan F. Triska (ed.), *Soviet Communism: Programs and Rules* (San Francisco: Chandler Publishing Company, 1962), pp. 110–122.

or labor. In turn, the place and effectiveness of the institutions on which they depend are related to sustained common purposes in the society as a whole. Thus the individual comes to have a stake in both stability and orderly change. He accepts the rule of law and submits disputes to the adjudication of courts and other institutions provided for that end.

When society is unable to control conflict by other means, it must employ force. The state normally has a near monopoly of force within a particular society. The very existence of this near monopoly serves as a threat which promotes conciliation and compromise in circumstances in which important differences in purpose might otherwise create a conflict dangerous or damaging to society. Yet the effectiveness of force in avoiding violent conflict within a society depends on the citizens' placing a higher value on law and order than on any other purpose. Civil war may erupt when other purposes come to have a higher value than order within the society. For this reason, domestic tranquility requires that the existence of force be continually complemented by efforts to sustain and expand the validity of common purposes. In this effort education and exhortation have a useful part to play. But in the longer run a necessary condition is that the population as a whole share in common and satisfying experiences. When, for example, one area of a nation remains economically backward and has in its midst an underprivileged and disfranchised group while the remainder of the country is experiencing economic and social progress, a violent conflict with the norms of society remains a continuing possibility.

At the same time, since force is concentrated in the hands of the state, restraint on its arbitrary use against the citizen represents a continuing problem. This danger is reduced when influence over the affairs of the individual is diffused among a multitude of organizations each serving particular functional or geographical interests. He thus retains the freedom to associate himself with one or another group. These groups, in turn, represent varying elements of power which must be taken into account in the actions of the state.

There is no reason to believe that the complementary roles of force and common interest are any less important in the international system than in the nation-state in controlling conflict, but effective control is, at present, infinitely more difficult to achieve in the international system.

Two main obstacles stand in the way of control of conflict on the world scene. First, force is diffused and no path appears open now for its just concentration. Second, cross-national diffusion of power is inadequate and action to create it does not engage the interests of any substantial body of men. Yet survival requires both effective restraint on force and the creation of common purposes in the international system. Many proposals for the establishment of world peace have emphasized the need for some form of world police force with a preponderance of power. The Soviet Union has often suggested, at least on paper, that the problem of force could be dealt with by general and complete disarmament. The diffusion of force could also be reduced by concentrating the forces of the United States and the Soviet Union, thus giving the combination a virtual monopoly. None of these solutions seems likely to be implemented in the present environment.

There remains the possibility of creating a substantial cross-national diffusion of interest and ultimately of power which would enhance restraint and contribute to the growth of a sense of community. From a practical point of view there is a wide variety of steps which could, on a relative basis, reduce the role of force in the transactions between the two nations. Many of these, it is arguable, even at present would serve the common interests of the two nations. Yet it is almost a definition of the nation-state system at its present stage of evolution that the citizens of different states do not find it easy to cultivate cross-national interests and enterprises.

Some would argue that while domestic subsystems are functionally significant, those in the international sphere cannot be. The grounds for skepticism are the nature of the Soviet state and the greater significance of internal as compared with cross-national interests.

Domestic subsystems in the West perform tasks which in their absence the national government would have to undertake, such as education, business organization, charity, medical help, entertainment, recreation, and communication. In the Soviet Union there is a concentration of control over these activities in the hands of the state.

Undoubtedly the monolithic design of the Soviet state is a most serious inhibiting factor, but material progress brings diversity and with it new possibilities for weaving a web of interdependence across national lines. Soviet society is already confronted by an array of problems which cannot be handled by a single hierarchy. Diffusion of influence at home provides the setting for increased common action across national lines. At the same time cross-national contacts will provide a stimulus to diffusion of interest at home.

Cross-national activities are, for a time, not likely to arise as wholly new enterprises but as extensions of present public and private internal programs. These domestic considerations are likely to continue to appear to be the most significant. Foreign trade, for example, while it may be subject to the influence of policies designed to maintain the health of the domestic economy, can also come to play an important role in the cross-national diffusion of interest. Similarly, arrangements for military cooperation even though limited will have a noticeable influence on the military outlook of the two sides.

Yet, in the longer run, creation of interdependence, in our view, is likely to come as a result of new tasks and new opportunities more than by the reallocation of old duties already being satisfactorily performed. Science and technology on a world scale are powerful tools in this effort. While there is no single path to adequate cross-national diffusion of power, its consequences when achieved, and to the extent it is achieved, will be restraint on the use of force. Only events will prove whether the web of common interest thus created is adequate for its time. Even in the American system, there have been numerous crises of restraint and one serious breach.

Any set of proposals for action is open to the challenge that even if achieved, they would be insufficient. Questions may be raised not only about the importance of the functions but also about the ability of the actors to create cross-national clusters of power— since in foreign affairs power is everywhere highly concentrated in the hands of the central government of the nation-state. Moreover, one may ask whether a cross-national organization may withhold power in the same way that a business or labor organization withholds power from a President.

Undeniably the state is today the most influential actor in the international system. Yet those who engage in cross-national action will remain citizens if not servants of the state. Their political task is both to create new enterprise and to influence the state of which they are a part to acquiesce in and indeed to support their efforts. Successful undertakings of this nature abound today in Western Europe but seem precluded in the Soviet-American confrontation because of the present conflict. Yet, is the impression wrong that nuclear weapons are bringing a steadily growing band of men on all sides to reassess their goals and modify their traditional outlook?

Further, it must be noted, the absence of salient and important cross-national purposes in other areas makes progress more difficult in the field of arms, since there is little experience and no model for collaboration in such a vital field. Existence of such purposes, and programs for achieving them, would provide a positive incentive for actions to reduce reliance on military force. Security based on arms control, as well as on arms, involves uncertainties and risks. The creation of positive interests which would profit from restraint of arms may be required to tip the balance. Otherwise, the known danger may be preferred to the unknown. Moreover, any system of arms control will almost inevitably involve the creation of a third system of social and political arrangements, tied to the two nations but in some respects different from either. Since arms control is a most sensitive area, constructive experience in other somewhat less vital fields would be valuable. Finally, the engagement in peaceful endeavors in cross-national structures will help to reshape the distinct historical and industrial experiences which make common understanding of the interaction of the two sides so difficult.

Interdependence, as an approach, emphasizes the need to work simultaneously and on a broad front on the two main obstacles to the control of conflict. On the one hand, there must be an intensive and steadily widening exploration and experimentation with the whole array of measures which may restrain or reduce the role of force. On the other hand, there must be an even more substantial commitment of resources and talent to the development of enterprises of understanding and action which will provide common experience for citizens of the two sides.[2] In short, competitive transactions between the two states in the military field must be reduced and restrained so far as possible, while transactions in areas giving promise of common achievement must be expanded by every possible means both for their own sake and for their contribution to an environment in which force may be more fully brought under the control of society.

Obviously, the present relationship between the United States and the Soviet Union is anything but consciously planned interdependence. It consists of vast areas of conflict, other areas of competition, and still others of limited tacit or explicit cooperation or common action. In the United Arab Republic, they are in competition. In Laos, whose future remains open to question, they have cooperated in attempting a new arrangement to reduce conflict. In each case, conflict has not occurred in undiluted form but contains elements of restraint.

[2] Some accept the desirability of the objective but doubt that it can be achieved. Brig. Gen. Sidney F. Griffin represents this view when he says, "Thus far, most such enterprises have led at most to expanded understandings of each other's experience, but not in sharing of experience. I do not think there is a real prospect for enough sharing of U.S.-Soviet experience in the future." Informal comments to author, Dec. 1, 1962.

Conflict among states, as among individuals, stems from incompatible purposes. Yet, most state purposes are mixed. At present, for example, each side is attempting to work toward world unity in the long run. At the same time each is much concerned with its survival. Thus the race to acquire the military forces necessary to impose a preclusive unity is restrained by the need to avoid provocation in the eyes of the adversary. Similarly, each side is concerned with its power and influence in third areas. Both, however, recognize that competition for influence must be conducted with restraint if the escalation of the conflict to dangerous levels is to be avoided. Thus, actions toward the goals of unity and the pursuit of power are moderated by the requirements of survival and the need for restraint. Moreover, each society has innumerable internal tasks which it seeks to accomplish. The Soviet Union, for example, is vitally concerned with the development of its agriculture. The United States is, or ought to be, devoting an increasing amount of its time and talent to the management of the vast urbanization process now taking place. Internally, the Soviet Union is concerned with the reform of Soviet law, while the United States is deeply committed to further progess in desegregation. Indeed, within each nation there are an infinite number of purposes being pursued by individuals and subgroups which do not impinge on the adversary and which are ill-served by the present conflict.

National Experience and the Need and Limits of Action

The purposes of a nation emerge from the totality of its experience, past and present, internal and external. In seeking to cultivate cross-national action in the field of arms or any other area, the differences which result from the unique experience of each state can be ignored only at the risk of frustration or failure. Equally important, similar experience provides the ground on which common action in the mutual interest may be built. Emphasis on differences may be prudent to avoid surprise, but the identification of areas of common development is essential for the creation of constructive enterprise.

The task of understanding the totality of Soviet and American experience which provides the opportunity and establishes the present limits of common action is a large one and has nowhere been systematically attempted. It is beyond the scope of the present inquiry. Clearly, however, there are three great clusters of experience which are relevant to the management and enlargement of a viable interdependence between the two societies. First are the general but germane historical experiences of each nation. Second are their common experiences with science and industrialization. Third are their experiences with each other directly and in third areas of the world.

The different historical experiences of the two are an important factor in their very different perceptions of what is necessary and equitable in many situations. Two examples must serve to illustrate the point. They are not by any means intended to encompass the range of diversity.

The Soviet Union, located in the center of the great Eurasian land mass, has suffered numerous invasions. As a consequence, it has come to see its security vitally involved in the establishment of friendly or subservient buffer areas all around its periphery. The United States, in contrast, located half a world away from the centers of conflict, has in the twentieth century twice found itself involved in world wars on foreign soil. Experience seems to have shown that its security is best protected by prompt military action in distant lands; hence, it has developed a world-wide system of bases and political influence.

Immigrants came to the new world in search of freedom either of ideas or of opportunity.[3] They undertook to settle and develop a virtually unpopulated continent. The task put a premium on individual initiative and enterprise. Governmental authority, in a sense, followed rather than preceded the creation of communities. In the realm of ideas, America borrowed first from the intellectual ferment that produced the French Revolution, but in time the substance of the democratic system was derived from the English liberal tradition. The American Revolution was a revolt against England, but only in a very limited way against European culture.

Russia, in contrast, has a history of centralized authoritarian government reaching back for centuries. It is a land, at least in its western parts, long since settled with highly organized communities. The modernization of the Soviet Union has been pre-eminently an undertaking of the state, which organized the energies of the people for a vast constructive effort. The central ideas guiding the undertaking represent both a protest against nineteenth-century European culture and a defense against the continuing threat from Europe. The writings of Marx represented a devastating critique of Europe as he knew it. The organizing genius of Lenin provided a means of defense against the West. Out of the Russian experience and the ideas and myths originating with these

[3] For a description of the notions of liberty bordering on license in the revolutionary period see, e.g., Arthur Pope, *The Morale of the American Revolutionary Army* (New York: American Council on Public Affairs, 1943).

men rose a new authoritarian state dedicated to the creation of an advanced industrial society.

The purpose in stressing the different historical experience of the two nations is to underline the scope and complexity of the task of creating a viable interdependence between them. The differences in history not only make for a difference in world outlook but also in the daily life and style of living at all levels of society. An appreciation of the entire range of diversities as well as a search for similarities will be essential in seeking stability in the relationships of the two societies.

Among those who have been optimistic about the possibilities of eventually getting along with the Soviet Union, reliance is often placed on the benign effects of the increase in the standard of living expected to result from further industrialization.

These expectations about the role of industrialization in mitigating the conflict between the Soviet Union and the United States may be justified by events but the effect is not inevitable. As the Soviet standard of living rises, it is said, the Russian people will be less interested in foreign adventures. They will have less to gain and more to lose. Moreover, as the people become more satisfied with life, the state will have less need for maintaining tight control over their actions. In addition, as industrialization takes place, the increase in education and specialization will multiply the number of group objectives and may open the way for a greater diversity of cross-national contracts and undertakings. Three points need to be made about this optimistic vista.

First, for the present and for some years to come, the differences in the level and maturity of industrialization in the Soviet Union and the United States will remain substantial. The United States has become overwhelmingly urban, while in the Soviet Union a massive rural element remains. The United States has reached the stage where the expansion of industry is no longer required at a pace that in any sense strains the economy. In the Soviet Union, in contrast, the drive for the expansion of heavy industry continues and the base is by no means adequate except possibly for the support of the military effort. The United States is affluent while the Soviet Union is barely meeting the needs of its people, although a gradual improvement is taking place. In these circumstances, the ability and inclination of the United States to keep the pressure on the Soviet Union may offset the benign effect of hard-won affluence. At the same time, it is undeniable that industrialization does open new possibilities for constructive action between the two societies. The range of freedom of the Soviet citizen, while still restricted, is increasing. Scientists and engineers envisage many possible common tasks. The two nations are increasingly involved in world affairs and in interaction with each other as a result of the advances of technology.

Second, the separate and distinct historical experiences of the two nations, in the absence of intervening common action, are at least as likely to result in continuing conflict between two fully developed industrial giants as they are to eventuate in true peaceful coexistence. The belief that the Soviet Union will somehow accept Western values after a long period of continuing conflict and advancing industrialization is, so far as can be seen, without adequate foundation. In the full power and vigor of a successful and largely isolated development, it is equally reasonable to believe it might simply assert more vehemently its unique and exclusive formula for organizing the world.

Third, while the past has made for differences in outlook and the present industrialization opens the possibility for growing similarities in values, the future outcome will be critically dependent on the experiences of the Soviet Union and the United States with each other. To wait and see if Soviet industrialization will soften its outlook, while continuing to rely overwhelmingly on force and engaging in world-wide defensive conflict to keep the Soviet Union at bay, is hardly more than to await an increase in the strength of an enemy.

The alternative, for which one may hope time is still available, is, first, to devise and to invest in areas which will provide understanding and common action in order that, as our adversary grows stronger, the common interest will prevail over parochial, even though continental, purposes; and, second, to seek by a variety of approaches to restrain and limit the means and occasions of violent conflict. For convenience, in contrast with the past policies, this alternative is termed a strategy of interdependence.

A Strategy of Interdependence

The Interplay of Purpose and Experience.[4] Purpose is central in the life of man, acting alone or as a member of a state. Man seems to differ from other animals in his ability to conceive purposes toward which he directs his actions. He has an innate capability for setting goals for himself. Intimately connected with this ability is man's pervasive inclination to attach values to all aspects of his experience in life. From the purposeful and evaluative aspects of man's behavior, two principles emerge for the control

[4] For a more complete analysis see the Appendix, "Human Behavior and the Control of Conflict," p. 370.

of conflict. First, there must be a continuing and vigorous search for common purposes, or common interests as they are referred to in foreign relations. One's own purposes or those of the adversary may have to be dealt with as fixed in order to act, but it is essential to realize that the very action will alter in some degree the values and purposes on both sides.[5]

Second, the infinitely varied capability of man to attach values to life's experiences requires that his opinion of what is needed or acceptable, threatening or rewarding, be recognized as an important reality. Thus, for example, the worth and reliability of deterrence or interdependence or any other approach to interstate relations is closely related to the extent to which, in the opinions of those who are involved, it serves purposes of value.

Man, however, does not live apart from his environment. His purposes and his values are shaped by his experiences. Experience may be divided into two main classes. First, experience may be thought of in its usual sense as consisting of those events and situations in which man plays a part. In this sense, the Berlin crises, the space race, the successes and failures of the aid program, and the problems arising from cultural exchange are part of the experience of the groups in authority in both the United States and the Soviet Union. Second, and in a less conventional sense, experience comes from devising and using instruments of power or from persuasion in coping with events. In this sense, weapons development, the creation of laboratories on earth or in space, and even the development of an organized set of policies or an

[5] For a description of the Department of State actor, see Paul Nitze, "Necessary and Sufficient Elements," in William T. R. Fox (ed.), *Theoretical Aspects of International Relations* (Indiana: University of Notre Dame Press, 1959), pp. 5–12.

ideology are relevant parts of experience. Both the events and the instruments help to mold men's purposes and determine their preference of means.

The crucial point to be understood, if the opportunities are to be appreciated and the pitfalls avoided in seeking to control conflict, is the nature of the interplay between man and his experience. As we have sought to manipulate and control the physical world, we have tended to think of ourselves as being in a simple subject-object relationship to the world. However, this ability to control our physical environment has in fact produced concomitant changes in ourselves. Man is a purposeful animal but his purposes and his values are in large part derived through interaction with his environment. As his environment is modified he himself changes. What he considers valuable will shift, depending upon the tasks he undertakes and the means he uses to accomplish them —in a word, upon his experience.

At the same time no man comes to a new task without an infinitely varied series of purposes and values generated from previous experience. His past experience and thus his values will be the consequence both of his participation in events, either directly or indirectly, and of his experience with a potentially wide variety of instruments for coping with life's problems. Thus, action on a particular occasion is a vector or a transaction of man and experience. Out of each such occasion will come new values and new tendencies for future action.[6]

The infinite possibilities inherent in this view of man in action

[6] For a persuasive presentation of the basic reasoning from which the above view of man is derived, see Hadley Cantril, *The "Why" of Man's Experience* (New York: The Macmillan Company, 1950).

account for the uncertainties of social prediction. They also suggest that whenever men interact with one another it can be expected that they will find conflicts of purpose and even disagreements over the best means of achieving what appear to be common goals. It is exactly this limitless capacity of man for attaching values to experience and thus of giving an infinite variety of meanings to experience that gives rise to the plurality of causes of conflict. It also helps to explain why no state has found an absolutely certain way to control conflict or any way at all to eliminate it completely. At the same time the role of experience in shaping men's values provides the opportunity for mitigating conflict and directing men's energies to new and constructive purposes.

Jean Monet, the architect of the European Common Market, summed up the practical man's understanding of the potentialities of new experience when he said, "Men change their minds because of the conditions in which they are placed, which are different from the conditions of the past." [7]

New instruments of destruction, nuclear weapons and missiles, are leading men to change their minds about the value of war. The existence of these weapons provides the setting in which the tanks of the great powers are used to squirt water at each other across the Berlin wall, and in which a delicately calculated quarantine takes the place of prompt application of force to curb the irritating antics of a small state on our very borders. Yet, together with increasing proof of the impotence of force, a lingering belief continues in its utility. Old purposes, old instruments of power, old patterns of behavior struggle for new forms in which their importance may be reasserted. Man changes, but the claims of the

[7] See John Brook, "The Common Market—II," *New Yorker*, Sept. 29, 1962.

past must be faced if the promise of the future is to be fulfilled.

The Limitations of Coexistence. In their struggles with each other the two great powers have sought to substitute coexistence and the cold war for a hot war. These moves represent progress in that they signify a recognition, on both sides, of the costs and futility of nuclear war. Neither is sufficiently adaptive to the world environment being created by science and technology to give great promise of avoiding catastrophe in the longer run.

Military interdependence between the United States and the Soviet Union exists and is recognized. Both admit the power of nuclear weapons and the desirability of avoiding war. What is missing is a full understanding of the need for, and ways of, working together if war is to be avoided. War is not seen as certain and its costs are not wholly and vividly visualized. For the leaders and people on both sides, working within the existing state structures to enhance power and influence is widely accepted as adequate or as the least evil option.

Interdependence also exists because of scientific and technical advances in communications, transportation, and many other fields outside the military. These advances permit and facilitate a global political conflict. While both sides wish to avoid general war, the global competition for power and influence continues.

Thus the conditions necessary for control of conflict are not only those which pertain directly to the management of military forces, but those which pertain to the whole environment in which the competition is taking place. New conditions, situations, and structures must be created to ensure common restraint on military force and to open the possibility of a future which both may live to enjoy. Interdependence exists; the great powers are confronted with the mutual task of making it a constructive force in the world.

The Soviet Union has proposed coexistence as the basis for relationships of the East and the West. The limitation of coexistence is that, while it recognizes interdependence in strategic nuclear weapons, it seeks to deny the need for, or reality of, interdependence in other areas. Coexistence often conjures up an image of the two adversaries pursuing parallel paths until one, the West, collapses from its own contradictions. Coexistence seeks to keep alive an exclusive vision of unity. By inference, it denies the reality or vitality of the society of two-thirds of mankind. At the same time it maintains that the Soviet Union retains the right to support wars to reshape new nations. Coexistence is designed to permit the Soviet Union to pursue its self-selected tasks, including that of expanding Communism, without taking undue risks. In this approach there is a constant tendency to underestimate the effect of its action on the West. Even as it seeks to undermine capitalism, it strengthens the forces in the West intent on more extreme forms of conflict.

Despite these fundamental limitations the idea of coexistence represents a movement in the right direction toward facing the consequences of the nuclear armed world. The long-run importance of the shift for Soviet society is easy to underestimate in the West.[8] To admit the possibility that we exist together is to open the possibility that our fate may be interdependent. If it is indeed interdependent, working together as well as competitively will be necessary to manage and shape it.

[8] It is hard for Americans to appreciate the emotion of the Russian lady who told the American scientist, "It has been difficult for a Marxist to accept even peaceful coexistence; it meant giving up a lot that one had come to believe."

It is in just this respect that coexistence, as presently interpreted by the Soviet state, is most deficient. At best the Soviet view of a joint endeavor is a collaboration at arms length. Often it is designed to provide an advantage to the Soviet Union without taking sufficiently into account the need for a comparable advantage for the United States. Even when mutual agreements have been arrived at, as is the case in the exchange program, many Soviet participants seem to be driven to exploit every opportunity to gain an advantage. In part this may be an "underdog" response stemming from the recent hardships and poverty of Soviet society. But since the Soviet Union is now a powerful nation and perhaps soon will be an affluent one, it may be possible for the Soviets to learn to identify the cumulative mutual advantages to be gained from restraint, cooperation, or from common endeavors.

Criteria for the Implementation of a Strategy of Interdependence

Control of conflict in the international system is a process which must be learned. Identification and cultivation of common purposes are necessary. Survival is a common purpose, but in the midst of the myriad of other aspirations and goals of both sides it may be inadvertently sacrificed. Therefore, it is essential to create a web of subordinate purposes which serve the interests of both sides. How to achieve this must be learned gradually by experience. Thus a strategy of interdependence is concerned with the whole range of action by which the two sides learn by experience the scope of restraint which must be developed and the areas of endeavor which bring mutual reward. The entire relationship of the two powers must be dealt with, not merely one or another element of their interaction. Neither disarmament nor cultural exchanges, neither military power nor economic influence can be sufficient. They must be handled and used in proper proportion. The goal is experience by both sides which contributes in a significant way to the control of conflict. To be effective the total experience must meet five criteria.

First, experience must contribute to the *convergence* of values and purposes in the two societies.

Second, experience must be *germane* to the present stage of development or interrelationship of the two sides.

Third, experience must be *material* to the control of the conflict—that is, it must contribute to the restraint of force or to the cross-national diffusion of power.

Fourth, experience must be *sufficient* across the entire breadth of the relationship. Thus, resources for the conduct of positive programs must be as adequate although certainly not initially as great as expenditures for the creation of instruments of force.

Fifth, experience must be *cumulative*. New and expanded cross-national arrangements and organizations within which transactions can gain a momentum of their own will be required.

Convergence of Values. The prospects for the growth of constructive interdependence between the two nations find encouragement in some of the individual transactions which have taken place in fields in which the two states have permitted contacts. For five years now exchange of individuals, groups, exhibits, and cultural material has been taking place on a reciprocal basis between the two nations under agreements carefully negotiated by their governments. Meetings and travel have also been arranged on the initiative of citizens of the two countries. From farming to art, from science to religion, interested individuals have managed to make more of the occasion than their states, bent on competitive coexistence or the cold war, intended.

In these engagements of Russian and American citizens, achievement of common action for a common purpose appears to conform to a kind of law of inverse relevance. The more remote the field of action, the more distinct the symbols of communication from the polemics of the confrontation between the United States and the Soviet Union, the more likely the success of the joint undertaking. Thus the fields of music and art have provided some of the finest examples of the possibility of cross-national action.

The possibilities inherent in all fields for satisfying achievement resulting from common action for a common purpose may be illustrated by an example from the field of art. Yuri Faier, Soviet conductor of the Bolshoi Ballet, met with the American orchestra which he was to lead throughout the Ballet's tour of the United States. Faier is nearly blind, and excitement was lent to the occasion by the hope raised by several American specialists that his sight might be partially restored by an operation. But the business of the day was strictly musical. As he was led to the podium, Faier called out the name of the first cellist, and, when he arose, seized him with one arm and pounded his back with the other. They were old friends and had worked together on Faier's previous visit. Several other musicians also got bear hugs.

Faier then removed his coat and went to work. The first number was *Spartacus*. Faier beat time and the orchestra played smoothly until there was a false entrance by the trumpets. Faier looked pained. He shouted in Russian. From then on it was any good conductor rehearsing any good orchestra, with the usual give and take between maestro and musicians. At the end of the first part of the rehearsal, Faier bowed to the brass section and said, "Das ist gut." A murmur of approval went through the orchestra. Flushed with linguistic success, Faier started calling out some numbers in the score in English. A trumpet player, not to be outdone, commented, "Horosho," meaning "good,'" when he reached an understanding with Faier about a mixup in six measures. "Très bien," said Faier to him.[9] Later, conductor, orchestra, and dance troupe teamed up to put on a series of reportedly sterling performances.

Two lessons must not be lost. First, a common purpose, give and take between the participants, respect for the skills each brings to the task, developing friendship, and the sense of excitement and satisfaction that results from positive accomplishment are important. Second, cooperation in the arts, while contributing to a convergence of values, is unlikely by itself to be decisive in the relations between nations. As an eminent American musician pointed out: "For decades Americans revered the great German composers of the eighteenth and nineteenth centuries—yet this had no relevance to the two wars with Germany in this century." Ballet music as such is clearly not sufficient for the control of conflict between the United States and the Soviet Union, but the symbolism of the art or of an artist, like Pasternak, Yevtushenko, or even Benny Goodman, may be important. In the nuclear age, art may play a

[9] The description of this incident is based on a story in the *New York Times,* Aug. 29, 1962.

role in avoiding wars that in an earlier time it could only help to make less inhuman.

Germane to the Present Stage of Development. Some forms of cultural exchange are, of course, germane to the development of relationships of the United States and the Soviet Union. When these occur, often at the initiative of individuals, the official response of one or the other state is likely to be ambiguous or resistant to the free development of the cross-national transaction of its citizens.

The experience of Professor H. J. Berman of the Harvard Law School, while visiting lecturer at Moscow University, illustrates the point. Soviet law has in the past few years been undergoing substantial rehabilitation. Increasing emphasis has been placed on protecting the rights of the Soviet citizen. Efforts have been made to carry out these changes without interfering unduly with the power of the state in Soviet society. Law, as a consequence, is highly germane to the present stage of Soviet development. During his stay in Moscow, Professor Berman began a series of twelve lectures on American law at Moscow University. Early lectures were crowded but attendance began to drop off and students told Berman informally that they were being criticized in some quarters for being too interested in the course. In order to avoid getting the students into trouble, Professor Berman felt it necessary to halt the series after the seventh lecture. The opportunity given Professor Berman to deliver the lectures represents the workings of coexistence. The inability of the students to continue to attend them suggests a lack of acceptance of the minimum kind of interdependence that is required for survival in the nuclear age.

Agriculture is a field highly germane to the Soviet-American confrontation. The United States has much to offer and the Soviet Union a great deal to learn. The Soviet Union is desperately trying to increase the quantity and efficiency of its agricultural production. In a minimum way, due perhaps largely to the efforts of a single individual, the United States has accepted the desirability of Soviet agricultural progress. As a consequence, on a quiet Sunday, Konstantin G. Pysin, Soviet Minister of Agriculture, found himself slogging through the muddy fields of Iowa watching the newest farm machinery demonstrated and visiting a commercial fertilizer warehouse and an experimental automatic air-conditioned pig shed. As the *New York Times* reported, "The world of nuclear tension seemed as far out as a Soviet cosmonaut. It was Iowa corn all the way." [10] One of the Soviet party was asked what he found most interesting in the United States. His remark may well serve as the motto of interdependence for Soviet-American relationships. He said, "That is a very great question—now we have to get to work." [11]

The host of the day was Roswell Garst, whose farm in Iowa has become a mecca for Soviet agricultural experts since Garst entertained his personal friend, Premier Nikita Khrushchev, there in 1959. Garst on this Sunday, in his shirt sleeves, was at the top of his folksy, down-to-earth, Dutch-uncle lecturing form. "As the spirit moved him he draped an arm over the Minister's shoulder. They leaned on the fence together. He lectured on the shortcomings of both Soviet and American agriculture. And when he said that the biggest lesson both American and Soviet agriculture could

[10] *Ibid.*, Sept. 17, 1962.
[11] *Ibid.*

learn concerned the use of waste, such as corn stalks for feed, the Minister said: 'Bezuslovno!' That means, 'Absolutely right.' " [12]

Until the present time United States expressions of interest in the progress of Soviet agriculture have rested largely with Garst. The official exchange program has accepted a small but significant number of Soviet technicians who have come to the United States to learn better methods of farming. Some American agricultural experts have gone to the Soviet Union, but, if one can judge from their comments, more for the purpose of finding out what was wrong than with any thought of helping to correct it. Agriculture is indeed germane. It could be of great material importance if the United States were willing to help and the Soviet Union were willing to accept help. For such transactions to meet the criterion of sufficiency, they might well have to be on a scale, both materially and technically, at present undreamed of on either side.

In building a viable interdependence it is as important to seek to find fields in which we can ask the Soviet Union for help as it is to identify areas in which we are ahead. Electric power, in modest degree, might be such an area, although it has nothing like the significance to our present stage of development that agriculture has to the Soviet Union's. Still, at least, in certain regions and types of power, the Soviets might make a contribution. Secretary of the Interior Stewart L. Udall toured the Soviet electric power developments. On his return, he pointed out that the Soviet Union is one of the leading countries in the development of water power and Americans have "much to learn" from Soviet specialists in this field. Udall was reported as also bringing back from the Soviet Union one other significant impression—and that was the

[12] *Ibid.*

value of exchange visits. Reports from Moscow suggest that the feeling was reciprocal. The second highest member of the Soviet Ministry of Power Station Construction was quoted as saying of Udall, "You are an open man with a Russian nature and you talk from the heart," [13] which is the highest compliment a Russian can bestow on a visiting American.

On further investigation by specialists, power may not turn out to be significantly germane to our development, but at the moment the possibility stands. It is of particular interest because it would represent a positive contribution from the Soviet Union. Another indication that technical gains for the United States may be possible is suggested by the fact that the President of General Electric International visited Moscow to negotiate for manufacturing arrangements for certain Soviet technical products. Still, such initiatives represent only a trickle at present. They will have to approach the dimensions of a torrent before they obviously become material to the control of conflict.

Material to the Control of Conflict. Experience which contributes to restraint on the use of force and to the creation of cross-national increments of power are the two key elements in this criterion. Normally, one thinks of arms control, reduction, or elimination as most relevant to the restraint of force. In the short run this may be correct. Face-to-face negotiations by representatives of the two powers, the experience of the last fifteen years suggests, is only one of many relevant forms of experience for achieving progress. At the level of discussion, the Pugwash experience represents a remarkable and fruitful innovation of a technical-policy character which helped to provide the setting for achieve-

[13] *Ibid.,* Sept. 9, 1962.

ment of the Test Ban Treaty. On issues as complex as armament a vast exchange of information and ideas is required before either side is prepared for negotiation in the conventional sense. On the whole, premature negotiations are counterproductive.

The Cuban "quarantine" of 1962 represents another kind of experience contributing to the restraint on the use of force. While it is too early to foresee the ultimate outcome, and while only a little learning is possible from each crisis no matter how grave, the lessons of the most recent one may be significant. Surely, it was one of the precipitating factors in the achievement of the test ban. The Soviet Union has learned that the geographic expansion of strategic forces will be resisted. The American people have learned somewhat more about the threat posed to the Soviet Union by our overseas bases. Both have learned that it will be wise to consider the acceptance of opposition governments. Third areas have probably learned something about the dangers as well as the prestige of missile bases. Whether both sides are really willing to formalize their new understandings in more than a temporary *détente* remains to be seen. Resistance to the expansion of force as well as the search for means to regulate its control are both part of the experience necessary to its restraint.

The hazards of resistance are, of course, substantial; thus in the intervals between crises experience, action which contributes to cross-national understanding and endeavors may be of great value. Cultural exchange as has been suggested can play a useful role, but much more is needed in the way of great common endeavors. Space is a prime field for such activity. The modest program of cooperation between the Soviet Union and the United States hardly represents more than cultural contact supplemented by an exchange of statistics. Bolder achievements are necessary if space is to play a material role in the control of conflict rather than representing merely another dimension for its conduct. Agriculture has already been mentioned as possibly making a material contribution. Other areas will be discussed in subsequent sections. The point here is that action must eventuate in a significant improvement in the restraint on force or in the creation of cross-national power elements if it is to be material.

Sufficient—Equal to the Purpose. The balance of the entire range of interaction will play a major role in the ability of the United States and the Soviet Union to control conflict. The balance in their transactions will be significantly affected by the allocation each makes for national power purposes and the control of conflict. At the present time there is an overwhelming reliance on military force as a method of restraint and also as a means of settling conflict. The single-minded reliance on military force is reflected in the allocation of resources and talent for the various modes of interaction between the two adversaries. In the United States, for every dollar spent for the development of interaction which seeks to devise and implement common actions, a thousand dollars are spent for competitive purposes and ten thousand dollars for purposes of preparing for conflict. The disproportion is probably even more extreme for the Soviet Union. States will use the instruments available when they are confronted with incompatible purposes; thus the present allocation of resources seems likely to contribute to the cumulative possibilities of armed conflict however much, in the short run, it may appear necessary to prevent aggression. Substantial resources will be required to shift the emphasis in the Soviet-American confrontation from conflict to one in which experiences of mutual gain predominate.

The tendency of the United States is to seek small changes in the hope that they may have cumulative effects. This is unlikely to produce the desired results in the absence of substantial investment in programs designed specifically for constructive cross-national purposes. Moreover, even significant efforts in one area are likely to be frustrated unless there is an effort along the entire front of interaction with the Soviet Union. Since there is no single cause of conflict, points of friction must be tackled more or less simultaneously if success is to be achieved. Just as in the military area it is judged impossible to imagine the exact situation which will require force, so also in the case of constructive investments, the exact opportunity for their use cannot be wholly envisaged and a similar large-scale effort is needed. While in the military field systematic planning and investment have been generally accepted, a similar approach has rarely been the basis for action on other fronts. Little progress in the nonmilitary fields can be expected until a policy of systematic planning, action, and investment is adopted.

Government investment alone will not be sufficient; the channels of trade must again be opened. This will require a major shift in the present policies of the United States in the field of trade and in Soviet policies in equally important areas. At the present time, even though there is a large and growing trade between the Soviet Union and Western Europe and an even larger volume of trade between Eastern and Western Europe, the United States continues to limit its trade with the Soviet Union to the minimum.

The situation, at least up to the time the negotiations for the sale of wheat were begun, had not changed greatly since Anastas Mikoyan's visit to the United States in the late fifties. At that time he was interested in buying various steel shapes and forms. American businessmen were very much interested in making the sale. The businessmen went to Washington to talk to the appropriate Secretary of one of the major departments to obtain permission to export the material. They were told that permission would not be granted.

United States trade with the Soviets has been restricted for a variety of reasons. American businessmen have been hesitant to initiate contacts. Pressure has from time to time brought our European allies to comply with our standards. Yet without trade, without Soviet exposure to public-spirited American businessmen, and without the opportunity for American businessmen gradually to acquire a first-hand understanding of both the limitations and the strengths of the Soviet economy, all other measures may be insufficient. The strength of the two societies lies in their industrial establishments and those who manage the enterprises. In many respects their occupation provides a common experience which is extra-political. Unless they in some degree come to appreciate their mutual experience, other measures for the control of conflict may not suffice.

The scope of present exchange programs is noteworthy but, alone, they are unlikely to do more than open the door to an opportunity. There have been visits of representatives or citizens from the two countries displaying their talents, competing, talking, seeking new knowledge, and even occasionally engaging in common undertakings in a wide range of fields. In advertising, agriculture, electric power, journalism, law, literature, meteorology, music, religion, science, space, sports, and other fields, travelers have found common interests with their opposite numbers on the soil of the adversary. Moreover, tens of thousands of books and other publications move each year between the two nations and find their way into the hands of the scientists, scholars, and students in the universities and centers of research. American movies, limited in number, are seen on the average by one hundred million Soviet citizens.[14]

A good beginning has been made at correcting stereotypes, advancing common understanding, and identifying common interests of specialized groups but, despite the range of activity, significant constructive action remains for the future. The door is ajar but plans to capitalize on the opportunity are for the most part missing from the files of government. Individuals either lack adequate resources or if they have them await the lead of government. Conflict and the gaining of national advantage at the expense of the other remain the dominant mode of thought. Specific suggestions are made and sometimes explored but they come to nought in the absence of an approach to interdependence on a broad front. Trade, public investment, increased resources for arms control, and political settlements are all essential parts of a coherent and sufficient effort.

Cumulative Creation of Structure. A strategy of interdependence envisages a step-by-step approach, but on a broad front, to the creation of conditions in which the United States and the Soviet Union will find it in their self-evident interest to work together both constructively and in the restraint of the use of force. Such

---

[14] Estimate by Department of State representative.

a result will be impossible to achieve if transactions of importance are limited to heads of state and the diplomatic corps. Planning is needed which will mark out broad areas of approved interaction in which both government officials and private individuals are encouraged to take the initiative in devising constructive tasks with their Soviet counterparts. What seems to be required is for the government to achieve increased influence over *events* by reducing somewhat its direct control over *instruments*. The desirable form of organization for the creation of viable interdependence appears to be in a certain sense acephalous. Initially, not so much the cooperation of heads of state is needed, since they must continue to stand guard over each nation's security, as the acquiescence in the common action of others. Constructive interaction of many others is needed, not alone for conversation and understanding, but in order to devise meaningful common tasks and arrangements.

A kind of acephalous organization is essential because mutual action requires a degree of inventiveness and initiative not present in normal state relations largely confined as they are to questions of national security and power. Interdependence requires the invention of new ways of thinking about "the enemy." Area by area, it requires the application of domestic norms to alien groups. New models of competition and of common action must be developed. Neither checkers, chess, nor chicken, which are the most widespread present models of the interaction with the Soviet Union, will suffice. A whole variety of "non-zero sum games" [15] will be

[15] See Anatol Rapoport, *Fights, Games, and Debates* (Ann Arbor: The University of Michigan Press, 1960), pp. 174–179, for a discussion of non-zero sum games.

required which involve an increasing number of individuals on each side of the contest. Such an effort will, as has been stressed, demand substantial resources and, at this point, the state will play a positive role and have appropriate controls.

The experience of joint effort cannot spring full grown from the brow of Zeus. At least two levels of action will be required to generate and implement the development of common rules, procedures, or codes of competition for common enterprises in the mutual interests of both sides. At each of the two levels there are likely to be both psychological and structural obstacles to be overcome before the new conditions can be created. Each step in the process must be sufficiently limited that it does not represent a major shift in the power of either state in its relationships with the other. At the same time, if the total effort is finally to succeed in creating significantly different conditions and thus changing men's minds, it must be carried out on the broadest possible front. Somewhere along the spectrum of transactions, a movement forward must be taking place at all times.

At the first level of action, each sector of the front need be manned by only a few individuals. Indeed, it probably must be, since only a few individuals capable of the initiative required are likely to be found on either side. These few men in each main field of human endeavor face a demanding task. First, in the absence of nuclear war, they must by an act of imagination anticipate the consequences of the present course. Second, they must visualize the changes required and possible in their area of competence. Third, they must commit themselves to the task of devising the new conditions and structure which will permit their fellow men to see where their new self-interest lies. Fourth, they must identify and learn to know their opposite numbers in the other camp. Fifth, jointly they must find a permissible structure in which a steady exchange of views can take place. Finally, from this exchange there must emerge step-by-step proposals which will create the conditions of common action within which a far larger number of talented but perhaps less creative men will find it gradually possible to change their views of what is valuable.

At the first level there is no substitute for the creative few who by a leap of imagination see the new conditions which must be brought into being if man is to adapt to his increasingly interdependent environment. But this is not enough; practical step-by-step measures must be devised which can be taken by common men whether at the top or just beginning the climb. Once this is done, the task at the second level is to provide the new structure with adequate resources and manpower and to a large extent to let common experience work its effect on men's purposes and methods.

Arms control, space, communications, weather, industry, trade, social sciences, and other areas are all in urgent need of such an approach. Not formal arm's-length agreements between impermeable states are required but men facing common tasks and seeking to create a common structure of action. There is no single cure for conflict. Physicists and psychologists, physicians and politicians—all are likely to make a more constructive contribution if they work from their own area of knowledge and seek to forge the links of common action, than if they seek to devise general cures for the whole spectrum of conflict.

Two complementary outlooks are necessary for the success of these efforts. First, there must be an appreciation of the fundamental nature of political power, which is no more than the ability to persuade others to work for one's own objectives. In a modern state it need not be and frequently is not exercised exclusively through bureaucracy or other organs of the state. A scientist who conceives a Geophysical Year and arouses his colleagues throughout the world to see it carried through is engaging in constructive political action beyond the scope of all but the most powerful statesmen. Each man of talent has some potential for political action which will contribute to the control of conflict. Together their efforts can be sufficient. Anything less may not be adequate for survival. Second, in a man's particular field of competence it is hardly necessary to guard against overoptimism. He knows the intractable nature of the problems, the difficulties of progress, and the never-ending character of the task. Time is always needed. In the control of conflict, a substantial period of time will be required for the myriad efforts to be initiated, planned, accepted, and implemented. Perhaps a decade or more will be required before a cumulative momentum is created.

The environment for a substantial positive effort at the creation of the kind of interdependence which could lead in time to major changes in Soviet-American relations would no doubt be enhanced if a *détente* between the two powers could be achieved. Such a *détente* based largely on the existing *status quo* seems a possibility. However, some argue that a fundamental settlement of outstanding political differences is a necessary, although not a sufficient, condition for genuine restraint and growing interdependence.[16]

While every effort to improve strained relations by diplomatic means is to be welcomed, progress in resolving the underlying

---

[16] Professor Robert Paul Wolff, University of Chicago, unpublished correspondence with author, Nov. 15, 1962.

issues seems likely to be limited until substantial common interests in other areas have been developed. Therefore, it is argued that investment in interdependence must be made even in the absence of settlement of outstanding historical differences. Not only compromise, but action which reduces the relative importance of present conflicts, is needed. In the meanwhile, force will continue to be our major reliance and war our continuing hazard.

New Directions—Old Obstacles

The United States and the Soviet Union are engaged in intensive and massive interaction in the field of military power. They are taking part in varied but limited transactions with one another in many other areas. Both are involved with Europe—East and West. Both are seeking influence in the underdeveloped areas of the world. Interdependence suggests that there is a common interest in managing these relationships with restraint.

Interdependence argues that it is possible and necessary to modify the present pattern of interaction between the United States and the Soviet Union and to open the door to a new *communitas*. Modern science and technology have made the task urgent but have also provided the means for working at it. The modern nation is no longer impermeable against attack, nor can it bar common action by committed men. The goal is to exploit self-evident individual and national interests which will help to regularize the competition and mitigate the conflict. The approach must be highly pragmatic and practical and must move step by step toward the goal.

No act of importance, whether it be a threatened use of force or a promise of positive cooperation, is likely to be without risk. Each must be weighed and analyzed with care, although prolonged evaluation—inaction—has its own risks. If every pertinent question were answered before a new weapons system was procured, none would ever be built in time. In the same way, if every objection to a project intended to be mutually rewarding must be answered to the satisfaction of all, the building of interdependence will never be feasible. In both cases action is required in the face of some uncertainty. A prudent management would invest substantial resources in the instruments of positive interdependence while providing funds for adequate military force. Moreover, it would make sure the resources for both are weighed in the same scales. This is not now the case.

In the present circumstances, the restrictions on the activities of individuals from both sides are severe, but the greater impediments appear to lie on the Soviet side.[17] The United States must use this advantage if interdependence is to be managed effectively. At the same time the rate at which progress can be made depends upon the receptivity of Soviet citizens and their ability to persuade their government that common action is in the mutual interests of the two countries. Progress as a result is likely to be slow but not impossible, provided that important tasks can be devised which do not appear to undermine the Soviet state.

The United States, scarcely less than the Soviet Union, is prone

---

[17] The asymmetry may gradually be reduced. As Lord Home, then British Foreign Minister, said in an interview, "When you see those thousands of young scientifically trained technologists growing up and visiting the outside world you can't help feeling they will not submit very much longer to being prisoners of Marxism. That stuff is intellectually sterile and the young Russians are not intellectually sterile." *Observer*, London, Sept. 23, 1962.

to rely excessively on force. A more serious deficiency is that it is inclined to underestimate the task of creating a viable sense of interdependence which will reduce the necessity for the use of force. While affluent, we have only recently become a world power and are only now acquiring the prudent concern for the interests of other world powers that is required. Having cast off our isolation we are only gradually coming to understand the limits of our ability to shape the world environment by our own unaided efforts.

2 Community and the State

"What permanence the new-won peace might have; what stature the United Nations could attain; even what the future course of civilization would be—answers to these questions now clearly involve . . . the ability of East and West to work together and live together in one world."

DWIGHT D. EISENHOWER
Crusade for Europe

The Search for Unity in the Nuclear Age

OUT OF the ashes of World War I emerged two visions of a new world order—Lenin's and Wilson's. Both held out the ideal of the unity of mankind, but on radically different terms. Men of every nationality have been influenced by one or the other vision—and often by both. Nevertheless, diversity not unity continues to be the mark of our time. Tension and conflict are widespread, yet the possibilities of a decent life for all are greater than ever before. Today mankind stands sadly in need of a way of living and working together despite its diverse visions.

In the 1920s and 1930s the United States and the Soviet Union coexisted while busying themselves with internal tasks. During World War II they combined to put down a third vision, foreign to both. For a moment in the excitement of victory there was an illusion among many in the West that the two sides shared the same vision of unity. Almost immediately the profound differences of history, culture, and ideology reasserted themselves as the two continental giants found themselves virtually alone and facing each other on the world stage. Each saw the common interests of mankind in peace and well-being. Each noted imperfections in the present order. Neither was entirely clear how they could best be overcome. Each, however, envisioned a world community, of men or nations, a new *communitas* to give expression to their ideal of unity. The issue between them was in whose image it would be constructed. Would it be Communism under the leadership of the Soviet Union? Or would it be a free association of independent states under the leadership of the United States? Thus posed, the issue, if history is the guide, could lead in time to a third world war far surpassing in scale and violence those which had gone before.

If there is a possibility that the past will not repeat itself, that an Armageddon may be postponed, it rests on the striking discontinuity which arose in weapons technology subsequent to the end of World War II. The production of large amounts of fissionable material, the construction of thousands of nuclear weapons and, finally, the introduction of intercontinental ballistic missiles have increased the effectiveness of each side, should it choose to devastate the other, by something of the order of 1,000,000 to 1.[1] Great efforts have been made on both sides to find means of con-

---

[1] To obtain a rough indication of increased effectiveness the following method was used. Nuclear weapons represent an increase of approximately 1,000,000 over the TNT bombs of World War II. Missiles represent an increase in speed of delivery of approximately 100 over manned aircraft. Speed as well as explosive power is related to effectiveness.

Power involves moving a load in space over time. Thus the relationship:

tinental defense. Such success as they may have seems unlikely to repair the breach created by nuclear weapons and ballistic missiles. The consequence of these developments is that both the United States and the Soviet Union can penetrate each other's borders at will. In our day the utmost strength coincides with the utmost vulnerability.[2]

The magnitude of the force that may be applied is not the only change resulting from the discontinuity. The existence of nuclear forces has given rise to a degree of interaction between the two sides hitherto unmatched except in wartime. Vast world-circling and overlapping intelligence systems have been created to collect and sift information on the development and readiness of opposing forces, minute by minute. Information flows in an ever increasing volume between the two sides, but the need is insatiable. Never in the history of man has the interaction between two potential antagonists been so intense and systematic as that which

---

P = power $\qquad$ L = load in tons $\qquad$ D = distance $\qquad$ T = time

$$P = \frac{LD}{T} = LV$$

LV = purpose load in equivalent tons TNT destructive power

In World War II: $V_1 = 500$ mph

$\qquad\qquad\qquad L_1 = 10T$

At present: $\qquad V_2 = 15,000$ mph

$\qquad\qquad\qquad L_2 = 10,000,000T$

Thus: $\qquad\qquad P_1 = 10 \times 500 = 5000$ ton miles per hour

$\qquad\qquad\qquad P_2 = 10,000,000 \times 15,000 = 10^9$

And: $\qquad\qquad \frac{P_2}{P_1} = \frac{10^9}{5000}$ or 2×10^5 or 2,000,000

Assuming present efficiency to be 0.5 of World War II gives a factor of 1,000,000 to 1 at present as compared with World War II.

[2] John H. Herz, *International Politics in the Atomic Age* (New York: Columbia University Press, 1959), p. 22.

is presently occurring in the military sphere between the United States and the Soviet Union. Their preparation for a possible war has the intimacy of a duel; yet, should it come, it may be as dehumanized as the calculations of a computer.

The flow of information between the two antagonists is but one facet of the increasing breadth and intensity of interaction in the modern world. Communication, not only of facts but of knowledge and values, has vastly increased the influence of the antagonists on each other and on all the rest of the world as well. Not merely weapons but ideas may be sent around the world within the hour. Moreover, in this age the mobility of men has been dramatically enhanced. The mind of man is increasingly concerned with the earth as a single system and with the larger systems within which it moves. World enterprises for space, in the oceans, for weather, for communications, for transportation, and in other fields are under way or being planned.

In the face of world-circling weapons and world-permeating communication, the need for the organization of a world-wide political community grows more urgent at the same time that the "security dilemma" of the modern state grows more acute.[3]

The power of the state to protect its people is in jeopardy. In the absence of higher authority which would protect each from

[3] *Ibid.* John Herz points out that the security dilemma "is a social constellation in which units of power (such as states or nations in international relations) find themselves whenever they exist side by side without higher authority that might impose standards of behavior upon them and thus protect them from attacking each other. In such a condition, a feeling of insecurity, deriving from mutual suspicion and mutual fear, compels these units to compete for ever more power in order to find more security, an effort which proves self-defeating because complete security remains ultimately unobtainable." See pp. 231–243.

the attack of the other, a general feeling of insecurity exists. Insecurity fosters mutual suspicion and fear, and compels the state —and especially the most powerful—to seek further force and power in an effort to achieve security. In the end, in a world where there are more or less equal contenders each having nuclear weapons, this proves self-defeating because complete security remains unobtainable—unobtainable because no state can achieve a monopoly of power and none can afford to give up the race. Thus the security dilemma. While the security dilemma is as old as the state system, it has been given new poignancy by the potentiality for mutual annihilation.

In earlier times the security dilemma did not usually result in an unlimited search for power, and, even when a universal goal was asserted, the state was unable to achieve it because both the territorial and the technological bases were limited as compared with the expanses of the earth. Today, world-wide *communitas* is becoming feasible technologically, but is excluded by the weapons in the hands of the opponent—weapons which are fundamentally discontinuous with those employed in the past.[4] Yet the radical changes occurring in human communication, mobility, and enterprise contain as much promise as do the new weapons a threat.

The political consequence of the discontinuity in weapons is to place a premium on restraint in pursuing national objectives, in-

[4] One indicator of the discontinuity is suggested by the fact that there is now in existence in the arsenals of the two major powers the explosive equivalent of 10 tons of TNT for each individual on earth, whereas at the beginning of World War II the per capita share would scarcely have been excessive for medical and commercial use. For the current estimate, see P. M. S. Blackett, "The First Real Chance for Disarmament," *Harper's Magazine*, Jan. 1963, pp. 25-32.

cluding the separate visions of unity. Thus far, the dimensions of the restraint required are but imperfectly perceived. Moreover, restraint is not enough. Nuclear weapons have created a tenuous but vivid sense of common interest between the United States and the Soviet Union—but it is as yet a negative solidarity arising from fear. The task ahead is to design and construct a community of interest, positive interest and feeling.

There is, of course, little consensus on the ultimate form that a world political community will take. While the United Nations and related activities represent progress as compared with the past and reflect a growing awareness of the need for common action, they also demonstrate a continuing reliance on national power and an imperfect commitment to unity. The point of view of this inquiry is that the task of the present is not so much to devise the structure as to lay the foundations of a world political community. The means are at hand to create a fabric of ideas, interest, and enterprise which can in time provide a basis both for world order and for the renewed security of the state. To spin the cloth a myriad concrete undertakings will be necessary, perhaps not one of which will add greatly to our security, but all of which in varying degree and circumstance may be important to it. Each individual and nation has a useful role in the undertaking, but a special responsibility rests on the two states which together divide a predominance of power in the world. They must avoid being so bemused with their security dilemma that they neglect the positive promise of the advance of science, technology, and enterprise on a broad front. Interdependence between the giants need not threaten their security; it can provide a rational basis for its re-emergence.

Community and the Ideal of Unity

The idea of community is central to the discussion which follows. The community includes more than the state or any other association which may operate within it. The community encompasses the entire range of sentiments, patterns of behavior, and interests of a people who in important ways share a feeling of solidarity. What constitutes a community is thus a matter of the sentiments of those who inhabit it. It defines those who are within and those who are without. Nevertheless, the sense of community is always a matter of degree. Solidarity may be intense or loose or casual. An individual may belong to different communities—a city and a nation. Finally, the feeling of community originates in two interwoven but distinct ways: first, by the sentiments derived from attachment to a group and, second, by the interests which arise from the participation in common tasks or enterprises.

Historical instances abound to illustrate the complex, ever changing sense of solidarity on which a feeling of community rests. When the feeling of solidarity exists or can be created, the transition to more extensive communities is made with remarkable ease. Thus in feudal Japan a larger sense of community developed which permitted the separate clans to give up their special privileges in what they believed to be the interests of their country. In the building of the Persian Empire, Cyrus, by a combination of skill, humanity, and wisdom not only aroused a sense of self-sacrifice in the original tribe from whence he sprang but later made great progress in establishing a sense of solidarity throughout the empire by providing for a common standard of service in war and advancement in peace. Alexander's attempts at the development of a sense of solidarity through the mass marriage of ten thousand of his Macedonian officers to Persian women seem to have been less successful; but had his death not been so sudden, his policy might well have had a more important effect on the gradual growth of community in the western Mediterranean.

The Roman Empire, of course, is a classic example of a sense of community induced by the extension of authority by force and made legitimate by a common body of law. Centuries later the Holy Roman Empire in the Rhine-Danube valleys continued to be sustained in part by a sense of solidarity. Revolutionary France was pervaded and invigorated by a sense of solidarity which for the first time affected large masses of the people. In our day the British Commonwealth stands as the best example of extremely diverse elements linked by a subtle sense of community.

Locality has through history most often been the basis of a sense of solidarity. The people of a village or city have a sense of belonging together and develop a distinct civic character. At the same time, they may see themselves as part of a more extensive community, frequently, in the modern world, a nation. As members of a nation, while living in widely separated localities, they may share common customs, history, and sentiments which provide in the outlook of all a kind of solidarity—a sense of community.

In Western civilization the sense of community is losing its exclusive attachment to familiar localities and is coming to be used in referring to a people sharing the basic conditions of a common life, although usually still expressed in terms of geographic location. It is in this sense that community is used in referring to European Community, Atlantic Community, or World Community. The emphasis on these uses is obviously on the sentiment of solidarity or on common interests, rather than on simple geography. In a sense the larger communities of the modern world seem to have their center everywhere and their periphery nowhere.

Community need not connote an absence of differences. Important shared sentiments or interests may provide a sufficient sense of solidarity despite different styles and purposes among the groups within the community. However, means for the expression, modification, and adjustment of differences must exist short of the explosive conflict which rends the fabric of solidarity.

The basis of community solidarity is as varied and complex as man.[5] The feeling of community stems from the experiences of men in living and working together in family, firm, state, and a vast array of other associations.[6]

As men participate in the life of a community, two main streams of experience contribute to a feeling of solidarity. These may be termed the *traditional* and the *instrumental*.[7]

Traditional solidarity arises as a consequence of attachment to a group. From birth the individual is a member of social groups. From his experience of belonging the individual develops a senti-

[5] Hadley Cantril, *The "Why" of Man's Experience* (New York: The Macmillan Company, 1950), pp. 21–49.

[6] For an extended treatment of the community as distinct from the associations which may operate within it, see Robert M. MacIver, *Community: A Sociological Study* (New York: The Macmillan Company, 1928).

[7] Emile Durkheim, *The Division of Labor in Society*, trans. George Simpson (New York: The Free Press of Glencoe, 1949). Durkheim describes the dual phenomena as it appeared in the late nineteenth century as "mechanical and organic solidarity."

ment of likeness, of identity. The rapid changes occurring in the modern world highlight the shifting relevance of various groups to the individual.

Within the larger community may be found different associations through which individuals seek to realize shared purposes. From the viewpoint of the individual, certain of these associations may for a time take on the character of community in which his whole life is lived.

The family, for the child born into it, is of such a nature. Family life is for the very young a nuclear community which prepares him for life in the greater community of the nation. But while his sentiment of solidarity with the family may continue as he grows older, his interest in its functioning will normally, in the modern world, diminish. In time, he will leave to participate in the activity of the larger community. Should he fail to perceive the differences in behavior appropriate to the larger community, his life may be confused and incomplete.

The locality in which the individual is born and raised may for a time mark the borders of his world. Both the opportunity for mobility provided by modern society and the complexity of its economic organization have tended to reduce the significance of one particular locality for adult welfare and livelihood. Yet traditional solidarity may continue. The sentiment of likeness may linger after the intrinsic purpose which gave rise to it has largely disappeared.

The momentum of the traditional sentiment of likeness would not be seriously troublesome were it not for the fact that in acquiring it men also learn to exclude the "unlike." When the individual attaches himself to a group, he divides people into "we" and "they." These distinctions may continue long after they have lost their instrumental purpose. Yet traditional sentiments, despite the impediment they represent to change, are unavoidable and even necessary since they lend stability and predictability to social life.

Instrumental solidarity arises initially not from attachment to a group so much as from involvement in a common task. Prior to the industrial revolution and the spread of Western civilization, traditional and instrumental solidarity tended to evolve together. Over generations, group sentiments and group interests grew up side by side. Thus in feudal Japan the attachment of the Samurai to the system and the function they performed in it developed together. In the modern world, however, the rapid advance of science and technology has tended to disrupt the traditional grounds of solidarity and to create different functional interests requiring new and broader associations for their successful achievement. In this light the current sophisticated interpretation of mutual deterrence may be viewed as an improvised and probably temporary arrangement which reflects the instrumental interest in survival brought about by the two-sided possession of weapons of mass destruction. Yet, deterrence in its more primitive sense is at least as old as man and seems likely to play a role in his future.

The impact of technology has often been unanticipated. The creation of new associations and organizations to cope with its consequences have almost always followed rather than preceded technical advance. Moreover, where traditional groups have been strong, they have not infrequently resisted as best they could the disruptive effect of industrial and technical advance. Resistance to change, control of change, monopoly of the fruits of change are all variations on the behavior of ruling groups and others faced with the disruption of traditional sentiments and the creation of new associations whose basis of solidarity is functional interdependence based on the pursuit of new common interests rather than only traditional sentiment.

On a world scale two forms of association have not infrequently been confused with the community. The first of these, which will be considered in subsequent sections, has a long history and is now manifesting itself throughout the world. It is the modern state within whose borders are occasionally found several national communities of much earlier origin. The second is a phenomenon more imprecise whose prominence in present-day thinking is due in large degree to the work of Karl Marx and the many intellectuals whom he has influenced. Of these, the most important was Lenin.

Lenin's vision of the future was based on a belief in the community of interests of a class, the working class. Relying on Marx he vastly overestimated the sense of solidarity resulting from the division of labor and the advance of industrialization. The emphasis of the Communists has been on instrumental solidarity of the working classes. "Workers of the world unite" remains their slogan. Economic determinism of a pessimistic bent postulated a growing cleavage between labor and capital. The productivity and creativity of modern science and technology were underestimated, and the adaptability of existing institutions when confronted by the startling possibilities of material progress was grossly miscalculated. The monumental magic of production sufficient to provide steady improvement in the life of all diffused the anticipated conflict.

Lenin's genius was to link the instrumental solidarity of inter-

ests of a class with the traditional sentiment of solidarity of a people, the Russians. Out of this synthesis emerged the Soviet Union
as we know it today—a multinational state glorifying the working
class and led by an elite whose power rests at once on the imperfect
traditional solidarity of the peoples who inhabit the vast spaces of
the Soviet Union and on the workers and peasants whose contribution and participation is increasingly important to the nation's
goals.

Yet, as a model of the world community, Lenin's vision of the
Union of Soviet Socialist Republics has been found wanting in
three respects. First, the interests of the ruling elite, the "new
class," as they have been termed by Milovan Djilas, are at least distinct from, if not always in conflict with, those of the workers
and peasants in the Soviet Union.[8] The new class is concerned
with the security of the state and with the development of the
economy. For both goals, sacrifices are required by the bulk of
the population. The inevitable difference of interest between the
educated, leading stratum and the less educated rank and file of
every radical movement was first pointed out by Waclaw Machajski at the turn of the century.[9] Once in power the interests of the
new elite intent on changing the conditions of society and the
masses intent on its traditional life continue to diverge for a time.
Ultimately, as is suggested by Crane Brinton, when the fever of
revolution has passed, a period of "thermidor" may occur in which
a new level of integration is achieved.[10] This plateau, however, is

[8] Milovan Djilas, *The New Class: An Analysis of the Communist System* (New
York: Frederick A. Praeger, 1957).

[9] Waclaw Machajski, *Intellectual Worker,* cited in Max Nomad, *Apostles of
Revolution* (New York: Collier Books, 1962), p. 10.

[10] Crane Brinton, *Anatomy of Revolution* (New York: Random House, 1960),
pp. 251–279.

attained only as a consequence of a merging of older traditional sentiments with the new instrumental values. In the case of the Soviet Union this has meant a return to greater emphasis on the traditions of the nation as contrasted with the newer identification with workers of the world.

Second, the instrumental solidarity of workers *qua* workers was overestimated in Communist ideology. Internally, the increasing achievement of the goals of Communist society, such as improved educational opportunities and industrialization, has provided new careers for the brighter sons and daughters of the workers. They have been assimilated in large numbers into the new class and serve the purposes of the Soviet Union. The credibility of their claim to represent the vanguard of the world proletariat is weakened. They are more often successful managers and technicians than revolutionaries. Their attachment to the Soviet Union limits their ability to identify themselves with the local and national aspirations arising throughout the world.

Moreover, the solidarity of local nationalism in the context of relinquishment of empire by the European nations has proved far more significant than Marx and his disciples anticipated. New nation-states have sprung up by the score in which the clash of classes, while important, is far more for the control of the independent territorial state than for the right to join unreservedly in the workers' world community under the hegemony of the Soviet Union. Even within the "socialist camp" this trend toward national community is obvious and apparently growing. In addition, the rapid progress in industrialization and steady improvement in the level of living of the workers of the Western industrial nations has blurred the common interests of workers as such while it has immeasurably broadened the basis of their relationship with each of the national communities.

Third, the Communist outlook, focused sharply on the need for heavy industry, tends to underestimate the complexities of human nature once the basic economic requirements are met. The state may by coercion and investment play a predominant and even effective role in putting in place the major foundations of a modern society, although many in the West judge the human cost in the Soviet Union too high. But as the society modernizes, man's capacity for expressing his individuality in a growing variety of ways as artist, scientist, tourist, merchandiser, and consumer seeks space to assert itself. These capacities need an increasing range of associations through which they may find expression. The needs of the community must reassert themselves even if in no other way than under the aegis of the state. Communist ideology may be adequate for the "take-off," in Walt W. Rostow's phrase,[11] but its content must undergo substantial change as the peaks of affluence are approached.

In contrast with Lenin's bold achievement, Wilson's vision of an organization of a world community of nations seemed at the time ephemeral. His dream miscarried at the outset when the United States Senate refused to ratify American entry into the League of Nations. Despite the dismal fate of the League, the central idea which it represented proved more durable. Following World War II the United States took the lead in the creation of the United Nations. A second rejection was guarded against by reservations, particularly the great-power veto which, negating any thought of

[11] Walt W. Rostow, *Stages of Economic Development* (Cambridge, England: Cambridge University Press, 1960), pp. 7–9.

coherent governance by the United Nations, still permitted all nations—or as it turned out, nearly all—to participate in a new form of world association which moved as far as the existing sense of need and of community permitted. It is hardly necessary to recall that the Soviet Union was at least as adamant in its insistence on the veto as any state in the West.

In the intervening years the aspiration of mankind for unity—shared alike by all great religions, all great worldly movements, and many men, great and small—has continued. Achievement of the goal has continued to be denied. In part this is the consequence of the natural tendency of the human race toward diversity. In part it is the specific result of the conflicting visions of unity held by the representatives of various nation-states and particularly the United States and the Soviet Union.

As so often has been the case in the past, proponents of unity find themselves not united but divided—with force remaining the final arbiter. The United States and the Soviet Union each emerged from World War II with a vision of world unity as part of its tradition. Until that moment the former had had little inclination, and the latter had had little opportunity, to try their hands at achieving it. In the subsequent fifteen years, the influence of the United States has expanded around the globe and the power of the Soviet Union has reached new heights.

It is not surprising that both Soviet and American leaders assert that the world is entering an era in which conditions will permit, even demand, that the international community be organized on a single set of principles. What would be surprising, were it not for the nature and intensity of the conflict between them, is how little progress has been made toward hammering out principles and procedures which provide a common ground on which both may stand.

The Soviet view of the coming victory of Communism on a world scale is by now so well known to Americans that it does not need repeating. Under Khrushchev the assertions have become more optimistic and expansive. "Your grandchildren," he tells us, "will live under socialism." The laws of history, he says, make the triumph of socialism inevitable. At the same time all good Communists must do their part to bring it about, including, when necessary, supporting "wars of liberation."

The American view of the need for unity finds many expressions.[12] Some stress the importance of universal nonviolent resolution of conflict; others rely on the universality of science; while still others emphasize the unity envisaged as flowing from a "victory" over world Communism by whatever means. Since World War II the American formulation has often displayed traces of each of these lines of thought, but has most frequently been couched in terms of a struggle for a world community of free nations.

The Kennedy-Johnson Administration, as did the previous one, has stated in different contexts and with varying nuances its belief that the goal is a world organized on common principles and that the issue is drawn.

Secretary of State Dean Rusk has said:

[12] For the view of the advocates of nonviolence, see *Speak Truth to Power* (American Friends Service Committee), a study of international conflict; for the scientist's view, see Eugene Rabinowitch, "The Role of the Scientist in the Community," an unpublished paper prepared for the Tenth Pugwash Conference on Science and World Affairs in London, England, 1962; and, for the conservative's view, see Barry Goldwater, *Why Not Victory?* (New York: McGraw-Hill, 1962).

We bear worldwide responsibilities. . . . We can be safe only to the extent that our total environment is safe. By environment I mean not only the land and waters and air of the earth but the adjoining areas of space, as far out as man can project instruments capable of influencing significantly the life and affairs of the planet. . . .

The world in our century is passing through the disintegration of the international order that prevailed in the last century toward a more comprehensive order in the next. . . . Our goal is a free community of nations. . . .[13]

Secretary of Defense Robert S. McNamara, in discussing the forces of change abroad in the world, has pointed out that, "The globe has shrunk to the point where we are all each other's neighbors," suggesting we must be as mutually and intimately concerned with world order as with the maintenance of law and order in the neighborhood. Speaking for the United States, he said the ultimate objective of the free world is "to establish a system of peaceful world order.[14]

Walt W. Rostow, counselor and chairman of the Policy Planning Council in the Department of State, has been more explicit. In his speech at Purdue University in March, 1962, dealing with the American strategy on the world scene, he said, while discussing the world-wide forces of change, "The ultimate question at issue is whether this small planet is to be organized on the principles of the Communist bloc or on principles of voluntary co-

---

13 Dean Rusk, "America's Goal—A Community of Free Nations" (Washington, D.C.: Department of State, Series S-No. 9), speech given at Davidson College, Davidson, North Carolina, Feb. 22, 1962.

14 Remarks made by Robert S. McNamara at the commencement exercises of the University of Michigan, June 16, 1962, as reported in *News Release* (Washington, D.C.: Department of Defense), pp. 4-5.

operation among independent nation states, dedicated to human freedom. . . . the outcome will be determined by whether the elements in the world environment . . . are more successfully gripped and organized by ourselves and our friends than by the Communists." [15]

The statements cited suggest that, whatever the intermediate ends our power and policies must serve, the ultimate objective is a coherent world community. The ideal of unity has deep roots in American history and psychology. Our experience as a federal union, our present relationships throughout more than half the world, our belief in the opportunity for progress resulting from the fruits of science and technology, our basic regard for the value of the individual—all lend weight to the search for a united world. But above all the necessity of resolving international conflict by other than nuclear means is borne in upon us as the age unfolds. While there may be many sources of the aspiration for unity, it is this nuclear threat that is forcing unity in the present age.

The chief obstacle, it is often said, is the absence of a sense of world-wide community adequate to provide the basis for order and justice throughout the globe. Yet even if such an outlook were general, the structural changes required would be difficult.

No doubt there has as yet been insufficient development of common traditional sentiments on a world scale. The democratic ideal which provides for participation of each individual in the exercise of the powers of government, while widespread, is by no means universal. Although educated men everywhere tend to share a

[15] Address before the Purdue Conference on International Affairs, Purdue University, Lafayette, Indiana, March 15, 1962, quoted from *Department of State Press Release*, No. 170, p. 7.

common and scientifically based map of the world of nature, all men by no means have the information to view nature through the eyes of science. Although the use of political power to foster economic progress is generally accepted, opinion on the most appropriate means remains divided. The well-being of the individual citizen is a widely heralded norm of action, but agreement is lacking on the means by which it shall be attained.

The instrumental interdependence spawned by science and technology also remains fragmentary and open to further development. Communication networks remain to be completed for carrying information and new knowledge to mass audiences. While technology has moved from the use of wind and water to electrical and nuclear resources, the application of the new forms of energy to world-wide enterprises has only begun. Control of the weather and management of the oceans lie in the future. While outer-space spectaculars have been achieved, the use of space for human purposes lies before us.

But these are only partial reasons for our present predicament. So far as they apply, they would seem far more of a barrier to the relationship of industrial states with the underdeveloped nations still seeking national unity and the means of modernization than to relations among the more advanced states themselves.

The nub of the problem lies elsewhere, as it has for the last hundred years. It lies in the relations among the industrial states—some more, some less advanced—who hold different views of the nature of the evolving community. These differences in turn stem from other differences regarding the origins and use of power within society, the role of science and the arts, the means of controlling production for the ends of society, and the willingness of leaders and ruling groups to make the seeming sacrifices involved in achieving world order. Specifically, for our time, the issue lies between the United States and the Soviet Union.

Yet the conditions for the growth of a sense of community seem far more ripe in the relationships of the United States, the Soviet Union, and their momentary mutual responsibility and classical intellectual mentor, Europe, than are the relationships of any of the three with the tropical or Asian borderlands inchoate and still struggling to assert their own internal sense of unity. This fact has important implications since the unity or lack of it among the advanced nations is likely to be the controlling factor in the immediate future.

To stress the essential community of the three—Europe, the Soviet Union, and the United States—may appear radical in the present context of conflict. But consider a moment, whence came the common fund of ideas now prevalent in both the United States and the Soviet Union? Where, with the possible exception of Japan and a few outposts of the British Commonwealth, has modern industrial civilization advanced so far? Where, but in these three areas—Europe, the United States, and the Soviet Union —are so large and broad a mass of men finding the opportunity for modern education? In what other area are the students in institutions of higher learning numbered in the millions, engineers in the hundreds of thousands, and scientists in the tens of thousands? Where, but among these three areas, is the overwhelming proportion of the world trade to be found? If the sense of community among these three is insufficient to permit men to find or found the associations required to keep the peace and manage the growing interaction, what then are the prospects for assimilation of China, the new giant whose people equal in number those of all three elements of what may be called, with much truth, the "Greater European Community."

Differences there are in abundance in the Greater European Community, within Old Europe as well as between the two new wings; differences not only in history, stage of development, and present outlook but, perhaps most significant of all, in the readiness to engage in new forms of association for the management of both its threatening and its promising interdependence. But these differences alone would not be the barrier they are, were they not entangled with the power and interests of the states which make up the area.

The State—Order and Development

At the heart of the problem of achieving order and progress in the Greater Community lies a confusion about the nature of the state. This confusion results from the rapid changes occurring in the life of modern nations as a result of the advance of science and technology and the paramount significance of the state as an instrument by which society accommodates and manages change and maintains order. In these times there is a constant tendency to view the state as *the* association for meeting the needs of the community rather than as *an* association, differing from others in certain critical respects, but *an* association nonetheless.

The tendency is most marked among those Communist nations that have undergone revolutionary changes in their political life but which have not yet entirely achieved the material basis of a modern society. For them, what began as a tactic has become a dogma. The tendency may also be noted among the many other nations throughout the globe which have avoided violent revolution but, while aspiring to a modern industrial society, have not yet achieved it. Even among the advanced industrial nations of the West there is considerable dispute about the proper role if not conception of the state even in internal matters. In external affairs there is an almost universal claim of sovereignty and widespread clash of interests.

All would, no doubt, admit to a threefold responsibility of the state in the spheres of order, development and, of course, security. Whether its responsibilities are exclusive or, if not, what should be their scope, are matters on which there are wide differences of opinion.

Order is highly valued in the community, at least by the old and the wise. It is well that it should be. Order is exceedingly difficult to attain, yet once it is achieved many other values may tend to overshadow it. Nevertheless, the achievement of other goals continues to depend on the maintenance of order. Order is the first business of the state. The state's responsibility for order is what makes it a very special instrumentality of the territorial community.

Historically, the state has been characterized by its ability to suppress the chaos which results when private-interest conflicts are unresolved, together with its ability to afford protection against external interference for the individuals who accept its authority. Thus, in an earlier period, absolute monarchy was accepted, with all its drawbacks, because it was better than brigandage and civil war or invasion and conquest. To illustrate, in England the state became viable when the King's Peace came to be more highly valued than the issues of private or local disputes. Hence, the origin of the *posse commitatis*. The community rallied to support the *King's sheriff*. Until there was order, many other ends of the community were impossible to achieve. Only as the state became effective in maintaining order could power give way to authority. Once order was established, diversity could gradually be accepted and the community could by degrees become more liberal and pluralistic. In this process the fluctuations were substantial and setbacks not infrequent.

In the transition from chaos to order, the role of force has frequently been significant. The community from time to time has had to choose or to acquiesce in the exercise of central force over fractional violence. The state not infrequently became operative when centrally controlled force became effective in suppressing private and local violence. But even after order has been initially achieved, the community remains an equilibrium of force. If state power is abused a revolution may occur. All states have been limited by the fear of inducing a violent reaction in the community. Yet all states continue to experience various forms of violence, some stemming from the conflict between special or local interests and others from the state's imposition of order.

Most states, of course, contain within them fractional groups or communities whose interests frequently work to limit the exercise of the power of the state. These subgroups may be geographical in character, such as the states of the union, functional, such as labor movements or manufacturers associations, or ideological, such as parties and religious groups. Not only do these subcommunities limit the power of the state to maintain order but they may, on occasion, engage in open and protracted civil war when the state is unable to maintain order. In the course of the evolution of modern states, the prevalence of civil war has been decidedly impressive, and violence has nowhere been wholly eliminated.

Thus, the evolution of the modern state may be described as follows. A central authority is established (as, for example, in the United States) or establishes itself (as, for example, absolute monarchies or the Soviet government) over a community which will tolerate it. Not infrequently, the community accepts establishment of state power because the alternative is chaos or subjection to foreign rule.

In the twentieth century, the pressures for change have been a significant factor in provoking disorder. Conversely, economic and social progress has been an increasingly important factor in establishing and maintaining order.

In a traditional society in which little change in the material conditions of life or in the range of opportunities open to the individual is occurring, order may be seen by all as the harmonious relationship of long-established elements of the community. However, beginning with the first stirrings of the industrial revolution and gaining momentum to the present time, science, technology, and enterprise have introduced an immense complication into the task of maintaining order. The achievement of order in society is less and less a question of stability of relationships and more and more a question of prudent accommodation to changes in relationships which are continually being introduced by improvements in man's ability to manage his environment for the attainment of a startling array of new purposes.

With the initial improvements of the material and social conditions of life—which seem inevitably at first to be mainly for the benefit of the few—the many, their desire and expectations increasing, lean toward valuing development or progress more than order for its own sake. Thus, the accomplishments and errors of modern states over the past hundred years may be seen as a result of their attempt or failure to make the achievement of order serve the more inclusive modern purpose of development. Men have accepted imposed order when it promised development which would improve the material and social—the human—conditions of life. When order failed to bring progress, or brought it only for the few, they were willing to disrupt it in the interests of development. The maintenance of order while seeking development has been further complicated by the unavoidable time lag involved in creating the material conditions for change. A necessity of modern order is that it compel or induce the community to invest in the future at a cost to their current satisfactions if not opportunities. Thus, development must unavoidably include a concern for intangible values as well as material resources.

Order in our day, then, depends not so much on the power to enforce acceptance of established relationships, as on the art of fostering arrangements which permit the community to obtain satisfactions from working for future achievements while still gaining adequate but not unlimited rewards in the present. Although order for its own sake may, indeed, permit the flowering of new institutions and associations which make development possible, the potential and actual scope of the changes which flow from science, technology, and enterprise make it far from certain that this will suffice.

Fortunate is the society that manages to maintain an equilibrium of interests in which the power of the state recedes and a variety of individual interests find expression, while order is maintained and development continues unimpeded. Development generates new interests, new sources of power, which tend to come into conflict with traditional centers of power. At some point the burgeoning society may erupt into civil war—either because the central authority is unable to impose restraints on traditional interests or because some new interest becomes irreconcilable and unsuppressible. Conflict within the community is a normal condition, as Hobbes and many others after him have pointed out. When the range of interest groups is relatively stable, the goal of the state in exercising its responsibility for order may simply be to maintain or to re-establish a harmonious relationship between traditional elements.

Fixation on order for its own sake is likely to produce chaos or the police state internally—and in the international sphere, war—rather than order. An Indonesia or a Congo may appear to contradict this point. The need for internal order in these traditional, even primitive, societies may seem to the onlooker or to the participant so overwhelming that thoughts of development must be abandoned. To a degree, in these cases, order for its own sake must have first call on the power of the state but even here the promise of development, of advancement, may play a significant role in gaining the acceptance of the authority of the state by key groups.

In sum, it is hardly possible any longer to find societies on the face of the earth in which the satisfaction of the aspiration for development, whether by promises or performance, does not play a part in the effective achievement of order. In the more advanced states, development normally has a predominant place in the maintenance of order with a minimum of violence. Only in the most affluent state does there appear again a tendency to stress order for its own sake—and even here more frequently in foreign relations than in domestic affairs.

Order, meaning the absence of chaos, may have made the development of a high level of civilization possible within the industrialized states, but science, technology, and enterprise, positively supported by the state, brought it about. In turning to the external relations of states, we will be well advised not to confuse the necessary condition with the sufficient conditions of order—or, as it is more widely spoken of, world peace.

East-West Relations—Order and Development

A vast array of American leaders from Edward Teller through Dean Acheson to Walt W. Rostow and many others of more extreme political views have pointed in one way or another to the importance of development for the maintenance of order in the free world.[16] While there is no doubt that development within the underdeveloped lands and within the West will make a contribution to world order, it is equally apparent that action which is concerned entirely with the free world can cope with the major source of disorder—the East-West conflict—only indirectly and probably marginally.

The gravest threat, not only to the uncertain world order that

[16] See Edward Teller and Allen Brown, *The Legacy of Hiroshima* (New York: Doubleday and Company, 1962); Dean Acheson, *Power and Diplomacy* (Cambridge, Mass.: Harvard University Press, 1956); and Walt W. Rostow, *Stages of Economic Growth* (Cambridge, England: Cambridge University Press, 1960).

presently persists but to national security and internal order of the two great powers, is the nuclear forces each possesses, now poised for launching against the other. Any form of order may be preferable to chaos, but a nuclear war should it occur would be the surest guarantee of chaos no matter which side first picked itself up from the nuclear dust. Moreover, even if nuclear war is avoided for the time being, the behavior required of each side in "solving" intermittent crises by relying on force, or the threat of force, or by accommodating or retracting only when it finds that its force is inadequate, is both highly dangerous and not in the long run conducive to the growing need for order.

So immense is the difficulty, clearly perceived by prudent statesmen, of maintaining any human order that their wisdom is frequently measured by the degree to which they cherish and strengthen whatever minimum of order exists at the moment. Thus, when there is an absence of major violent conflict in the international system, they are likely to be reasonably satisfied with the existing state of affairs. Wars of liberation or counter-revolution may be accepted as unavoidable disturbances within an otherwise reasonable degree of order.

A certain pessimism about the possibility of avoiding war is warranted. Wars have occurred as a clash of dynamic and *status quo* states, as an outcome of a clash of interests of similar states, or when one state misjudged its power, as well as in many other circumstances. But optimism about avoiding war may also find its validation in history. Over long periods of time most states have found it possible to live at peace with at least some of their neighbors.

Yet with respect to internal order, communities the world over have found it necessary to provide or accept the state's responsibility and generally to place in its hands a near monopoly of force for this purpose. In addition, as states have developed or adopted the elements of Western civilization, they have gradually learned that, despite an apparent monopoly of force, order was best maintained when it served the goal of development, broadly conceived.

In the international arena a monopoly of force seems unlikely to be achieved in the near future. Such order as exists in the East-West confrontation rests largely and precariously on mutual deterrence based on strategic nuclear forces and, in lesser degree, on limited war capabilities. Since, in internal affairs, order which serves the development of the capabilities of the nation and the individual has proved most effective in avoiding chaos and violence; since both the United States and the Soviet Union now advocate, and in some degree implement, policies which rely on development as a means of preserving order within their bloc or association of nations, one may ask whether increased emphasis on their mutual development would not serve their interest in maintaining order—that is, ensuring their security and avoiding nuclear war. If order which seeks to serve the goal of development is fruitful and important within the nation, the bloc, and the alliance, is it less essential in providing a stable relationship at the center of the world conflict in the confrontation of the two great powers?

A prudent man may ask, Is it possible to generate at the center of the world conflict—which has no operational center—the prerequisites of order which permit the commitment to development? Admittedly, it may be a close decision. In place of the formal and legitimate center of authority found in the established state, there exists only the precarious brutal order imposed by the threat of mutual nuclear annihilation in the international system. Men have sought order to end chaos, but the chaos of nuclear war, if it should occur, may be sudden and complete. Men have also found unity in the face of direct and visible common danger, but nuclear weapons remain remote and silent until the moment of use. Today the prerequisites of order depend in remarkable degree on man's higher faculties, the ability to foresee the consequences of a nuclear exchange and to draw the lessons in advance. The leadership of the nuclear powers, given an opportunity to learn their job, have an advantage in this regard; the facts, the figures, and above all the possibility of having to face a decision to use nuclear weapons, help to drive home the mutual danger and to move them toward a common view of the threat to the world.

But what is true of the leadership in power never seems to be quite so true of their internal opponents. The opponents are at once deeply dependent on the prudence of the leadership and rebellious against it. Almost always, it seems, they believe the leadership could do better by being bolder, more aggressive, more imaginative.

For this reason a common commitment to development may be a prerequisite to continuation of even a modicum of order in the international system. Such a commitment or its absence will also have much to do with determining who will lead—the designated leaders or their opponents. If the leadership on both sides seek out forms of enterprise and common action which engage the minds and lives of their citizens, the promise of a better future will strengthen support for their leadership. If they do not, their opponents without the burden of the deadly responsibility for nuclear weapons will be able to claim that they could do more by acting in bolder fashion—with the continuing risk that their claims will be believed.

Moreover, the salient characteristic of development in the present period—larger opportunities for both sides rather than redistribution of a pie of constant size—strengthens the motive for using the nuclear order of the moment to pursue development which will provide a more stable basis for order in the future.

The commitment to development must in the end include both common enterprises in the international sphere and a reasonable concern for the internal health of the antagonist's economy and society. The Soviet Union has begun to show interest in the prosperity of the West, but the contribution of Western economic progress to stability and thus to the security of the Soviet Union has not been fully accepted. Conversely, many political writers in the West have observed that a state may be tempted to engage in external adventure when this serves to sublimate internal discord, that is, to reinforce the goal of order and conformance internally. Yet the Western attitude toward the economic progress of the Soviet Union remains ambiguous.

To the extent that internal development contributes to order and to the degree that the existence of internal order reduces the temptation of external adventure, each side has an interest in the orderly development of the other. Not that a commitment to development will eliminate all conflict; differences will continue to arise over the kinds and rate of development and the distribution of the fruits of growth. But as new opportunities continue to expand, as the range of choice is increased, the recognition will grow that order which emerges from development is the opposite of the order of some traditional societies in which one man's gain is another's loss.

A widespread aspiration for unity exists in today's world. The means are at hand for advancing toward the goal. The maintenance of order and the growth of a sense of solidarity are both essential to the life of the world community. Development which provides new opportunities for common action serves both order and solidarity. Along this road lies unity. There are, however, many obstacles to be overcome.

3 Barriers to the Control of Conflict

"Interdependence is the only alternative to a world that destroys itself."

SIR ALEC DOUGLAS-HOME

Environment of the International System

AMONG some men of all states there is a lack of humility which leads them to believe that they have discerned the absolute answers provided by natural law, revelation, or by history. There is also a common drive of men for consistency or, perhaps more accurately, simplicity in their world outlook. While barriers to the control of conflict may stem from such human attributes, they also arise from the complex interactions of larger social systems which men have created.

A strategy of interdependence does not provide an automatic guarantee against war between states. No strategy can do that any more than a democratic state can guarantee against the rise of a tyrant. Vigilance and wisdom are needed to maintain peace and freedom abroad as well as at home. Yet the tragedy which befell Germany and France in the first half of the twentieth century need not be repeated with the United States and the Soviet Union in the second half.

The prospect that the United States and the Soviet Union may avoid a repetition of the earlier European tragedy rests on four factors in their relationship. First, the power of nuclear weapons which both now have in abundance. Second, the geometric increase in the potentiality of science and technology to improve man's welfare and to link societies together in common tasks. Third, the present American posture in the international system which combines industrial superiority with a desire for stability. Fourth, the gradual growth in comprehension of leaders, especially in the United States, that stable relations between nations involve interaction and integration and that the fostering and management of this process is their principal task in the international system. There is in short a discernible increase in sophistication in the understanding of conflict control.

Yet while general war may be avoided, the outcome is by no means certain. The use of nuclear weapons in a general war would result in hundreds of millions of casualties. Nevertheless, such a war is conceivable. Some powerful voices on both sides continue to argue that since such a war is conceivable, the survivors—even though they may envy the dead—can and must be prepared to pick themselves up from the nuclear dust and continue to seek to prevail. Nuclear war is after all manageable, they suggest. Others hold out the hope that if sufficient resources are invested in weapons development, the megafold discontinuity in warfare may somehow be overcome. Clearly, if one side makes such an investment, the other must attempt to match it. But the interests of both will be served by the continuation of the restraint on the conduct of general war which has been imposed by nuclear weapons. Several kinds of restraint will still be required.

While the United States and the Soviet Union have attained

their superpower states in roughly the same period, the United States has maintained a lead in the development of nuclear weapons systems. The traditional response to weapons superiority has suggested to some the idea of supremacy. A more considered view is that the nature of these new weapons is such as to deny rational use for that end. Yet, the nature of man does not necessarily preclude their use. Bismarck saw the need for Germany to exercise restraint in seeking to achieve its aims, but those who followed him were not so clear-sighted. An absence of a restraint today can bring the world to the brink of catastrophe, but the consequence of the use of nuclear weapons is borne in on even the rashest of statesmen and works to hold him back. This was not true of the pre-World War I weapons which had been used on many occasions without vast harm to society.

The political and social consequences of general nuclear war must never be allowed to sink from sight. Here the lesson of history is relevant. One of the factors contributing to World War I was that in 1914 few grasped the nature of modern war. Everyone thought that war could be fitted within the existing framework of civilization as earlier wars had been. Judgments may differ as to what will survive in event of general nuclear war, but civilization with its present freedom, variety, and richness is an unlikely candidate.

Nor can the view be accepted that the simple avoidance of general war is a sufficient goal of strategy over the longer run. Here again the experience of Europe before World War I bears witness. The tendency of statesmen and their people to believe that because one or another crisis has been surmounted by a show of strength or by the limited use of national force all other crises can be handled in the same way must be resisted. Standing up to the Communists is necessary, but to neglect the circumstances of each particular encounter is to court disaster. The support of all counter-revolutions is no more sanctioned by justice or prudence than is the support of all revolutions. Limited wars today, as in the instance of the Balkan wars before 1914, may teach a false lesson. Conflict may escalate now as it did then. Moreover, the history of the twentieth century suggests that reliance on arms alone gives no assurance of maintaining the peace. The arms buildup which preceded World War I is capable of being repeated again with no certain prospect of a different outcome and with the promise of a far more deadly one.

The restraint imposed by nuclear weapons is reinforced by the opportunities being opened through science and technology for intercontinental integration of the endeavors of mankind. Today the numbers of scientists and engineers have increased a hundred-fold over the period in which the conflicts of World War I were being generated. Whereas the task of technology in the earlier period was to meet basic human needs in Europe and to provide the means of unifying the nation-state, it is now opening the possibility of controlling man's environment on a world scale.

Basic industries like steel, whose expansion represented one of the major European undertakings of the prewar period, have now reached the point where they can easily meet all the requirements of the advanced states and the foreseeable requirements of those still lacking an industrial base. The psychology of scarcity, which was well founded in previous times, is being gradually replaced by an understanding of the present potentialities for abundance. The shift of the population from agriculture to industry and from rural to urban areas continues apace. A common metropolitan culture is emerging on a world scale, but especially in those states which are furthest advanced into the industrial age.

At the same time the immense contribution of science conducted on a world scale is gradually becoming more widely perceived. The International Geophysical Year demonstrated the value of world-wide coordinated observation and reporting. Similar activities for exploring the ocean's secrets, for predicting and ultimately controlling the weather, for penetrating the earth's mantle, for investigating the Antarctic, are under way and many more have been conceived. But it is not only the world-wide efforts to understand and ultimately to control man's natural environment that are significant. Man as a world inhabitant will come to be understood. A world biological study period has been launched. Beyond that lie the expanding efforts in many countries to broaden and deepen the understanding of man himself as an individual and as a social creature. We now believe—*know* is hardly too strong a term—that substantial investments on a world scale in each of these areas, as well as in fields of more immediate interest to society such as communications and transportation, can produce results of great benefit to man—both in meeting his needs and in resolving his conflicts. Despite these prospects it would be wrong to suggest that the consequences of the world-wide activities of science and the enterprises of technology which it spawns are automatically benign. A world-wide communication system, for example, may seek to divide and differentiate men as well as to integrate their goals and purposes. Here the perception and intention of states and other international actors play a major role.

In the nineteenth century commercial and financial relations

among the peoples of Europe increased substantially, but interdependence as a conscious state policy was nowhere steadily ad-
hered to. The industrial class was on the rise, but a dispropor-
tionate share of state power remained in the hands of traditional
groups. Force continued to be thought of as the primary means of
expanding the influence of a state. In the first half of the nineteenth century France sought by force to assert its right to supremacy on the continent of Europe. The prospects of French
success in this endeavor may be seen in retrospect to have passed
their zenith shortly after mid-century. For a time in the second
half of the century the peaceful integration of Germany into an
interdependent European society might have been possible if
capabilities comparable to those of the present had been available
and statesmen had been less satisfied with balance-of-power
policies.

Soon, however, the modern capabilities of Germany began to
outdistance those of France. The growing power of Germany was
reflected in the rapidly developing concentration of population in
the urban areas. By the end of the first decade of the twentieth
century, with sixty per cent of its population in urban areas and a
strong industrial base, Germany had a choice of spreading its
influence by peaceful means or seeking to dominate by force. Out
of Germany's interaction with the other European nations of the
time its search for a place in the sun became a pursuit of supremacy—ultimately by force. In the end, the balance of power
was shattered, but supremacy by force was denied to Germany as
it had been to France.

Today the United States has a superiority in means of influence
in the world *vis-à-vis* the Soviet Union, which may be compared

with that which Germany enjoyed in relation to France in the prewar period. United States superiority is not a new development. The shift of the American population from predominantly rural to predominantly urban long antedated that of the Soviet Union. By 1920 the United States was more than fifty per cent urban and the trend has continued. The Soviet Union has also gradually become a highly industrialized state. However, not until the late 1950s was more than fifty per cent of its population to be found in urban centers. At the present time the United States has an advanced and integrated economy capable of generating the resources for both a high level of internal welfare and a high level of national power, while the Soviet Union continues to find it difficult to meet all its requirements for both national power and welfare.

Since the United States already has a primary role in world affairs, it has no need to seek a place in the sun. It seeks stability while accepting change and supporting progress. But equally significant, since the power of the United States is paramount, it has an opportunity to play a leading role in the integration of the rising capacity of the Soviet Union into the modern world. The decade or two ahead may provide an unique opportunity in this respect. The discontinuity in warfare introduced by nuclear weapons compels the choice of an integrative policy. Science and technology provide a vast array of means which were unavailable in such abundance in an earlier period. The knowledge to ensure sound and growing economies which increasingly meet the needs and desires of the people, and with which to avoid some late twentieth-century version of Hitler is available. Germany's fatal choice may be avoided.

Yet, while the decision to seek to maintain its influence through integrative measures lies first of all with the United States, it is one which must be increasingly shared by the Soviet Union and others. If, as is its inclination, the United States chooses cooperation and nonviolent forms of competition, there remains a question whether the Soviet Union will do the same. The outlook for Soviet behavior is cloudy. The future is obscured by the deficiency of consent in the Soviet system. The Soviet Union, while it has achieved great industrial power, is still in midpassage in becoming an advanced state in all respects. The point at which the goal of production becomes civilized by the higher objective of seeking to meet the infinite variety of men's desires has not yet been reached. Moreover, a confusing ideology continues at times to mesmerize the ruling elite.

In both the Soviet Union and the United States a more widespread and profound understanding of the nature of action and thus of interstate relations in the international system will be required. Fortunately, there are signs, however limited, that an appreciation of the true nature and scope of the interactions determining the issue of peace or war is growing. The citing of a single cause—whether Communism or capitalism—to explain the conflict is becoming less credible to citizens on both sides. Recognition of the consequences of undirected interaction has led to an emphasis on peaceful coexistence and has constrained the cold war. Evidence that the two giants may come to appreciate that they are involved in a single process of differentiation and integration is suggested by the steady search for common interests beyond mere survival.

Yet many problems remain to be dealt with. Let us now turn to examine some of the obstacles which the United States must continue to take into account. In the following sections, salient and important aspects of the present environment are examined. They include: (1) developments in Soviet society, (2) Communist ideology and Communist power, (3) preclusive versions of world unity, (4) the United States policies of containment, (5) the dilemma of permanent military supremacy and the problem of superiority, and (6) crises and the balance of terror. The final section provides the transition to the program of common action.

Developments in Soviet Society

Societies in the early stages of a revolution, in seeking to bring order out of chaos, have not infrequently abdicated or submitted to the state's assertion of near exclusive responsibility for order. In these circumstances the order derived from law may give way to order induced by terror. Not only the regulation of outward behavior required for the tranquility of society, but common standards of virtue, as well, become the state's concern.[1] In these circumstances the state may even become the judge of who is sufficiently virtuous to wear a mustache, as in the French Revolution, or a beard, as in a more recent revolt. Among the states of Greater Europe, the Soviet Union bears the largest continuing burden of the confusion of private virtue with public order. However, in the Soviet Union, as the revolution has receded into the past, the tendency of the state to be accepted as administrator and judge of private virtue has ebbed.[2]

[1] Crane Brinton, *Anatomy of Revolution* (New York: Random House, 1960), p. 190.

[2] For example, the inner life of the family has become increasingly immune to the arbitrary intrusion of state organs. Indeed, despite a continuing desire to

Within a society, as development provides wider opportunities for choice by the people, it contributes to the maintenance of order. But the demand for an excessive rate of material growth on the part of those who control the state may lead to the need for increased coercion and intervention to maintain order. Only when sufficient development has been achieved to serve the objectives of the elite and to provide increasing fruits of the process to the people at large can the control be relaxed.[3]

In the Soviet Union, the drive for development continues, although its objectives are broadening to take somewhat greater account of the current requirements of the Soviet people. Indeed, an industrial base has been created which year by year could significantly enhance the well-being of the Soviet people, even while permitting the base to expand, were it not for the continuing and growing requirements for security and competition with the West.

Thus it is, that as the objective of security impinges on the need for order, the extension of the Soviet state is most apparent. Security, since the Soviet leaders do not yet feel that it has been

---

draw women into the economy, it may be fairly said that the family has become, as it were, a Soviet institution, a stable force pointed to with some pride—a sharp contrast with the early days of the Soviet state. The role of the secret police has indisputably been curtailed and many of its activities subjected to the accountability of "socialist legality." True, emphasis on the creation of the "new Soviet man" has increased, but even here the emphasis is on the persuasive influence of environment and training in inducing the new morality rather than on the direct coercive intervention of the state.

[3] So urgent was the desire for development of the industrial and military base in the Soviet Union under Stalin, that the state—whatever its form—would have inclined toward intervention in a myriad of ways in the life of the individual. Since the urgent desire for development was accompanied by an outlook that set no limits on the role of the state, intervention went beyond that previously experienced by other states in the process of industrialization. The history of development in the Soviet Union has left its legacy to the present.

achieved and perhaps believe that it cannot be attained until the world-wide triumph of Communism, appears to continue to demand both vigilance and control over their people.[4]

When a community has been rent by revolution and the revolutionaries come to power, their interest in order and, particularly, a new system of order, is likely to be intense. At such times the public attribute of lawfulness and the private attribute of virtuousness are likely to be assimilated as an area of state action. Similarly, when development of the material basis of society is a most urgent national task, frugality is a national asset and wanton wastefulness a public offense or, if property is the possession of the state, a crime. While state interference to ensure order and development has a tendency to be limited by the influence of the national community, the requirements of external security have no such built-in corrective.

The consequence of forty years of Communist rule in the Soviet Union, it appears, has been to increase the richness and complexity of the community life and the prosperity and well-being of the

---

[4] The direct and indirect intervention of the state on the occasions of potential contact of Soviet citizens with foreigners has two origins. The first is derived from a continuing sense of doubt about the reliability of its own citizens—in short a concern with domestic order. The "nationalities question" has posed a continuing problem for the Soviet state and was compounded by the annexations following World War II. The Soviet Union, while dominated by the Russians, is composed of a complex of nationalities including conquered and potentially rebellious peoples. The degree of central authority which has been maintained reflects this fact. However, when and if the legitimacy of the Soviet state becomes accepted by the citizens, its intervention on this ground to ensure the respect of its citizens may be allowed gradually to disappear. The second, which derives from the conflict of the Soviet state with other states, and particularly with the United States—in short the fear and anxiey which stem from a concern with the security of the Soviet Union—may be expected to continue as long as that security in the opinion of state officials remains threatened.

people, while the fundamental values of the society remained relatively constant. It is, perhaps, too soon to estimate where the growing complexity of Soviet life will lead. Already, one may conjecture, it is manifest in the efforts of the state apparatus to decentralize, in the emphasis on regionalism, and in the separation of agricultural from industrial development. But these are only beginnings, and for good cause, since the period of general affluence, if it arrives, is still in the future.

If other industrial states are to be taken as a precedent, the growing complexity of society will also produce a need for a flowering of new forms of association to give scope and meaning to the new potentialities. Science and the arts are already demonstrating some of the attributes of semi-autonomous association found in a free and modern society. Yet, at each step in the struggle to a new level of social integration reflecting the new conditions of life, resistance from established institutions may be anticipated. In a totalitarian state as this process continues, widespread internal violence cannot be precluded, nor can external adventure. Two illustrations will serve to indicate the continuing problem of order in Soviet society and its implications for the West.

Succession Question. The Soviet Union has made such dramatic progress as a great power that the lack of certain elemental attributes of internal integration may occasionally be overlooked. The most startling is the absence of an accepted constitutional and procedural method for selecting a head of government and ensuring a "safe" term in office. Even among the Communist Party elite, who have a growing stake in order and stability, there is as yet no apparent consensus on how this should be accomplished.

While there has been a widespread revulsion against the bloody purges and "cult of the individual" of the Stalin era, power appears to continue to reflect successful conspiracy—conspiracy no less, though it may be more creative and less coercive.

Today no Soviet statesman has tenure of office for a specified period, no legitimate procedure exists for succession, and tenure is dependent on skill in the accumulation and exercise of power.

While it seems to follow from the absence of constitutional guarantees of tenure that the first call on the power of the Soviet ruler is to maintain his position against possible coalitions of conspirators, the task may sometimes be overestimated. In the absence of really critical failures of the regime, the very lack of established methods of succession may create a common interest in maintaining the *status quo*. The uncertain consequences of change in considerable degree may offset the inclination to conspire. Still, a wholly legitimate succession has yet to take place and Khrushchev's experience must surely sustain the view that constant vigilance is required lest an opposition combine to displace him. Indeed, many of his actions may be read as efforts to broaden and especially to diversify the base of his power.

The next succession will be of great significance not only for the Soviet people but for the West as well. It may well display the degree to which the desire for an orderly and peaceful change in Soviet leadership is a real and growing common interest at least of the Soviet elite. Concern for legitimacy among the new class is an important sign of concern for the sentiments of the community —however limited and inarticulate. For the West, the consequences of the Soviet achievement of orderly succession at some future date remain ambiguous. Establishment of a community of

interest among the elite will reduce in some degree the requirements for the accumulation and maintenance of power at the
center. The government may thus be freer either to meet the demands of the people or to place new demands upon them, to collaborate or to compete with the West. Stability and predictability
may be enhanced—the direction of effort will depend on the tasks
and opportunities at the time.

Resource Allocations. Annually in the Soviet system there is an
effort—a struggle—to increase the resources available to the Soviet
citizen, as a consumer. While the results of the annual argument
over allocations to consumption as against heavy industry and
military requirements may be meager in the eyes of the West, the
importance of the central issue is beyond dispute. Paralleling the
controversies over allocation of resources are the continuous attempts to improve administration through decentralization and
reorganization.

An increase in resources available to consumers and the decentralization of the management of the means of production will
have mixed implications for the exercise of Soviet power. As life
improves, the people will have increased regard for the state as a
legitimate instrument for development. Indeed, this is already reported to be in evidence as a result of the improvements in the
standard of living to date. National sentiments will be strengthened. At the same time a web of dependence is created between
state and society as differentiation grows and the variety of investment widens. Decentralization may break production bottlenecks
by freeing initiative but, at the same time, it creates new and
diverse centers of interest. The power of the nation may be increased but the ability of the regime to exercise power against the

interests of the community becomes more difficult and complex.

Whether a more affluent Soviet society will be more or less dangerous than the present one depends to a significant degree upon its experience with the outside world in the intervening years. The satisfaction the Soviet people find in their external relations depends in the first instance on them, but the West also has choices in shaping this future. Western policy can seek to delay and disrupt the development of affluence in the Soviet Union on the grounds that economic growth will strengthen Soviet power. On the other hand, the West can choose to act in ways which will minimize disruption or even assist in the development of Soviet society.

Communist Ideology and Communist Power

Grave doubts remain in the West about the role of faith and the place of force in the outlook of the Soviet state—internally, in the bloc, and with respect to the free world. What about the claims of Communist ideology? Will the continual search for expansion ever cease? Is Communist political faith open to rational political controversy? Is a prudent search for mutual security possible? The cues from recent events and pronouncements provide only half an answer. War between capitalism and the socialist camp is no longer seen by Communist doctrine as inevitable in the nuclear age. Coexistence is possible, they assert. But is there evidence of a growing appreciation of the need for a change in outlook on both sides which would permit the emergence of a sense of solidarity essential to world order?

Communist ideology in the Soviet Union contains an important element of utopianism.[5] Its emphasis on man's ability to modify his environment derives, of course, from the long-prevailing belief in Western civilization in the inevitability of progress and the gradual perfection of human society. Out-of-power Communist movements have often emphasized change and revolution. In power, their steady tendency has been to stress internal evolutionary progress bordering on conservatism—though conservation of Communist gains. The role of ideology similarly shifts. Out of power, it is a lever for arousing the masses to action and for setting priorities of the radical elite. In power, ideology tends to become a ritual for maintaining conformity, although efforts continue to use it to mold opinion in support of the regime. In both cases it provides one means for reinforcing group unity.

Many tenets of early Communist ideology have undergone a radical transformation in content in the years the Communists have exercised power in the Soviet Union. The utopia of the aspiring revolutionary can never fit the manifold tasks and complex experiences involved in running a nation—particularly a large and heterogeneous one. Attempts to fit life into a utopian mold are bound to create conflict and in the end must be abandoned if progress is to continue. The history of the Soviet Union in the last forty years may be viewed in one perspective as a constant tug between utopia and experience. Experience is gradually winning out, but the pace of change is not all forward, nor has it occurred in all sectors of thought and action at the same rate. Internally, where experience—success and failure—serves as a daily check on reality, the decline of the vitality of ideology is most marked.

[5] Karl Mannheim, *Ideology and Utopia: An Introduction to the Sociology of Knowledge,* trans., Louis Wirth and Edward Shils (New York: Harcourt, Brace and Company, 1936), pp. 239–247.

Decline in ideology is related to the fact that the questions facing Soviet society are no longer so much questions of either-or as of more-or-less. On these issues the advice of the expert is as likely to be useful as the voice of the agitator. To counteract the decline of ideology the party organization has been given assignments and resources not only to reinvigorate ideology within the party but to carry its efforts to the broad masses of the people. Organizational effort and indoctrination are designed to maintain an intense purposefulness in the party and the people. Yet organizational effort, while it may have a certain success, seems unlikely to prove an adequate substitute for a system of ideas—an ideology which captures the mind and moves to action.[6]

While Communist dogma and the Soviet state remain at present opposed to the emergence of autonomous associations, the growing complexity of the society suggests the possibility of their eventual emergence. In the years immediately ahead, continuing tension seems likely as one group after another seeks to assert its freedom to pursue specialized goals as well as to influence the outlook of the party and state apparatus.[7]

Diversity and diffusion of responsibility are the antithesis of

[6] Zbigniew K. Brzezinski, *Ideology and Power in Soviet Politics* (New York: Frederick A. Praeger, 1962).

[7] For example, cybernetics, in the Soviet Union, may be viewed in one perspective as a scientific approach to the establishment of harmonious relations between various subgroups and diverse interests in Soviet society. While conforming to the broad Communist goals for the "good society," it substitutes philosophical speculation about values, mathematical-systems theory, empirical investigations, and man-machine engineering for dogma. While its ultimate achievements may be long delayed, the undermining of dogma seems likely to remain a continuing tendency. At the same time, for some in the Soviet Union cybernetics may be of special interest because it seems to promise more effective means of planning and control.

Communist ideology, in contrast with the partial and complex belief-systems prevailing in the West. In order to be effective such an ideology must simplify experience, establish a claim to truth, and lead to a commitment to action.[8] Experience, when some progress is achieved, underlines the unevenness of change in directions desired, the complex and uncertain consequences of action— in short, the complexity of man and nature. Though the motive for action may remain, it cannot help losing, as in the case of Christianity and Islam, some of its religious and proselyting fervor. Religious fervor without the promise of life after death must face the test on earth. Modern communications permit comparison of the ideal and real, virtually on a daily basis. The decline in fervor, which required centuries for Islam, may be occurring in decades with Communism.

Responsibility in the exercise of earthly power, while it may confirm the need for commitment and action, reinforces both the value of being cautiously pragmatic in seeking further gains and the need to conserve hard-won achievements.

The Communist Bloc. The solidarity of the Communist bloc has a high priority for Soviet interest and power, but the very success of the Soviet Union in imposing its system on other areas, as well as the rise of Communist China, has fragmented ideology.

While at first expansion gave new vigor to Soviet ideology, the longer-run consequences have been to diffuse and complicate it. The different stages of development of the various Communist states have produced different problems requiring solutions which could not always be equated with the Soviet experience. In some

[8] Daniel Bell, *The End of Ideology* (New York: The Free Press of Glencoe, 1960), p. 372.

of the countries the background and environment for the growth of the Communist movement has also encouraged an outlook as similar to Western socialist movements as to the Russian experience. Communists in these areas have in several instances tended to move away from the simplifications of Soviet ideology and to view the problem of social change not in either-or categories but as a continuous world-wide process requiring a gradual and continual transformation of social consciousness.

The splintering of ideology reflected in the competition of Moscow and Peiping, in Poland's European outlook, and in other ways, presents some of the same problems faced by Christianity in its missionary work. The doctrine of the "various roads to socialism," which seeks to rationalize these differences, lies along the path to increasing diversity within the bloc. When national differences and local differences are sufficiently accommodated in doctrine, the door is open to long-run differences in outcome.

Thus in terms of ideology as well as power it is important to distinguish, within the bloc, the place of the Eastern European satellites from that of Communist China. The satellites are as much European as Communist societies. They may be viewed as the eastern end of a European bridge between the Soviet Union and the United States. Communist China, on the other hand, gives rise to a different kind of bond between the two great powers. China represents the nearest thing to a potential common aggressor presently found on the face of the earth. China's potentiality for this role seems likely to increase, however unevenly. With a population equal to that of the Soviet Union, Europe, and the United States combined, the only thing it lacks is an industrial base. In time and at great cost, this can be provided by its own efforts.

At present China represents an imperfect asset from the viewpoint of Soviet power. Chinese efforts to influence or "capture" Communist movements throughout the world must be countered or offset. Chinese potential for endangering or involving the Soviet Union in a war in the Far East must be kept in check— although occasions are conceivable when such conflict might appear to Soviet advantage. It is in the longer run, however, that China represents the greatest threat to the Soviet Union.

While for the Soviet Union a Communist China is preferable to a China associated with the West, an unlikely contingency so long as China aspires to the leadership of the Communist movement, in the long run adequate means for the containment of China may become more important than the particular cast of government. Thus the Soviet Union and the United States may, if they are prudent, find it desirable to develop their common interest in the restraint of China. Only on this basis does it appear feasible to find ways of peacefully integrating China into the modern world even in the very long run. For the Soviet Union to be faced with the task alone is to court disaster.

In Eastern Europe the situation is radically different. The Soviet Union has a vital interest in maintaining friendly governments in these areas, but no single state or combination is likely to represent a major threat to the Soviets. Since possible defection to the West must be prevented, the threat of unrest among the people must be dealt with. The power of the Soviet state may be adequate for this task, but constructive policies which permit economic and social progress and participation in the growth of Europe will be most effective.

Eastern Europe provides an important catalyst for the modification of Soviet opinion and behavior. These countries also provide a modest counterweight within the bloc to the competitive and militant policy sought by Communist China. At the same time the desire and need of these nations for greater freedom in the pursuit of their own social and economic policies may lead, as in the case of Poland, to a decentralization of Soviet control which contributes to the experience necessary if the Soviets are ever to participate in the creation of a Greater European Community, let alone a world community.

While a strong and coherent Western European community is in the American interest, one which seriously reduces and curtails transactions with Eastern Europe may not be. Berlin is a thorn in the side of the Soviet Union, but it could also be a dangerously short fuse which could set off a general war. Berlin is symbolic of the United States commitment to prevent an unfavorable resolution of the German question, the issue of Germany itself, and many of the weaknesses in the European community and also of the present lack of community in the world's great industrial complex extending from the Urals to the American heartland and beyond. Final settlement of Berlin may well turn out to be impossible without the development of common sentiments and interests which assign the issue the modest place in the scheme of things that it deserves and would then be seen to have. Attempts at settlement of the future of Berlin may prove to be as dangerous and costly within the narrow context of Berlin, as would the problem of Cuba in the context of Cuba alone. Meanwhile, of course, opportunities for suitable adjustments in Berlin's status to minimize friction should be taken as feasible, but these are not to be mistaken by either side as a settlement or as opening the avenue to exclusive action. Finding feasible actions in Berlin is difficult and intractable because their influence on the outcome of the larger issues is uncertain.

All this is to suggest that a growing sense of community in Europe—East and West—is necessary and desirable for the control of conflict. Further, in the period ahead the creation of a community of Europe depends on the continued commitment and involvement of the two great and still in a sense psychologically remote neo-European powers—the Soviet Union and the United States.

For events to move in this direction a further loosening of Soviet exclusive control over the European satellites will be necessary. The determination is largely in the hands of the Soviet policymakers. In the field of economics continuing expansion of the freedom of trade is necessary. In foreign affairs a more viable and reassuring relationship between the United States and the Soviet Union must somehow be evolved. The Europeans, both East and West, and the United States may have a significant influence on creating the conditions for the relaxation of Soviet control. Such actions, while they may be necessary, will not be sufficient. A change in Soviet outlook and policies will also be required.

The Soviet Union in an effort to preserve the solidarity of the Communist bloc has been led to take account of the growing diversity of Soviet practice. The interests of the Soviet Union have led it to ignore or modify ideology to serve the current requirements of the Soviet state. To break the link with Soviet state interests would lessen its appeal internally, while to maintain the link may weaken its appeal abroad. The value of an ideology is that while it represents a simplified or abstract vision of reality, it is a reasonably satisfactory explanation of the trend of events, a guide to action. If the reality it must reflect is too diverse, the simplicity is lost. Yet when ideology is divorced from experience, it loses its power to guide and gain commitment to action.

In the Free World. Beyond the bloc, Soviet power is presently engaged in seeking to disrupt and impede the efforts of the United States to increase the strength and cohesion of the free world. The Soviet Union is also seeking to assert its own right to positive participation in shaping the environment of the developing areas. Two approaches are used. Everywhere the Soviet Union supports Communist parties intent on building up their strength and ultimately attaining power. In key countries as the opportunities have been presented the Soviet Union also has extended assistance to the government in power.

Among the developing areas of the free world, Soviet ideology continues to seek to play the role of a lever of social change, which it did much earlier in the Soviet Union. As a long-run threat to the West its effectiveness may be doubted, since the erosion of the vitality of the ideology at home reduces the effectiveness of its representatives in securing commitment to action abroad. As the domestic role of ideology becomes more heavily weighed in the direction of conservation of the gains of the past, its relevance to societies seeking to achieve initial and rapid modernization may decline. (Here a distinction may be drawn between Soviet ideology and the Communist ideology of Red China. The latter may continue to retain an appeal among some of the impoverished developing countries. To the extent that this is true, it will represent a challenge to the Soviet Union as well as to the West.)

As the gap widens between the Soviet Union and many more slowly developing nations, the have–have-not syndrome will undercut the direct application of Soviet ideology even when Soviet industrial organization practices may be adopted. Finally, while the twenty-year program of the Soviet Union looks forward to the advent of Communism and a decline in the role of the state, in fact, the state has been enshrined to a considerable degree as the reflection and carrier of the ideology. Resistance to an ideology identified with a foreign state in this age of nationalistic feelings is likely to be significant. A Moscow party functionary or bureaucrat when sent abroad and adequately backed with resources may foster subversion, but his effectiveness as a revolutionary leader will have some of the same limitations as political representatives of the West.

Furthermore, the emerging nations seem to have a tendency to develop a kind of nationalist ideology of their own, often parochial, frequently eclectic, taking ideas from East and West alike to weave a scheme suitable to their particular environment. Moreover, Soviet ideology seems to have been led to concede that in the stable democracies of the West some new kind of transition from the bourgeois stage to the socialist stage must be contemplated. Such a conception, as Brzezinski points out, "comes dangerously close to abandonment of Leninism." [9] But equally important, men of the underdeveloped areas claim to be building societies of a socialistic type and actually doing it through democratic and highly pragmatic means. They are using neither Soviet nor pure capitalist

[9] Brzezinski, *op. cit.*, p. 129.

methods. If they should succeed, they will not only cast new light on the processes of social change but in some degree articulate the alternative philosophies to which present evidence suggests they now tend to adhere.[10]

While the Soviet propaganda and its economic and military aid programs designed to influence the free world do not match those of the United States in terms of total expenditures, its costs are annually in the hundreds of millions. Everywhere, they are intended to enhance Soviet influence. Occasionally, a specific economic purpose may be served. However, in the strategic locations where the bulk of the resources are directed, they appear to have the specific purpose of weakening or countering the military posture of potential antagonists of the Soviet Union—particularly the United States and its allies.

Since the free world, under the leadership of the United States, is engaged in seeking to maintain and enhance its military posture, strengthen its economic foundations, and resist the advance of Communism—the result is division and conflict. The interplay of forces tends either toward a shattering of society and a polarization of the population or, where local political power remains viable, toward a society not identical with the United States or the Soviet Union. In either event the short-run consequences, at least, are not the intended ones.[11]

In a discussion of Soviet interaction with the free world, Germany deserves special mention. The Soviet view of Germany

[10] Ralph K. White, "The Cold War and the Modal Philosophy," *Journal of Conflict Resolution,* Vol. II, No. 1, March, 1958.

[11] John H. Kautsky, *Political Change in Underdeveloped Countries: Nationalism and Communism* (New York: John Wiley and Sons, Inc., 1962), pp. 57–90.

reflects a historical anxiety. Strengthening of Germany in any way is seen as evidence of hostile intentions. Twice in a generation, Germany decimated the Russian people and sought to destroy the power of the Russian state. In the face of a German threat, actual or anticipated, the Russian people and the Soviet state may be counted on to react almost as one. In the light of present German resurgence, the dead past leaps to life. Soviet interpretations of the threat from Germany are not, and cannot be expected to be, wholly rational. A powerful Germany is seen as an instrument to be turned against the Soviet Union. An alliance with Germany is always subject to being viewed as an alliance against the Soviet Union. At the same time, Germany continues to be viewed as a threat in its own right, either alone or as the dominant force in Western Europe. Germany is feared both as a catalyst of war and as an independent instrument of aggression.

Yet the Soviet Union has not been willing to join with the United States and the European nations in the creation of a viable Greater European Community, which in the long run is the only means of providing a constructive role for Germany and of protecting both sides against *revanchist* tendencies. The Soviet view of Germany's actual power at a given moment often appears colored and exaggerated by the destruction and death wrought in the past, mingled with continuing anxiety for the future. While this may be more representative of the popular view than the official one, even the latter may be affected by the memories of past danger and destruction.

To summarize, while ideology may serve to enforce conformity within the Soviet state, and while it may continue to serve as an instrument of Soviet foreign policy in developing areas, the ideology seems likely more and more to come to serve the organization rather than the organization the ideology. In short, as the ritual of a political movement, Communist ideology may have a long life and even an expansive old age, but as a vibrant religious-political abstraction it may, in many parts of the world, begin to wane.

Meanwhile, Soviet experience with the West continues to provide an inadequate corrective to the oversimplifications of ideology. The tendency of Americans to view Soviet Communism in black-and-white terms, while lessening, has not yet disappeared. The abstract images that the two societies tend to have of each other is a dangerous luxury in the nuclear age. The remoteness is aggravated by the policies of the Soviet regime which seek to maintain the isolation of the Soviet people from the complex and progressive reality of the industrial states of the West. But even here the erosion of ideology seems unavoidable. The regime cannot escape the experience of transactions with the West.

In order to accelerate the advance of the society, the new elites in science and technology require access to the science of the West. Unavoidably, they acquire more accurate knowledge of the West as well. Even among the masses, barriers increase curiosity. Despite restraints imposed by the regime, opportunities to acquire a more accurate understanding of the changing West are seized upon. Moreover, as modern communication becomes more effective, the opportunities at all levels of acquiring knowledge tend to increase in spite of the obstacles placed in the path. Perhaps it is time for the Soviet regime to reconsider at the highest levels the danger and declining value of secrecy.

The Preclusive Version of Unity

Today the Soviet Union, while a leader in asserting the need for world unity, is a major barrier to the achievement of an enlarged sense of community among the people most affected by the advance of science and technology. Communist ideology elaborated the vision, but the Soviet state is being called upon to provide the means. Yet, as we have seen, the Soviet state—from the very center of power in the Kremlin—is faced with the task of adjusting to the needs of a series of communities whose interests even at the center are more than those of the state. In essence, the adjustment called for is the displacement of policies of force by the politics of consent.

The Soviet elite's allegations about United States behavior are best understood in the light of their faulty concept of the kind of unity that is practically and conceptually possible in the modern world. The Soviet assertion that the United States opposes social progress and national independence movements throughout the less-developed areas may be seen as only in part contrived, but as more significantly a reflection of opposition to all manner of change and stability which do not accord with a particular preclusive and parochial view of the nature of world unity which may be achieved. If, as is asserted, the Soviet Union is the guardian of the historically progressive forces, United States opposition, or even dissent from Soviet views, is by definition divisive, counter-revolutionary, and regressive. Obviously, an examination of the history of the twentieth century will show that the record of the American attitude and action has been, on the whole, on the side of human freedom and progress—both in intention and in effect.

The United States can hardly be expected by the rulers in the Kremlin, as well as others, to acquiesce in revolutionary trends when only those trends which enhance the power of the Kremlin are defined as revolutionary. Many interpretations with voluminous quotations from Marx and other Communist theorists have been given for Soviet declaratory policies in this respect. A simpler and equally useful explanation suggests that the leaders of the Soviet Union, seeing the need for some kind of world unity to ensure survival and to open the way to the almost unlimited progress that science and technology now permit, are using the only model of unity with which they are familiar, with which they have experience—the Soviet state with its integral single-party apparatus.

As long as the Soviet Union seeks world unity on its terms, then, it is argued, the United States must give a high priority to the creation of a more coherent free world which will be so strong that it will resist Communist blandishments. Present United States strategy places a major emphasis on the creation of a new set of relationships with all parts of the world outside the Sino-Soviet bloc. Highest priority is given to the internal cohesion of the so-called hard core of the Western world which now includes North America, Western Europe, and Japan. The North Atlantic Treaty Organization (NATO) is to be strengthened and Western Europe fitted ever more closely into American strategy. In addition, the relationships between the northern and southern halves of the free world are to be measurably strengthened. The economic output of the southern half of the free world is to be visibly increased. The northern and southern halves of the free world are to be linked by a variety of extranational organizations. Strong national communities able to resist Communism are to be everywhere created.

But what is likely to be the course of the dangerous conflict in the intervening decades or generations? The strategy for the development of free-world strength was conceived not long after the end of World War II when the intentions of the Soviet Union became visibly threatening and when the growth in its scientific and technological capabilities was still grossly underestimated. It was also conceived before the desire of many nations on both sides of the Iron Curtain to pursue independent paths to the future was so clearly discernible as it is today. In the 1960s it has become apparent to all that there are non-Communist and non-Western nationalistic forces in nearly every nation of the underdeveloped world who seek to maintain access to the technology and support of both the West and the Soviet Union while they pursue their own unique pattern of development and growth. Europe, too, shows signs of developing its own vision of the future. Moreover, as was previously discussed, there is a growing "polycentrism" within the Soviet bloc which has had to be taken into account by the Soviet Union and which the West would also be wise to recognize. At the same time, the growing economic power of the Soviet Union, while it is still considerably inferior to that of the West, must be reckoned with on a world-wide basis.

The consequences of seeking to build an expanded free world at the same time that the Soviet Union seeks to expand the influence of Communism and Soviet power throughout the world seems at best likely to be a world-wide contest—and not one world but two, both guarded and supported by world-circling military weapons. But, as third areas seek to maintain their independence by playing one side off against the other, the result is likely to be international instability and conflict which involves the great powers and, as the preparations on each side are advanced, possibly military conflict.

Because of the emergence of powerful new forces in the world and because of the dangers inherent in the strategies presently pursued by the United States and the Soviet Union, it is arguable that it is what might be called in the West "compelling prudence" but what in the Communist lexicon would be referred to as "necessity" for both to seek to develop a new set of relationships which will broaden the basis of the restraint exercised by each in the coming period of instability, when new atomic powers will seek to assert themselves and when new nations and clusters of nations come to play a larger role on the world scene. If the Soviet Union cannot be excluded from the world and if the international system is growing more complex, then it will be in United States interest to seek to develop with the Soviet Union an understanding of their common interests and more extensive common efforts to achieve them in order that the dangers to both may be reduced.

The United States Policy of Containment

Since the end of World War II the mind of America has been divided. Containment—division of the world—has been the dominant mode of action. World unity has been a basic underlying aspiration. The troubled subconscious of America has avoided facing the dilemma of containment in the light of day.

The imperative and growing demands for military containment

have shaped national action throughout the last fifteen years. The cogent argument of urgent necessity brought acceptance of an enlarged military establishment as the key instrument of containment. Patriotism, love of country, permitted acquiescence in the increase in power of the state out of all proportion to the influence of the individual. In return the state has promised security based on military deterrence. After more than fifteen years it may be useful to ask: Who is secure? Whom does containment contain?

Through the postwar years the dream of unity, although repressed, has not died. Under the darkening shadow of vast military preparations, the United States has continued to grope toward the building of the free associations which will bring unity and a stable world on the basis of consent. Containment largely set the boundaries of these efforts and shaped their substance. They have been designed to strengthen the unity of the free world. What are the results of the search for half a unified world?

At the end of World War II, the United States envisaged the possibility of settling outstanding disputes and differences through the mechanism of the United Nations; military forces were demobilized, and the nation sat back to enjoy the peace. The illusion was swiftly shattered by the re-emergence of forces which up to this very day have governed the multistate system. Stalin, like the Czars before him, sought Soviet aggrandizement along the periphery of the Soviet land mass. Motivated by a historical fear of further invasions of Russia, by a suspicion of capitalist states, and by a desire to expand the sphere of Communist and Soviet power as a distant preliminary to achieving the goal of a Communist world, Stalin sought to extend Soviet hegemony in Europe, in the Middle East, and in the Far East. As Soviet aims came to be understood in the West, the major lines of United States policy took shape and the task of mustering means for implementing them was begun.

The most immediate threat appeared to be in Western Europe, which lay prostrate and devastated as a result of the war. The strong Communist parties which existed in a number of states were making capital out of the economic chaos. In 1948, to meet this crisis, the Marshall Plan was launched, seeking to meet the threat from within as well as to provide the basic economic strength required if Europe was again to play its role in world affairs. In 1949 NATO was created as a vehicle for bringing force to bear in Europe. United States troops were committed to the Continent, and the long task of rebuilding European military power was begun. Both the Marshall Plan and NATO had as one of their major purposes the creation of a unified Europe in which the ancient conflicts between France and Germany would be subdued and which, with United States backing, could again face the colossus to the East. During the early period the American lead in atomic weapons probably played a role in containing Soviet efforts at aggrandizement, but the need of the Soviet Union to rebuild its shattered economy seems also to have been a significant factor in its restraint.

Confronted with the evidence of United States determination to resist in Europe, Stalin turned to the Far East and fostered the last major move in the postwar period to extend Soviet power by military means over a peripheral area. Events in China and the explicit statements of United States officials that South Korea was outside the area of vital American interests seem to have stimulated Stalin's desire to extend Soviet influence in the Far East and, at the same time, lulled his instincts for avoiding risk. South Korea was invaded, and the United States promptly responded by landing military forces. The Korean experience had a powerful influence on United States policies in the succeeding years, and one may conjecture that its influence on the Soviet Union has also been significant.

The United States learned the need for a more concrete and inclusive conception of free-world unity and the necessity and cost of nuclear restraint. The policy of containment led to military pacts in the Near East and Far East. Following the Korean War, "massive retaliation," relying on the superiority of the Strategic Air Command, was briefly in vogue as a means of deterring aggression both large and small. During the middle 1950s, as Soviet nuclear power increased, the recognition of the need for American restraint grew. Attention turned to alternatives to nuclear retaliation as a response to limited aggression—but no significant action was taken.

The launching of the first Sputnik in 1957 symbolized a potential military capacity which unless matched seemed to threaten the very bastion of free-world unity. It also signaled the beginning of the argument whether both the United States and the Soviet Union could eventually have invulnerable retaliatory capability whose existence would tend to drive the conflict to lower levels of force.

The threat to the United States was most alarming. While official reports as early as 1954 had perceived the potential threat and recommended action, only after Sputnik was the need for strengthening and accelerating the development of United States nuclear forces based on missiles as well as airplanes at last fully accepted. While action to reduce the threat to the bastion of unity was taken immediately following Sputnik, adequate conventional forces to protect the unity of the free world, without provoking nuclear war, were longer in gaining support.

A dispute began within the government on the question whether conventional forces should be strengthened in order to meet limited aggression on its own terms. Although efforts were made as early as 1956 by the Department of the Army and representatives of the Department of State to give added emphasis in national security policies to the building up of conventional forces, it was not until 1958 that the log jam was broken and significant efforts to enhance the ability of the ground forces to meet local aggression on its own terms were undertaken. Despite the delay, by the end of the 1950s, considerable progress had been made in reshaping United States ground forces to make them more effective in a limited war of the scale of the Korean conflict, but much remained to be done.

When the Eisenhower Administration came into power in 1952, it had rejected the term "containment" as a description of its security policy. Containment, the term popularized by George F. Kennan, described the strategy followed by the Truman Administration and was designed to meet the foreign policy of Stalin's Russia. It advocated meeting force with force all along the periphery of the Soviet Union, thus "containing" the Soviets within the area they held at the end of World War II. Prior to taking office, the Eisenhower Administration had spoken of the "liberation" of Eastern Europe and, in the Far East, had talked of "unleashing Chiang Kai-shek." Both of these policies turned out to be merely declaratory and the Eisenhower Administration continued to follow the policy of containment throughout its term in office, although not accepting the word.

During most of the Eisenhower Administration, the United States relied mainly on its nuclear supremacy as a means of containment. The opportunity to rely on nuclear supremacy was extended beyond its natural technological life by the changes that were occurring in the Soviet Union with the leadership of Malenkov and then Khrushchev. The transition was characterized for a time both by significant changes within Russia and by restraint with respect to the outside world; however, following the launching of the first Sputnik in 1957, Soviet foreign policy took on new dimensions and new pretensions. Whereas formerly the Soviet Union had spoken of being encircled by the capitalist West, it now talked of zones of peace. Stalin's policy of peripheral aggrandizement was replaced by a new Soviet style and emphasis whose horizon was again the entire world. At the same time, recognition of the power of nuclear weapons led Khrushchev to abandon the doctrine of the inevitability of war between the Soviet Union and the West and to emphasize peaceful coexistence. The Communists did not give up the goal of a unified Communist world but gave greater emphasis to the need for restraint in attaining it. To Khrushchev, peaceful coexistence seems to connote the maintenance of substantial strategic military strength to deter attack and continuing efforts to maintain and increase Communist power and influence until finally Communism achieves world-wide predominance.

The United States response to Khrushchev's policies has been a continuing but uneven effort to build up the military force with which to resist the perceived threat of aggression by the Soviet

Union. At first this power was visualized as being used for containment; but later, as American power increased, the purpose became one of deterring Soviet aggression before it began. While building its own forces, the United States also sought to increase the strength and coherence of the free world by maintaining existing military alliances and expanding the economic organizations of the free world and by providing resources for the development and support of nations unable to go it alone.

The Eisenhower Administration also made two attempts to negotiate with the Soviet Union at the highest level, one inconclusive and one abortive. In addition there were exploratory discussions from time to time on such issues as arms control and disarmament. The gain from all of these conversations, designed as much to maintain communication as to achieve agreements, was at best modest and many argued that the consequences were negative. Nevertheless, the dialogue between the United States and the Soviet Union was maintained.

In the meantime, the Soviet Union made a remarkable recovery from its wartime devastation and became recognized by all as the second most powerful industrial nation in the world. With the growth of Soviet power, the requirements for deterrence assumed the center of the stage as the principal problem of United States politico-military policy in the last years of the Eisenhower Administration, although hope for a *détente* lasted until shortly before the U-2 incident. While the practical possibilities of the Eisenhower Administration to advance world unity ended with the incident, the dream remained strong. Even at the very end, in his farewell address, the President said, "Down the long lane of the history yet to be written America knows that this world of ours, ever growing smaller, must avoid becoming a community of dreadful fear and hate, and be, instead, a proud confederation of mutual trust and respect." [12]

When the Kennedy Administration came to power, it too was permeated by a desire to make progress toward world unity, but its concern for what it viewed as deficiencies in the implementation of the policies of containment proved at least as powerful. The Kennedy team was agitated about the "missile gap" which had been an important issue in the campaign. Of scarcely less concern was the belief that inadequate preparations had been made to cope with limited wars. Based on certain prior studies of advisory groups and on its study after taking office, a decision was made that military expenditures for both purposes must be increased in order to cope with the nuclear and conventional threat posed by the Soviet Union. While at first these steps were believed to be necessary because America must "come from behind," a number of events intervened which both underlined the importance of the effort and modified its objective.

In the first year in office, the Kennedy Administration experienced the trauma of the Bay of Pigs, Khrushchev's toughness and rigidity at Vienna, and the Soviet-East German threat to Berlin. From these and lesser events came a dawning United States conviction that to express concern about its defenses was to invite Soviet belligerence. Out of this conviction grew a new American attitude, starting in mid-1961. In his Report to the Nation on the Berlin crisis, July 25, 1961, President Kennedy announced that he

---

[12] Dwight D. Eisenhower, "Farewell Radio and Television Address to the American People," Jan. 17, 1961, *Public Papers of the Presidents—1960–61* (Washington, D.C.: U.S. Government Printing Office), p. 1039.

was sending a request to Congress for an additional 3.2 billion dollars for military expenditure in the current fiscal year, including a request to increase the authorized strength of the army to one million men, as well as for modest increases in the navy and air force. John J. McCloy, who was with Khrushchev at the time, was reported to have said that when Khrushchev "got the message" he "exploded." Sensing the impossibility of a settlement and faced with the flight of the East Germans, he responded with the Berlin wall. Later, as the crisis grew, Kennedy called up the National Guard units and took a number of other steps designed to strengthen the American position in the continuing Berlin crisis. Then came public discussion of the great "windfall," the disappearance of the "missile gap" resulting—as is widely understood —from an intelligence breakthrough. The disappearance of the "missile gap" was followed in due course by talk of supremacy as a continuing goal of United States policy.

The Dilemma of Permanent Supremacy and the Problem of Superiority

Thus, in less than two years, the United States moved from agitation about its inferiority to confidence in its present supremacy—and thence in some quarters to an insistence on the possibility and requirement for permanent supremacy. On the latter point, however, prophets were by no means unanimous and advisors did not all speak as one.

Permanent supremacy as an objective presents many difficulties. It provides no terminal point for limiting military requirements. One can hardly have enough supremacy. Pursuit of supremacy seems bound to aggravate the arms race as the adversary seeks to reduce the gap. Assessment of supremacy is difficult because of rapid technological change and the problems of intelligence collection and evaluation. Moreover, a sense of supremacy may dull the sensibility to the continuing need for restraint.

Supremacy suggests an ability to take the initiative in the use of force. Yet, in the nuclear era, supremacy must ultimately rest on strategic nuclear weapons systems. Not only their threatened use but the willingness actually to use them would be required for a major initiative. But technically supremacy does not mean and probably cannot mean the ability to knock out all the strategic nuclear weapons of the opponent. Secretary McNamara testified in early 1963 that an all-out nuclear war between the United States and the Soviet Union would result in one hundred million American fatalities. Thus a willingness to employ American supremacy in a major way would ultimately mean a willingness to commit the nation to immense destruction. While a response to aggression which would have this consequence might in some circumstance be unavoidable, for what conceivable political objective would an initiative costing a hundred million American lives be rational? If supremacy has no rational use, of what value is it?

In place of supremacy, the Kennedy Administration systematically sought to provide the United States and the West with the kind of military power at all levels, from guerrilla action to general nuclear war, required to deter any aggressive activities by the Soviet Union and, indeed, by the entire Sino-Soviet bloc. That administration built on the substantial foundations provided by the Truman and Eisenhower Administrations, both as regards weapons in being and in terms of the substantial increases in funds which had been provided for research and development. The military budget was increased by over fourteen billion dollars in two years.

At the strategic level, United States nuclear capabilities are being expanded, hardened, dispersed, and made more mobile. A substantial investment is also being made in the improvement of the command and control arrangements to permit more deliberate action in the event of conflict. These efforts have required the expenditure of four billion dollars on an annual basis over and above the twelve to fifteen billion which was being provided for strategic nuclear capabilities previously.

Substantial investments have been made in the strengthening of conventional forces. They have been reorganized, expanded, and steps have been taken to give them the capability of swifter response in the event of conflict. Again, something in the neighborhood of four billion dollars a year, over and above previous expenditure levels, is devoted to this purpose.

The improvement of United States capabilities for coping with guerrilla action has received the attention of the President and many other high officials of the administration. New resources for this purpose are thought to be approximately of an order of a billion dollars. This is a not insignificant amount in light of the fact that new tactics, techniques, and weapons would appear as important as massive resources.

The United States defense posture provided by present and past expenditures is superior to that of the opponent, we are told. Secretary McNamara has said that, while there is always a margin of error in calculating relative military strength, "the margin of error is much less than the margin of our superiority." [13] The Secretary has also pointed out that present authorizations provide for over one thousand land-based intercontinental missiles, plus over six hundred and fifty Polaris missiles in forty-one submarines, plus more than seven hundred B-52 and B-58 bombers, with a high proportion of the bombers on alert status at all times. These forces, based on conservative calculations, he has stated, will permit the United States to achieve practically complete destruction of the enemy target system even after the United States has suffered an initial nuclear attack. [14]

Generally, the present mood seems to be to view the posture of the West as one superior to the Communists, even though improvement in some elements of strength continues to be desired. At long last then, perhaps for the first time since 1954-56, the strength exists to implement the policies of containment and deterrence and to move from a position of relative strength. What then are the prospects for the future? Has stability been assured by at least relative attainment of an objective pursued since shortly after World War II?

Military forces in the present environment, unfortunately for stability, must continue to serve three purposes. First, they must deter aggression on the homeland. Second, they must deter or, if necessary, counter aggression anywhere in the world (or, as the Soviet Union would say, support "just wars of liberation"). Third, in event of general war, they must give promise that one's own side will, if not "win," at least prevail. The effect of these three

[13] Stewart Alsop, "McNamara Thinks about the Unthinkable," *Saturday Evening Post,* Dec. 1, 1962, p. 18.

[14] Robert S. McNamara at his news conference, March 15, 1962.

objectives when taken together is that military preparedness, quite apart from specific crises, has a tendency to escalate.

The fundamental factor may be the continuing determination of both sides to seek to use their military strength as an instrument in shaping the world environment in ways that are hospitable to their own view of the requirements of world order or unity.

The pure rational theory of mutual deterrence has a tendency to become fuzzy when discussed by practical men guided by practical time tested precepts.[15] From the American point of view there is a long experience with the aggressiveness of the Soviet Union. As a consequence, the United States feels that it must be prepared for the ultimate aggression. Conversely, the United States policy of nuclear or extended deterrence to defend its allies relies on the threat to strike first (i.e., respond to local aggression by intercontinental nuclear attack). Thus it is not surprising that the Kremlin feels that it must also be prepared. Mutual deterrence thus seems to require, at least under present conditions, mutual superiority since it implies the need to sustain a blow and strike back. The viewpoint, when seriously held by both sides, cannot but disturb the stability of any particular balance of terror.

While both sides may prefer to have a secure second-strike capability to not having it, a reasonable doubt remains whether either will be satisfied to stand still once it has been achieved. General

[15] Roswell L. Gilpatric, Deputy Secretary of Defense, for example, explains, "The reason we must stay ahead . . . is because we have foreclosed ourselves from the initiative in the sense that we will ever strike first." (Interview on ABC's "Issues and Answers," Jan. 21, 1961) Premier Khrushchev has said practically the same thing: "The Soviet Union will not initiate an attack, therefore, the Soviet Union must do everything possible to increase its military power." One need not doubt the veracity of either statement to note the curious and destabilizing effect of this line of reasoning when adopted by both sides.

war would be unbelievably costly. While its occurrence may be remote, the possibility that it could occur is believable. Thus, while the commitment to initiate it must be avoided, the preparations for waging it cannot wholly be neglected. Deterrence of attack depends in part on the will to use strategic forces if given no reasonable alternative. The will to use them depends on the estimate of all the consequences, including the possibility that one can prevail. If one is to prevail, superiority in some sense would seem essential. The lingering need to prevail is one of the factors that makes the limitation of forces required for a stable balance of terror, so difficult to define in terms to which both sides will adhere.

The military requirements for deterrence as well as to prevail can never be fixed in a hard-and-fast way. Intelligence myths, which have created mythical gaps in the past, cannot be wholly precluded in the future. Moreover, the continuous change in military technology, as a result of the developments of science, both pure and applied, creates a continuing apprehension that any temporary balance may be upset by future developments. Research and development must be pursued on a very broad front to preclude the possibility that the opponent will score an unmatched breakthrough. As new offensive or defensive weapons are developed, there is a steady pressure to include them in the operational arsenal. If one side begins to produce operational elements of a new weapon, even in a modest way, the opponent has no sure way of knowing either the exact capacity or the ultimate production intentions of the opponent. The best protection is normally judged to be to move to production oneself. While this need not be the course of events, the tendency of military advice is in this direction.

The need to prevail at each level of violence also contributes to the tendency of investment in military preparedness to escalate. War certainly remains a potential instrument of policy for the Soviet Union today. As a minimum they are on record as supporting wars of liberation. For the United States, as Secretary Mc-Namara said, "War has to be conceivable in support of vital national interests. Otherwise, you have no real national power." [16] War could come as a result of misjudgment of our response as a threat to our interests. It could also occur by other types of miscalculation or as an irrational act. If war could occur, so also could a general nuclear war.

The need to prevail, to reduce losses, and to emerge from the conflict with significant power represents an influence in all great defense efforts. Shelters, for example, gain much if not most of their support from the fact that war might occur and that, if it does, shelters would save some lives. Antiballistic missiles and other defenses gain support for similar reasons. Even the power of nuclear weapons will not force the nation to abandon all thought of victory, if war should be forced upon it. Thus the nice calculations of deterrence are always subject to other influences of which a significant one is the desire to prevail. When this occurs on both sides, as it is likely to over any period of time if the conflict continues unabated, the balance of terror is set a-teetering.

Finally, one must note the role of particular institutions. No invidious connotations are intended, but institutions normally exert influence in the direction of the purposes they were created to serve. When national policy relies overwhelmingly on the means provided by one institution, the role of that institution and

[16] Alsop, *op. cit.*

the industrial elements throughout the society which support it cannot but be enhanced.

Military force is the mainstay of deterrence. Thus a primary role in national policy must be played by the military elite. Their role, their influence, their prestige in national affairs is of necessity very great. Can they in good conscience be expected to be satisfied or, indeed, as the conflict grows more grave, accept mere partial preparations against the time of the possible failure of deterrence? Will they not come to feel, as Charles de Gaulle wrote:

> For them, armed power is something essential and, as it were, sacred. The ideal of their vocation is sacrifice which, by exalting the cult of patriotism, makes any thought of compromise impossible. Furthermore, the professional soldier, being in a constant state of preparedness, is only too ready to believe that war may break out at any moment. Consequently, nothing seems to him more necessary or more urgent than to accumulate the means which will make victory certain.[17]

Can we ask less, as the nations continue on their present course, than that the United States military establishment use its increasing influence to gain a posture which gives promise of "victory" if war should come? Should we expect less of the Soviet military establishment? The answer to both questions must surely be No. In the search for security the United States would do well to heed the warning of President Eisenhower, who said in his farewell address:

[17] Copyright 1960 by Criterion Books, Inc. Reprinted by permission of the publisher from *The Edge of the Sword* by Charles de Gaulle (New York: 1960), p. 110.

In the councils of government, we must guard against the acquisition of unwarranted influence, whether sought or unsought, by the military-industrial complex. The potential for the disastrous rise of misplaced power exists and will persist.

We must never let the weight of this combination endanger our liberties or democratic processes. We should take nothing for granted. Only an alert and knowledgeable citizenry can compel the proper meshing of the huge industrial and military machinery of defense with our peaceful methods and goals, so that security and liberty may prosper together.[18]

It would be in the interests of all if citizens and leaders of the Soviet Union were to heed the relevance of his words to their society, as well. Means, other than military, seem to be required if the way of life of either is to prosper for long.

Crises and the Balance of Terror

Ultimate reliance on nuclear weapons, the strongest ingredient of the balance of terror from the point of view of the state, is in terms of society its greatest weakness. Mutual deterrence may restrain the actions of states but only at the price of society's being from time to time willing to risk its existence.

The balance of terror is a product of the existing condition of the nation-state system. In this system conflicts of interest or purpose between states are presumed to exist. Force is the ultimate means for resolving conflicts of will between states. As these conflicts continue, crucial periods occur from time to time which are

[18] Dwight D. Eisenhower, *op. cit.*

commonly referred to as crises. Crises are marked by a turning point, best seen after the fact, from whence events lead on to war or more usually back toward lower levels of conflict. When crises of this nature occur, the balance of terror is believed to require that each side act rationally in order to achieve its objectives at the least cost. When purposes are clear, when information is complete, and when time is available, this is possible. Efforts on both sides to improve any of the three are therefore praiseworthy.

Unfortunately, as states confront each other the ideal cannot always be approached for any of the three. One's own purposes in nicely ordered array, let alone the perceived purposes of the antagonist, can never be entirely clear. Information is often incomplete or, when relatively complete, tardy. Slow-motion crises, while they are desirable and sometimes occur, are in a sense a contradiction of the nature of the true crisis, which is marked by a turning point that is unlikely to be of infinite duration.

Thus the balance of terror seems destined, from time to time, to be marked by crises in which action must be taken in the face of great uncertainty, resulting from the obscurity of purpose, the inadequacy of information, or from the compression of time.

Uncertainty is not the only source of potential failure of the rationality of terror. Deep-lying needs exist in men which they seek to meet. Many of these may not be effectively handled by the rationality implicit in the divided deterrent forces of the balance of terror. Killing may be a profound form of mourning for a lost existence. Sadism and masochism have been satisfying to some, even in high places. But these are extreme examples of a more fundamental point. In the behavior of all men and groups of men there are substantial elements of what for our time at least must be termed the irrational. The balance of terror with its excessive reliance on rationality seems likely sooner or later in the midst of a crisis to fail to cope with the irrational factor.

Moreover, crises have another aspect that further confounds the reliance on the balance of terror. In medicine the word "crisis" is used to denote the change in a disease which indicates whether the result is to be recovery or death. Over the centuries a great deal of knowledge about such changes has been garnered, but prognosis in some illnesses remains uncertain. On the conflict of societies possessing nuclear weapons, history is short and knowledge limited. A crisis, in the sense of a change lacking the drama of great tension but whose prognosis is war, can conceivably flow from reliance on the medication of terror and pass unnoticed until a later turning point. Then escalation which seems without purpose may happen and war without rational reason occur.

Today's balance of terror is sometimes discussed in terms of the old balance of power of the nineteenth century.[19] To cope with the tendency toward escalation in arms and escalation of crises, efforts are continually being made to provide for the balance of terror an environment comparable to that which made the balance of power workable. Power politics in the nineteenth century were facilitated by three conditions. These were: (1) a sense of common culture among diplomats, (2) the relatively limited military capabilities of the contestants, and (3) the relative passivity of the world outside Europe. Given these conditions the system worked, although it erred occasionally and failed ultimately.

Today, those who see no alternative to the balance of terror seek

[19] Arnold Wolfers, *Discord and Collaboration* (Baltimore: The Johns Hopkins Press, 1962), especially pp. 117–132.

to refurbish and adapt the earlier concept to the modern problem. Great emphasis is placed on continuing diplomatic conversations with the Soviet Union through calm and crises alike, but there is a danger that weapons may speak louder than words. To meet it, theorists urge the need for a common culture of terror which would permit the two sides to communicate more accurately, both by threat and by assurance about intentions and capabilities. Unfortunately, in the conversation of nuclear opponents, ambiguity is sometimes either necessary or unavoidable, just as it was in the old diplomatic language.

An infinite variety of suggestions have been made for limiting military capacity, not at the nineteenth-century level, of course, but at some "reasonable" level. Limited war, conventional big war, tactical nuclear war, limited strategic nuclear war, and no-city nuclear war all have their vogue—and all may, under carefully defined conditions, make their contribution to restraint. The cost if they do not is, of couse, immensely greater than that which could result from the failure of nineteenth-century diplomacy. Numerous suggestions are also made for limiting the force available to countries other than the United States and the Soviet Union. These are unlikely to come to fruition in the absence of agreement between two great powers. Even then the prospects are uncertain. The world is no longer politically passive as it was after the end of World War II. The test ban, for example, may continue to be resisted by France and China. Unfortunately for the policy of balance, the weapons are not limited and the world is not passive. Communication which ultimately relies largely on threat and counterthreat of the use of force remains prone to violence, and on a world scale. Limited agreements such as the test ban will ultimately be seen to require extensive areas of common action if the world's security is to be maintained.

The modern version of balance seeks to achieve rationality (i.e., certainty and predictability) in the threatened use of force and its employment. The common culture of terror is intended to achieve a reasonableness in the management of weapons on both sides. It concentrates attention on one element in the behavior of nations. When the times call for modification of values and the acceptance of new tasks, it promises that old habits may continue undisturbed. War still has its place, it suggests.

The difficulty with over-refined balancing of weapons is that it overestimates the fear of destruction and underestimates man's inclination to destruction. In the absence of direct experience, a people may not visualize losses wrought by war. When faced with the choice of modifying their prejudices or of having war, they may choose the latter. War serves as an outlet for both the individual and the community of which he is a part.

Those who in the absence of war are confident of their ability to manage nuclear weapons so that it may be avoided would do well to heed the words of Sigmund Freud in an exchange of letters with Albert Einstein prior to World War II. He said:

> You are amazed that it is so easy to infect men with the war-fever, and you surmise that man has in him an active instinct for hatred and destruction, amenable to such stimulations. I entirely agree with you. I believe in the existence of this instinct and have been recently at pains to study its manifestations. . . .
>
> With the least of speculative efforts we are led to conclude that this instinct functions in every living being, striving to

work its ruin and reduce life to its primal state of inert matter. Indeed, it might well be called the death-instinct. . . . The death instinct becomes an impulse to destruction when, with the aid of certain organs, it directs its action outwards, against external objects. . . .

Obviously, when this internal tendency operates on too large a scale, it is no trivial matter, rather a positively morbid state of things; whereas the diversion of the destructive impulse towards the external world must have beneficial effects. Here is, then, the biological justification for all those vile, pernicious propensities which we now are combatting. We can but own that they are really more akin to nature than our stand against them, which, in fact, remains to be accounted for.[20]

For many, war as a means of doing evil while feeling good, has no equal. War may provide excitement and adventure, contribute to social unity, free the individual from anxiety, and permit the release of aggression without guilt. At some point along the road of threat and counterthreat of the building of force and counterforce designed to achieve balance or, as it is frequently termed, deterrence, the appeal of war is capable of gathering a momentum of its own. Then the element of uncertainty which is admitted to exist in all rational calculations grows apace. Accidents are more prone to happen. Inadvertence may be misinterpreted as calculation. Aggression can be mistaken for defense, sadism for punishment and, finally, every act justified in the name of victory of the good over evil.

Yet, in the dangerous world in which we live, capacity for

[20] A. Einstein and S. Freud, "Why War," *Round Table: Emotions and World Problems,* No. 554, Oct. 31, 1948.

restraint in exercising power throughout the world, both to reduce the risk of a response which would endanger the United States and to enhance the credibility that our forces will be used, is desirable. Hence, a growing emphasis on the development of conventional capabilities backed up by tactical nuclear weapons may be necessary. Increased emphasis on countering Communist advances at the level of subversion and guerrilla action also may be valuable. Construction of a "hot line" between the White House and the Kremlin is also helpful, but all these measures are obviously means of handling the early stages of limited conflict, not ways of coping with the underlying causes.

A unique aspect of present-day crises is that no matter how inconsequential, if they involve the great powers, they are played out in the nuclear environment. A serious crisis finds possible resort to nuclear weapons frequently in the foreground. Cuba, for example, in which the United States had a variety of options, displayed many possibilities of swift escalation to the nuclear level. If a few more weeks had gone by and the missiles on Cuba had become operational, they could have dominated the subsequent events. Even the possibility of their soon being in place precipitated action. Reconnaissance flights off course, or ship captains who acted on their own, or any of a number of other elements in the crisis could have been misread and led to rapid escalation. When this possibility exists at the furthest extension of Soviet power, the infinite possibilities for crisis escalation in all the areas between may be imagined. This is not to suggest that the United States should not deal from strength, only that however resolute the initial act, it leads into the unknown and uncertain.

Each crisis of the past decade has had a sobering effect on those directly participating in the attempt to manage it. Others, not so directly involved, have not infrequently been tempted from lack of experience or the possibility of public approval to draw over-simplified conclusions. With the passage of time, it may become clearer to all that in the nuclear age any crisis involving the great powers is pregnant with the possibility of a nuclear exchange.

While there are many specific causes of the conflict between the Soviet Union and the United States, the most pervasive is the notion of the Soviet Union that unity must be Communist unity. To this notion the United States is opposed, and opposed mainly with force. In addition, the United States is becoming, under the pressure of the Communists, steadily more bent on shaping the world environment to accommodate its sole vision of the future, which though not exclusive gives only a distant place, or none at all, to the integration of the Soviet Union. Many view United States military power mainly as a means to permit their country to engage more effectively in the political struggle for the organization of world unity. The United States seeks the ability to organize the free world on its terms. The Communists have long sought to maintain a similar exclusiveness in the parts of the world which they control. The choice inherent in the promotion of exclusive visions of *communitas* was clear in Hungary and is clear today in Cuba—violence.

Military preparations, it is said, need not lead to war. The desire to deter aggression is a desire for peace. Deterrent forces are intended simply to restrain those who otherwise would impinge upon the rights and freedom of others. Were the goal of *communitas* not present in men's minds, were the advances of science and technology not making the possibility of achieving it more vivid each day, had the different visions of the goal more in common, the prospects for restraint in a sharply divided world would be better.

When an arms buildup occurs it must be either an end in itself or serve some higher purpose. The purpose of increasing United States military capabilities may be to keep the pressure on the Soviet Union. To what end? "We arm to parley," President Kennedy once stated. How is the pressure meant to work? One may ask if Communist states, because of their ambitions and because they are states, may not also arm to strengthen their negotiating position. The answer seems apparent. Neither side expects a settlement. Both expect the world-wide competition for the minds of men and the allegiance of states to continue. Both hope that nuclear war may be avoided; neither is sure that it will. Both expect to continue to strengthen their arms. And yet the gnawing doubt remains. Even assuming that escalation of arms can be restrained, can the inevitable crises be successfully handled in a nuclear environment without nuclear war? How many? For how long?

The lesson of Cuba should not be missed. As the century unfolds, the security of the nation may be possible only at the cost of accepting nonviolent or less violent competition kept within bounds. This will require the development of wider areas of common interest between the United States and the Soviet Union than exist at present. For these tasks, force facing force is the antithesis of unity. So far as force continues to be overwhelmingly relied on, there will be no unity and little development. Yet, while force cannot take the first step, neither can it be given up until many steps have been taken. Meanwhile, force—nuclear force—must serve as a substitute for unity, but in our age a dangerous and possibly fatal one.

Toward Common Action

In the current international system, force is fragmented with two opposing states, the United States and the Soviet Union, each having an immense concentration in its hands. For those in the state who must deal with the external world, it is apparent that the diffusion of force, while it may inhibit some forms of conflict, increases the danger of violence when conflict occurs. The search for unity or *communitas* may thus be seen as a Sisyphean struggle to fashion a near monopoly of force in the world, while avoiding conflict which would destroy it. Yet achievement of a near monopoly of force by any means seems unlikely in the foreseeable future. Thus the world is faced with the need to live with force which is diffused.

In the face of fractionated force some would place their whole reliance on restraint. Those who value restraint as an intermediate end, even though they see the opponent as seeking ultimately to impose unity by force, encourage the maintenance of diplomatic communication and the exchange of other selected personnel for information and intelligence purposes, but look with skepticism at common undertakings. Their objective is to delay and postpone the search for unity in the hope that something will turn up. They advise reliance on force but hope to restrain its use. For the key to the future they look to the wisdom of the past rather than to men's aspirations and new-found capabilities. War, since it has been part of the past, might somehow be coped with in the future —even a nuclear war.

Still others seek ways of achieving not only restraint but enhanced unity so as to reduce substantially, if not to eliminate, the possibility of nuclear war. Observing that the mutual dependence created by nuclear weapons has magnified the need for restraint, noting the increasing interdependence developing in other areas and the potential of science and technology for meeting the needs of mankind, they seek for means of accelerating and organizing common efforts across national borders.

To those who would rely on force, the search for cross-national diffusion of power may appear dangerous. To those relying on restraint, the advocates of force may appear overoptimistic. Yet, it is conceivable that the growing possibilities of interdependence, if cultivated and supported with resources, could lead to a strengthening of the sense of unity and provide a broader, more positive basis for restraint as the norm of international action. The initiative cannot be left wholly to the state. While the states must facilitate and support the effort, the task is one which requires the commitment of large segments of both the Soviet and the American communities. New cross-national associations and systems of influence are required, which in time acquire power to influence and restrain the actions of both states.

There is no easy path to the reduction of tensions or to the control of conflict. Men will not forget their past which is infinitely diverse. Nor will they be easily turned aside from their aspirations for the future. Their experience in the twentieth century thus far has underlined the need for world-wide unity to control conflict, but the devastation and decimation of two wars did not make self-evident the road to the future. Yet the themes of restraint and interdependence together with unity have been so persistent in this experience that they suggest where future attention and effort should be concentrated.

4 Common Interest and the Restraint of Force

Conflict and Mutual Interests

THE UNITED STATES emerged at the end of World War II as a great power. In response to Soviet aggressiveness, it fell gradually into the habit of couching its goals mainly in terms of hostility toward the Soviet Union. Yet despite the antagonistic statement of the ultimate goals, the two adversaries are slowly discovering that their present posture gives rise to a number of mutual as well as conflicting interests.

These mutual interests arise in a number of ways. One set of such interests—the need for both to view time as "on our side"— ironically springs from the fact that, while their ultimate goals are antagonistic, neither has a chance of attaining them so long as the other maintains its power. A second cluster of common interests arises directly from the threat which general nuclear war poses to the existence of each. A third set derives from the need of both to restrain the actions of other states and to cope with the aspirations of these states in a manner which does not bring the two great powers into conflict at times and in places not of their choosing.

A fourth set of common interests of the more positive kind derives from the fact that science and technology now make building the "good society" on a world scale a realistic possibility, though by no means a simple, swift, or certain one. Finally, the complex web of interdependence, which unavoidably arises from efforts to maintain the necessary restraints on international action while each state continues to pursue its efforts to expand its power and influence, makes necessary a mutual understanding surpassing in scope and depth that which has been required of nation-states in previous periods.

The terms of the present conflict prevent an easy acknowledgment of mutual interests. To do so, it is felt, might weaken the will of one's own people to compete or if necessary to fight and would also tend to erode one's influence among external friends or allies. Yet common interests are no less important because they are unacknowledged.

Time Is on Our Side

Both sides believe that "time is on our side." The need for such a belief arises from the fact that while the ultimate goals of the two adversaries are antagonistic, neither is certain of attaining his goals as long as the other maintains invulnerable strategic nuclear forces. At the present time, neither side can clearly foresee how world unity is to be achieved without the "consent" of the other while both retain their power. Neither has a credible program for obtaining that consent. Thus it is necessary for both to cherish the belief that time is on their side. While the belief fosters restraint in seeking political gains and in attempting to achieve a decisive military superiority, it has not as yet prevented dangerous competition and conflict in both areas.

The hope and the fear remain that a breakthrough in military technology might lead one side or the other to believe it possible to achieve unity by force. Thus intensive research and development on new weapons continue on both sides. Moreover, while in the direct confrontation between the two it may be in the interests of each to have the opponent believe that time is on his side, each must strive to prevent the other from appearing to represent the wave of the future in the minds of the elites or masses of third countries. Great advances by one side either in the field of military technology or in the political competition for the allegiances of third areas increase the risk that the other, abandoning its hope for long-run success, may lash out "irrationally" to prevent the ultimate success of the opponent.

Maintenance of the view by both that time is on their side encourages restraint in the face of unavoidable setbacks. The "loss" of Yugoslavia to the Soviet Union or Cuba to the free world, and China to both, may be put in a longer time frame. Those who argue that the loss need not be irrevocable will find support in the view that in the longer run it may be recouped. The longer-run view also argues against "premature" ventures in independent states or unstable areas such as Eastern Europe or Latin America. Finally, the view encourages a shift of attention and effort to fields such as space or the modernization of underdeveloped countries. Gains in these areas may be seen as contributing to victory in the long run but they do not in themselves necessarily represent true losses for the opponent. Above all, the mutual belief that "time is on our side" may provide the long years required for the development and success of common enterprises which might lead to a redefinition of world unity that would indeed be in the long-run interest of both. This hope is not entirely visionary, since no objective reason except for their present mutual hostility can be adduced why time should not be kind to both adversaries.

Restraint in the Soviet-American Military Confrontation

INVULNERABLE STRATEGIC FORCES

Both the United States and the Soviet Union have an interest in reducing the threat which general nuclear war poses to the existence of each. Agreement on actions designed to reduce this threat are limited by antagonistic goals, by intermediate political objectives, and by the need to prevail if war should come. Thus, both sides have an interest in the stability of the military environment—but not so much stability that it would thwart other objectives. The need for stability has given rise to a continuing discussion of possible methods of arms control and disarmament by which it would be enhanced. While the Soviet Union apparently continues to lag in missile production, there are some in the United States who appear to believe that stability may be enhanced by the development of mutually invulnerable strategic nuclear systems.[1] It is felt that such systems would provide the minimum requirements for deterring an attack on the United States without in turn appearing provocative to the opponent. Similarly, it is possible to envisage a Soviet strategic posture which, while invulnerable, would not be threatening to the United States. The sudden discovery of United States "superiority" at the strategic level has tended to obscure the interest in the posture of minimum deter-

[1] Stewart Alsop, "McNamara Thinks about the Unthinkable," *Saturday Evening Post*, Dec. 1, 1962, p. 18.

rence. It remains, however, for the longer run a valid and important area of possible mutual interest serving to guide common action.

Both sides envisage a continuing need for tactical nuclear forces and conventional forces in order to exert pressure to achieve or maintain political gains in third areas. Moreover, each side envisages the need to use whatever other instruments may be available to maintain or extend political power.[2] This attitude toward the use of force and political pressure throughout the world might easily give rise to unmitigated conflict which could lead by process of psychological and actual escalation to the threat of general nuclear war. In order to offset to some extent the antagonisms generated by the political conflicts throughout the world, each side has found it desirable to maintain a parallel line of policy consisting of peaceful declarations and occasional cooperative actions which would keep alive the hope that the conflict could be prevented from spiraling into uncontrolled violence.

The dual nature of Soviet policy in this regard is looked upon with distrust and suspicion by the United States. However, a more prudent view would be to welcome both the declarations of peaceful intention and also the acts, however modest, which would tend to support these declarations in the belief that it is desirable as a minimum that neither side engage in a policy of total conflict. Quite apart from ultimate objectives, it is in the interests of both

[2] Robert Strausz-Hupé, *A Forward Strategy for America* (New York: Harper & Row, 1961), presents one approach to an activist policy for America.

sides to encourage the dual policy of the other, not because it is preferable to wholehearted collaboration, but because it dilutes in some degree the tendency toward wholesale conflict.

The United States, until recently, has not devoted substantial resources to the development of peaceful initiatives. Where such gestures have been made, as in the case of the creation of the United States Arms Control and Disarmament Agency (ACDA), they have been far overshadowed by parallel actions on the military side. The financing, for example, of the disarmament agency amounted to no more than one one-thousandth of the increases in funds devoted to military forces by the Kennedy Administration. While the present ACDA also might be appropriately compared with a Pentagon "planning staff" and while an increase in its budget equivalent to the increase in military expenditures may be unwarranted at this time, a much more substantial effort will be required both for the development of effective arms control measures and for the stimulation of comparable investment on the Soviet side.

DISENGAGEMENT

The disposition or movement of forces which might give rise to a direct confrontation of the United States and the Soviet Union has been an area of concern to those who seek stability. There has been a continuing interest in modifying the disposition of forces on both sides so as to reduce the probability of anarchistic clashes which might lead to general conflict. This has led to a number of suggestions for disengagement on a regional or geographic basis. Some sixty disengagement plans have been suggested by the West and more than twenty by the Soviet bloc between 1957 and the present time. Despite rejection of the idea of disengagement by the last three Secretaries of State, including Dean Rusk, it has remained alive as a possible means of reducing the hazards of the nuclear age.

One difficulty with almost any disengagement proposal is the possibility that it might result in unforeseen shifts in political influence. Disengagement, when it involves the removal or reduction in forces in third areas, must be accompanied by some new form of mutual engagement between the United States and the Soviet Union which would maintain their relative political influence or which would provide an acceptable definition of the new terms under which the competition for influence was to take place in the area. The inability to devise acceptable terms for disengagement leads some to feel that direct confrontation of the two powers is more stable than disengagements which might encourage or compel unrestrained attempts to increase influence in areas from which forces had been withdrawn. It is on this rock that many of the proposals for disengagement have foundered, since they have inevitably appeared to the United States as a means of reducing its influence in the area and opening it to Soviet infiltration in return for a hypothetical increase in nuclear stability. Nevertheless, the drive of the smaller nations for independence of action may in the future require the great powers to develop a common approach to partial disengagement. They may find it desirable to seek to reduce their absolute level of military involvement in third areas, provided that the balance of their political influence is not jeopardized and the stability of the strategic environment is maintained.

DISARMAMENT

The continuing possibility of general nuclear war, however re- mote, and the desire to appear before world public opinion in the role of peacemaker have resulted in a quiet but continuous fixa- tion on the problem of general and complete disarmament since the end of World War II. The series of changes in position adopted by the two sides and the inability thus far to make any serious progress suggest that while there is an interest in disarmament there must also be serious impediments to it. No doubt an impor- tant reason for the lack of progress is that each side believes, as pointed out earlier, that time is on its side. Moreover, general dis- armament requires both sides to give up, in apparently irrevocable fashion, the idea that either may acquire a near monopoly of force and thus to abandon the possibility, however remote, that victory may somehow, sometime be possible through the political threat of force or its actual use.

Despite the inability of both sides to face the facts that a unique historical development has made successful use of force to over- come the adversary unlikely, one might have expected more progress with respect to partial disarmament which would not foreclose an attempt at military victory should the technology ever permit it. Partial disarmament, however, is made difficult not only by the range of unsettled political issues between the two sides which might be affected by even limited agreements but by the very different military and political requirements of each side. Despite these limitations, studies of the world environment which general disarmament and partial disarmament and arms-control measures must serve, as well as the means by which they might be achieved, deserve a somewhat greater investment of resources and talent than they are now receiving. An investment in this area helps to maintain the peaceful image of adversaries, it contributes to the maintenance of the peaceful element in the inevitable dual policy of peace and pressure, and it provides the kind of forethought about the future world order that is necessary in order to capitalize on any opportunities for arms control and partial disarmament which may arise.

The history of disarmament discussions since the end of World War II suggests that there are two interrelated issues of comparable importance on which action has foundered. The first question, which has received the most systematic attention, is, How can disarmament be carried out without jeopardizing the security of the parties to an agreement? Equally important and as yet unsolved is the question, How can disarmament be initiated? Obviously, if an acceptable agreement could be reached on how disarmament was to be carried out, the difficulty of beginning might be solved. Unfortunately, no agreement has been reached in more than a decade of negotiations. There are many reasons for the negotiating stalemate. Some of them suggest that if a beginning is to be made on disarmament, significant informal or tacit arrangements rather than formal agreements may be a necessary first step.

In a formal disarmament or arms-control agreement, each side is in fact attempting to optimize its remaining power after reduction or control occurs. Each side is also trying to ensure that the adversary's strength is eroded at least as much and preferably somewhat more than his own. The difficulty arises not so much in optimizing one's own remaining strength but in agreeing on what the effect of the adversary's actions will be. The problem is further complicated by the need of each side to avoid giving the impression to the public that, in fact, what is being discussed is the maximization of power at a lower level of force expenditures with only enough increase in mutual control to prevent conflict by accident or inadvertence. The dilemma posed by conventional arms control and disarmament negotiations suggests the possible need for an alternative approach.

One alternative approach would be for both sides to accept as given that at each step of downward revision each side will attempt to maximize its power at the lower-force levels and to build the disarmament procedure around that fact. Both sides should also explicitly, but not necessarily publicly, recognize the possibility that the occasion may arise when for a time they may find it necessary to reverse the process and actually increase expenditures, while at the same time both may wish to continue to avoid war. Both sides will also need to explore the difficulty for each of getting and reaching agreement within its own power structure on the equity and adequacy of the adversary's actions. Yet both sides may for different reasons desire a reduction in defense expenditures.

Faced with these conditions, tacit agreement to reduce military expenditures toward a lower level would still be possible even though detailed agreement on the composition of the reduction on the two sides could never be achieved. This alternative might be termed the statesman's approach as contrasted with the disarmament expert's approach. Each side retains its sovereign freedom of action. Year-to-year shifts in direction would be possible without abrogating a formal agreement. Competition for influence could continue. A climate in which mutual trust might lead to further action would be encouraged. Intentions could be tested by a wide variety of interaction. Both increased opportunity and necessity could encourage the gradual broadening of the means of verification. The environment created by the downward initiative might open possibilities for common action and experience on secondary questions now dealt with largely on a unilateral basis. Finally, the statesman's approach does not rule out, but actually contributes to, a setting in which limited formal agreements might become easier to negotiate. Let us examine, briefly, the present possibilities for such an approach.

Since the end of the Korean War, for almost a decade, annual United States expenditures for defense programs have remained around ten per cent of the gross national product (GNP). Economy waves and crises have come and gone, each reflected in some degree in marginal fluctuation of defense expenditures around the fixed proportion of GNP, but without in significant degree affecting the general level. In the meantime, total output of the economy in real terms has increased more than a fifth and defense expenditures have experienced a proportionate rise.

The decade has also been characterized by the presentation of a series of disarmament and arms-control plans. Each one has been discussed at length, and probably in increasing detail, within the United States government, with the Allies, and with the Soviet Union. On its part, the Soviet Union has also presented a series of proposals for discussion.

During the same period, the defense programs of our European Allies have shown an over-all constancy similar to ours but at a level somewhat less than half that of the United States in terms of the percentage of the GNP.

During the decade there also has been an immense flowering of strategic literature as well as official explanations of what strategy the United States was pursuing over the long run and in any particular year. The period was also marked by many significant shifts in the weapons systems and organization of forces. Continental defense measures were at first accelerated and then decelerated. Missile production expanded and aircraft began to be phased out. Conventional forces were initially cut back and later expanded again.

But during all this period, national defense expenditures continued to rise with GNP in a constant proportion of about ten per cent. Does this fact have any particular implications for arms control and disarmament efforts? It may have.

Most of the research and diplomatic investment in arms control in the recent past has gone toward negotiations with the Soviet Union to try to perfect a three-stage disarmament agreement in which the forces on each side would be gradually reduced so that neither side would obtain an advantage. In many respects, the present effort is not dissimilar from that carried on in previous periods. The obstacles to reaching a full agreement by this process, if not infinite, are almost so. They stem from at least seven sources.

First, the geographic position of each side is unique, leading each to place different values on different elements of its defense posture. Second, the political requirements, intentions, and styles of the two sides are diverse, which also leads to a divergent evaluation of the various instruments of force. Third, and related to the preceding points, each side visualizes somewhat different contingencies in which it might have to resort to force. Fourth, and of novel significance in the present era, the requirement that the main elements of military power be mobilized rather than latent, awaiting the call to mobilization, has resulted in the acquisition on each side of a large untried and ever changing investment in military capital resources whose current value in event of conflict is exceedingly difficult to estimate. Fifth, research and development is constantly lifting new or improved weapons into view on the horizon which further complicate the calculation of symmetrical reduction or control. Sixth, the Soviets have continued to rely on secrecy and to resist inspection, while the United States has remained relatively open to verification. Seventh, and more conjecturally, the constancy of the proportion of the United States GNP devoted to defense suggests a national decision on more general grounds than pure defense requirements, which, until discarded or modified, is bound to stand in the way of progress on disarmament, if not arms control.

Arms control in this context may be thought of as an effort in the direction of mutual management, both of the deployment and use of existing forces and of the marginal fluctuation and changes in the mix of the forces so as to avoid war by inadvertence and so as not unduly to disturb the relatively constant proportion of the GNP going into defense programs. For the purposes of arms control, certain kinds of limited formal agreements may have a place, but more important is a tacit understanding, now developing, that it is in general in the interest of each side to manage the forces in such a way as to avoid upsetting stability. Each side will, of course, assume that the other will continue to pursue its separate objectives by whatever means seem feasible and not too dangerous. This seems to have been the practice even before the arms-control vocabulary was invented. However, both arms control and defense analysis have been providing additional insights into the process.

Since, in the area of arms control, tacit agreements—if arrangements for good communication between the two sides are provided—are likely to work about as well as formal agreements, neither side has been greatly interested in the latter. Moreover, since understandings may need to be disregarded from time to time as new opportunities, new weapons technology, or other factors intervene, tacit understandings have the advantage of being not only more easily negated but more easily revived once the test of wills is over. Moreover, they can be disregarded in part without opening to the opponent the advantage which may then be gained by publicly terminating the entire agreements. In other words, tacit understandings are likely to be abandoned only to the degree required by a particular contest. Tacit understandings also have the advantage of being more fully in the hands of the top political leadership of each side. One of their great advantages, of course, is that in taking specific measures to achieve stability, each side escapes to a considerable extent the charge of giving in to the other, since there is no formal agreement to which to point. At the same time they may have the kind of instability that comes from personal rather than institutional relationships.

There can be no doubt that a great deal of such tacit parallel action has occurred over the past decade and that much of it is going on today. But it may be asked, Even though tacit agreement is useful for adjustment at the margins, is it not out of place when real disarmament is considered? Disarmament, it has been assumed, would mark such a dramatic turn in the cold war that people would expect and Congress demand a solemn, formal ritual of agreement to mark the occasion. Objectively, there seems to be no more reason requiring a formal treaty for the reduction of arms than for their control or increase. The United States has for the last decade followed the policy in the main of letting its military expenditures grow at the rate of growth of the GNP, but this was, of course, done without any question being raised about the need for a treaty with the Soviet Union. Why then a treaty to cut back armaments?

What would be required on the United States side would be a Presidential decision to the effect that some other formula was better suited to American security and development needs. What would be the nature of such a decision? After exploring the question with the Soviet Union and reaching a judgment on the probability of Soviet reciprocation, the President could decide, for example, either that military expenditures would no longer be allowed to grow at the rate of growth of the rest of the economy or that, if allowed to grow, they must be brought down to a level of seven or eight per cent rather than ten per cent of the GNP. But it will be asked immediately, Would not this require a detailed review of military programs? Otherwise it might be argued that budgetary considerations are determining security needs. The answer is Yes, but in a second phase of decision-making and for a somewhat different reason. The President has the responsibility not only to recommend the over-all level of defense expenditures but to approve what, in his judgment, represents the mix of specific expenditures within the total which will contribute most effectively to the security of the nation. But should not the total expenditure emerge from the review of specific needs? The answer seems to be that while this may be true in the kind of logic we customarily use in dealing with the relatively simple problems of daily life, national security expenditure levels are in fact never set quite that way.

During World War II, the total level of military expenditure was set at what it was calculated to be the rate at which resources could be converted to wartime production and later at the top limit of resources that could be diverted from civilian consumption. The World War II period thus found the United States devoting something like forty per cent of its GNP to defense purposes. In the Korean period a plateau of around thirteen to fourteen per cent was attained to handle the conflict, but more importantly to prepare against general war. In the interim between the two when the United States felt at peace the level was just above five per cent, or slightly higher than the level maintained by our European allies during the past decade.

But, it may be argued, even though over-all expenditure control has its place, the level that is fixed represents a highly complicated interplay between weapons and force requirements and budgetary and political considerations. In the end, it has been said, security considerations must prevail. This may be true in a kind of moral and subjective sense.

Yet, if the process is so complicated, if weapons systems are always changing, if shifts in the opponent's intentions and capabilities as well as many other factors must be taken into account, is it not curious that for almost a decade the amount that has been required each year was around ten per cent of a growing GNP? Even if one could explain the constancy in a world of uncertainty as a result of an infinite series of offsetting factors, a puzzling question would remain.

How was the ten per cent figure arrived at in the first place?

Would it be too simple to suggest that ten per cent represented a substantial cutback from the previous Korean plateau and was judged to be the level the American people would support over an extended period of time? Too simple, because after a decade of capital accumulation in the military field, one might then simply ask whether eight per cent would serve as well as ten per cent.

Suppose a President felt in his bones that eight per cent was adequate, how could he best achieve the reduction? The disarmament or defense procedure would suggest the detailed design of the first stage of a disarmament agreement in which United States reductions would be carefully matched by Soviet reductions in such a way that each side could agree that the other side had not gained an advantage. But then all the earlier-mentioned obstacles to agreement on specifics in a plan that was actually going to be implemented would arise and plague the negotiations. Each service and industry affected by the cuts could go to the Congress and the country. The political opposition could make capital of the weakness of the administration. The Senate would have to be deeply involved in shaping the treaty, would have to concur in the essential symmetry of the innumerable steps to be taken. Most troublesome of all, the President would have to unduly narrow his alternatives, especially if the agreement—as would be likely— were to include provisions about general and complete disarmament.

All this would be involved if one followed the conventional disarmament path even though at the outset the President might judge that eight per cent would serve national security about as well as ten per cent provided the Soviet Union did any of a number of things only part of which might be of a military nature, and which might include cessation of certain activities or refraining from some possible future actions.

Suppose—to make the situation more closely parallel to the disarmament case—the President felt that a reduction from approximately ten per cent to eight per cent of the GNP for defense expenditures was desirable provided the Soviet Union reciprocated in the downward movement. Suppose, in addition, the President wanted to maintain his options if the Soviet Union did not cooperate, that he wished to avoid becoming entangled with his opposition any more than necessary, and that in reducing expenditures he wanted to optimize the country's security at the lower level of expenditure. How could he best proceed?

First, he would need to set up highly reliable and possibly complex lines of communication, not only to his opposite number in the Soviet Union, but to the various influential Soviet elites. Prior preparations of this kind are essential, not only to suggest what he is about, but to provide means of explaining, interpreting, and providing supplementary information which would ensure that the opponents understood in as exact terms as possible what was occurring. In this process, methods of ensuring that the Soviet Union realized the United States was moving from strength and not from weakness or a false belief in the benign intentions of the Soviet Union would be needed.

Second, at home Presidential action might begin not with an emphasis on the intention to disarm or even to cut expenditures, but upon the value of a further tax cut. The obvious advantage of this approach is that in any society, but particularly in a democracy, few measures are likely to find such widespread public support. Once the tax cut is achieved, provided it is deep enough, the gap between expenditures and revenue ought to become more salient. Defense, representing by far the largest element in the Federal budget—nearly sixty per cent—would then be an unavoidable candidate for cutting in a setting of economic growth.

Third, analysis of alternative military postures at a lower level of expenditure would have to be initiated. Within the United States government, studies would be required aiming at a consensus on what mix of expenditures at the lower level would provide optimum security. Next, over the communications channels previously established with the Soviet Union, it would be desirable to establish as far as possible what would be the feasible and likely Soviet response to expect. These two lines of analyses would be joined at the Presidential level and shape the ultimate decisions about specific programs and activities. The discussions with the Soviet Union—while extended and carried on over a variety of channels—would not be negotiations in the formal sense. However, at some point Khrushchev would be given the opportunity to indicate his plans and later to explain and interpret them as they were or were not carried out.

The approach to disarmament sketched above seems particularly relevant where one side, as in the present case the United States, has marked superiority in certain weapons areas and where the other side may have an advantage in others. Moreover, each side keeps open not only the opportunity to maximize its security at the lower level of effort but also to make a place in its arsenal for new and improved weapons or for the research and development which may devise them. At the same time, since the trend is downward, the procedure could improve the climate of relations and open the way for a second round. Uncertainty would remain, however, about the possibility and character of such a second round. Arguments over the scope of the adversary's reduction would continue, but they would involve issues of judgment among the leaders of one side or the other, not questions of adversary compliance with the letter of an agreement.

While we have dwelt largely on the American side, the advantages on the Soviet side would seem to be similar, though not identical. The same element of initiative, optimization, reversibility, and simplicity would be open to the Soviet Union.

Obviously, for the approach to work, the two sides would have to be in agreement that a lower level of security expenditures is desirable, but that is also a *sine qua non* for a formal agreement. Beyond that the tacit approach seems much less dangerous and politically and administratively more feasible. It relies on the *de facto* interdependence of the two military postures and on the breadth and detail of the information now flowing back and forth on the general characteristics of that posture. To reinforce the comprehension that what seems to have been done has been done, the tacit approach would require strengthening of the channels for reassurance and persuasion. Beyond that the initiative remains on each side.

On the other hand, it need not cause unemployment among arms-control analysts and military planners, or the closing down of research and development establishments upon which the long-run security of the nation may rest. Rather it enlivens and enlarges their work. Each step of the downward movement will profit before and after the fact from detailed analysis and review. Invention of additional actions will be needed as well as suggestions for obtaining or providing further reassuring information. Optimization at a lower level will provide room for both creativity and controversy.

Suppose there were a tacit understanding to reduce defense expenditures by two per cent of the GNP, what would be the likely shape of the implementing actions? One of the advantages of this form of disarmament, it should be recalled, is that each side can continue to maximize its power at the lower level of expenditure. Therefore, insofar as possible the reductions on both sides could be expected to come from (1) more rapid abandonment of *obsolete* weapons systems and organizations, (2) reduction in the numbers of weapons which are in some sense *excess* to national requirements, (3) *stretch-outs* in production and to a degree in the development of, but not research on, future weapons systems, and (4) improvements in the efficiency of the armed forces.

Within these broad categories the particular mix of cutback on both sides would be affected by (1) the measures being initiated by the opponent and (2) the feasibility of cutting alternative programs in the light of contending interests at home and among allies or satellites. It would be presumptuous at this stage to suggest the intricate course of events. However, some categories among the approximately fifty thousand nuclear weapons which the United States is estimated now to possess would seem to be likely candidates for reduction.[3] Indeed, the process of reduction with respect to certain categories such as the Jupiter and Atlas missiles is already under way. A more rapid phasing out of the bomber force has also been suggested as a possibility, although in

[3] See *Verification and Response in Disarmament Agreements*, Woods Hole Summer Study, 1962, a study prepared for the United States Arms Control and Disarmament Agency (Washington, D.C.: Institute for Defense Analyses, Nov., 1962), p. 40, Annex Vol. I.

this case substantial internal political resistance might be expected.

While possible reductions such as these may arise from the obsolescing nature of the weapons themselves, the process may from time to time be speeded up and, as a part of a strategy of interdependence, make a contribution to the control of conflict. On the Soviet side another attempt to cut back conventional forces as well as to reduce its commitment of forces to some areas of Eastern Europe would appear to be a possibility. In the light of United States pressure to maintain the *status quo* and in view of the hazards of nuclear war, the present size of Soviet conventional forces would seem to represent in some degree an obsolescing or excessive asset in an environment of mutual reduction of military expenditures.

Stretch-outs represent another important contribution to the general reduction. The postponement of antiballistic missile and shelter programs would represent a contribution through the next few years. Slowdown in production of Minutemen and Polaris missiles could also serve this purpose. On the Soviet side a comparable stretch-out might be feasible in their various programs designed to offset present United States superiority. When a deficiency exists there are in fact only a few occasions when it is of vital importance to eliminate it by a particular date. Two or three years' extension normally appears to make little difference in the longer time frame in which both sides tend to operate—a mood that could be enhanced in the years of downward revision.

Cutbacks achieved as a result of increased efficiency represent a mixed picture. Efficiency which is achieved by increased reliance on nuclear weapons obviously has its hazards. In the communication of downward revision an important topic of discussion must be the avoidance of shifts which increase the danger of excessive acceleration if conflict should occur. The capability for rapid response is another form of effectiveness. Elimination of forces which lack this capability would, in general, seem a possible avenue of over-all reduction, while at the same time increasing the average effectiveness of the remaining forces. Certain reserve elements in the United States have been suggested from time to time as a candidate for reduction on these grounds.

Fundamentally, however, while it cannot be stated categorically without hard information, the trading position seems to be that in a period of downward movement the United States has room for adjustment in its nuclear forces, primarily the strategic element, while the Soviet Union has some military flexibility in regard to conventional forces.

In addition to the general reduction in the level of defense expenditure, disarmament and other measures for arms control and political accommodation could and should be pursued simultaneously.

The statesman's approach, in which each side retains full control over its own actions, does not eliminate the need for verification but it shifts the burden from the adversary who previously has had to demand proof of a reduction. In the approach suggested here, the party making a cut has the primary interest in providing the proof which will lead to continuing reciprocation by the opponent. Obviously, each side will wish to retain a maximum capacity to verify the adversary's actions to its own satisfaction, but the adversary must share this interest. The adversary must be as deeply concerned with how his own actions are being perceived as he is with a particular action of his opponent's on the slope of downward revision. Thus in the case of a reduction of future strategic delivery vehicles by one side or the other, as has been discussed, both sides would have an interest in establishing the proof that such a reduction had actually taken place.[4] Adversary claims of inadequate proof and possible cheating would still have to be dealt with, but opportunities for proof would be more abundant in the dynamic game here envisaged than in the usual static disarmament game. Similarly, reductions in conventional forces by one side would have to be carefully planned and some form of continuous observation might be required to convince the world and the adversary that the reduction had actually occurred as stated. But in both cases the responsibility and interest in providing proof would lie with the side making the cut. The adversary has no need to assume the task of extracting the proof although he will wish to do what he can to ensure that it is conclusive.

Even within a framework of a mere two per cent reduction in GNP devoted to military expenditures, certain difficult problems would be likely to arise. However, if on the initiative of one side or the other, they did come up, each side would be free to act in accordance with its interests in the light of all the information available to it from national sources as well as from those provided by the adversary. Announcement of the cessation of development and production of chemical and biological weapons might be a case in point. Informed opinion has held that complete assurance in this area is virtually unachievable.[5] While not a particularly likely initial candidate for action, if it did occur, a national de-

[4] *Ibid.*, p. 6, Summary Report.
[5] *Ibid.*, p. 7, Summary Report.

cision which took into account the relative value of the chemical and biological weapons in the total environment and the risks of undetected violation in event of conflict would be necessary. The decision could well be not to respond to the stated reduction in kind but in another area, while at the same time opening discussions on the nature of the arrangements necessary for the adversary to obtain a response in kind. Or, in the light of the present opinion that it is not possible to prove the nonproduction of such weapons, a decision not to respond at all might be reached.

As the initial downward revision proceeds, two specific complementary lines of action are desirable in addition to the establishment of the general range of channels of discussion and information flow suggested earlier. These are (1) the annual budget consultation, and (2) expansion of scientific and technical exchanges and enterprises.

ANNUAL BUDGET REVIEW

Consultations on the budget may be useful either before or after a downward revision in defense expenditures begins. Such consultations are an essential information device in the interdependent world in which the Soviet Union and the United States now find themselves. The present practice of devoting substantial resources to the analysis of the adversaries' expenditures without the opportunity for face-to-face confrontation places the statesmen at the mercy of the experts.

Independent expert analysis is not as conducive to stability as is analysis plus systematic mutual discussions, however formal they may be in the beginning. The requirements for making a coherent and reasonable presentation, the opportunity for questions, and the need for year-to-year consistency encourage moderation and understanding.

The suggestion, initially, would call for an annual review and discussion of East-West military budgets by a joint body of political representatives and experts similar to the yearly review of the national accounts by the Organization for European Economic Co-operation (OEEC) and of military budgets by NATO.[6] It need not imply that the review process necessarily involves a requirement that the national authorities modify their military budgets. Initially, the process would simply involve the various nations presenting their budgets in a common forum established for the purpose; the process would permit the representatives of other nations to comment on and ask questions about the size and composition of the budgets, seeking gradually to improve the adequacy of the information provided.

The proposal has a number of advantages from the American point of view. First, it would involve the Soviet Union in a mutual discussion of military budgets in a way that would create a suggestion of interdependence without actually threatening the autonomy of any state. Second, it would provide more adequate information about Soviet military expenditures and help to throw light on the rate and direction of Soviet actions in a period of downward revision, without involving direct intrusion into specific areas of the Soviet Union. Third, it would help to educate and inform third areas on the actual nature of the problem of arms

[6] The Soviets have in the past indicated that, at least in principle, they are willing to consider some such examination of their military budget. See the Soviet proposal introduced in the United Nations Disarmament Subcommittee on March 27, 1956; the text appears in Department of State *Documents on Disarmament*, Vol. 1, p. 607.

and arms control. Fourth, as the experience with annual budgetary reviews within nations and among nations has shown, it provides a good setting for opening up a whole array of other areas which lend themselves to common study and analysis. Fifth, it might have a dampening effect on the arms race without necessarily precluding national action where that seemed to be overwhelmingly in the national interest.

SCIENTIFIC EXCHANGE AND ENTERPRISE

In a relatively disarmed world, military research and development represents one of the most serious continuing obstacles to stability and still further disarmament. Steps therefore are required in the first phase of a downward revision of arms to begin to come to grips with this problem. Three approaches have been suggested: (1) the cessation or monitoring of testing and other actions which are necessary steps in the development of new and improved weapons systems; (2) substantial increases in exchanges of scientists and scientific publications which would help to lay the basis for an international scientific community and open the way to free movement of scientists in all the research facilities of the world; and (3) joint enterprises of both a positive and a protective nature, which would engage the talents of scientists and technicians of many nations.

Verification of the cessation or the peaceful purposes of development-testing represents a complicated technical problem. The spectrum is wide. In some instances verification by national means alone is entirely feasible. In other instances no means of verification whatever can presently be envisaged. In the statesman's approach to disarmament, verification of cessation of testing or other forms of development represents only a secondary, though still important, question which must be dealt with before he takes a specific step in the downward revision. Equally, he must consider the issue before he makes a judgment on an action his opponent alleges he has taken. It becomes a matter of discussion as they proceed along the path of downward revision. It helps to determine the score each gives the other, but is no longer an insuperable obstacle to further action, although continuing lack of adequate verification across the entire front of the adversary's alleged action could again become an insuperable obstacle. However, this seems unlikely at the initial scale of downward revision.

The positive requirements for substantial expansion of scientific exchange and common enterprise are discussed in a later section. (See Chap. 5, pp. 178ff.) Here we are primarily concerned with the steps which might be taken in the context of downward revision to reinforce a common perception of the actions taken and in some degree to lay the foundation for future action.

In this context, many of the steps which each side contemplated taking on a sovereign basis might well be preceded by a series of exchanges of scientists and experts in the particular field of focus. If nuclear weapons testing was at issue, not only the discussions of topflight scientists, as for example occurs in the Pugwash meetings, but of seismologists, radiologists, and many others might be desirable to clarify the situation in advance of action. Once an action is taken, further exchanges among the same or similar people would be desirable to reinforce the understanding that the action announced is being taken. Moreover, as specialized individuals from the two sides become better acquainted they should be encouraged to develop parallel or common research interests which would keep them in continuing contact.

In the longer run ideas and plans for joint enterprises might be expected to develop which would require government support and financing. Looking forward to this time the United States would be well advised to begin very early to devote an increasing proportion of research funds directly to this end.

The rationale for both enlarged and directed scientific exchange and increased collaboration in common scientific and technical enterprises is not only that they are beneficial in themselves but that this may be the only effective means of reducing the destabilizing effects of nationally isolated research and development. The power of new scientific ideas and technologies appears to be so great that only reassurance and verification which relies on an organic relationship of the scientific establishment of the adversaries is likely to be sufficient guarantee against surprise at increased levels of disarmament.

ECONOMICS OF DISARMAMENT

Even a brief discussion of limited reductions in military expenditures should perhaps touch on the concern in the United States over their impact on the economy. Support for a reduction depends in part on the confidence of the American people that alternative requirements for resources exist which will take up the slack when military requirements are reduced; otherwise, economic growth may slacken and unemployment increase. P. M. S. Blackett has made this point. He said:

> Another reason why it may be difficult for the American Government to adopt at the present time a policy of nuclear parity with the Soviet Union, as they have for total manpower, is the uncertainty as to the social and economic effects of such a drastic policy. . . . Perhaps the attraction to many

Westerners of arms control at a high level, as an alternative to drastic disarmament, may sometimes have had less to do with purely military arguments, than with a concealed fear of the economic and social consequences of disarmament. . . . Has it not been said by a wise American, "It seems necessary to convince the American electorate that we can spend as much on disarmament as we do on armaments." [7]

If arms reductions are to increase United States security, a concomitant increase in investment in other forms of strength may be required. Reduction of arms does not mean that a similar reduction in the nonmilitary investments required for a stable world order will be possible. On the contrary a substantial expansion in other forms of expenditure may be needed to shape the world environment in the United States security interests. Such investments are also required to maintain a continuing pressure on Soviet allocations of resources away from military expenditures and in the desired directions.

At present the United States budget is virtually bereft of funds intended to support a program of growing constructive interdependence with the Soviet Union or to influence Soviet use of resources in the direction of such interdependence. From fifty-five to sixty per cent of the total budget goes for the maintenance, operation, and buildup of military power. In contrast, less than .003 per cent is allocated to programs which contribute to Soviet-American constructive action. While ten per cent of the budget is allocated for nonmilitary resources designed to strengthen the free world, virtually none is on a basis which involves the Soviets

[7] P. M. S. Blackett, "The Way Ahead," unpublished paper for the Ninth Pugwash Conference on Science and World Affairs, Cambridge, England, 1962.

in common action. Of the ten per cent for free-world strength, more than half is for domestic space, education, and other programs carried out as competitive or countermeasures of Soviet actions, while the balance is for overseas development largely on a bilateral basis.

Thus along with a tax cut at the outset of arms reduction, certain significant shifts in resources used may be envisaged over a five-year period. These shifts would help both to create a secure world environment and to sustain economic growth in the United States. Four areas may be suggested as candidates for increased expenditures. First, there are shifts of resources within the United States designed to strengthen it for long-term competition and common action in a wide variety of fields from space to education. Second, there are shifts to new world-enterprises requiring Soviet-American common efforts. Third are shifts in American resources designed, on the one hand, to encourage shifts in Soviet resources toward consumption and, on the other, to provide the intricate web of understanding and communications essential to Soviet-American *entente* and common action. Fourth, shifts to economic development and cross-national nonmilitary security activities in third areas would be desirable.

Over a five-year period, programs designed to enhance domestic strength could be as much as doubled if political support in the country and in Congress could be found. Expenditures for world enterprises in space, the oceans, and elsewhere could rise from virtually zero to one or several billion. Resources directed to accelerating Soviet concentration on consumption could be substantial. Finally, if economic aid and loans were to develop a strong United States constituency, substantial additional resources could be made available to developing nations which now urgently need additional foreign capital. Arms reduction, a tax cut, and increased resources for nonmilitary programs on the American side would permit the Soviet Union to shift some of its resources to internal consumption and to participate in world-wide economic activities which would have a significant effect on the environment in which it must live. Whether the Soviet Union would respond can only be determined by its reaction to a series of preparatory and testing actions initiated by the United States. At the same time, nonmilitary security expenditures by the United States represent insurance against the economic hazards of reduction in arms if the private sector does not pick up the slack.

UNIFICATION

Ultimately, the diffusion of power and nuclear weapons in the world which is now taking place, as well as the nuclear threat the two great powers pose to each other, may provide the basis for still another approach to their common interests. If, as both idealists and realists tend to argue, the danger in today's world arises, in a fundamental sense, from the lack of a near monopoly of power in the hands of responsible authorities—the idealists pointing to the need for a world government and the realists pointing to a need for "victory" by the United States—then in logic a third approach is open. Because of the present antagonistic posture of the two sides, it has not received the attention that it would appear to deserve from hard-headed statesmen. At present the approach may appear so radical that it will be dismissed out of hand; nevertheless, its logical simplicity, whether in terms of power and force or in terms of peace and progress, is so compelling that it seems to warrant more systematic investigation than it has hitherto received.

Admittedly, the idea is not at present emotionally compelling and it runs against the overwhelming weight of conventional wisdom. Yet the reasons—good and bad—which actually prevent the two chief opponents from making common cause need probing in depth, if for no other reason than that in a multistate system they may someday find that they are again on the same side.

Today, the United States and the Soviet Union combined have for all practical purposes a near monopoly of force in the world. If the use and direction of this power could somehow be synchronized, stability and, indeed, even unity might be within reach. Men's attitudes clearly prevent such a present development, but in time and at a cost it is conceivable that they may come to view their interests as lying in this direction. The possibilities of such an eventuality arising make it desirable that steps be taken in the not-too-distant future to think through the implications of such a course of action and, if it seems a reasonable possibility among others, to take what steps may be open to bring it about in such degree and at such time as the opportunities permit.

Soviet and American Restraint on the Conflict of Other States

The two great powers, while they have many goals which divide them, also have a need and a desire to play a major role in the management of world affairs in order to avoid being drawn into the conflicts of third states which may involve unwarranted risks or costs or which may occur when the timing does not accord with the great powers' own longer view of history. This holds true even though the two powers are competitors, intent on using the other nations against each other. The diffusion of power now taking place in the world raises numerous specific issues in this regard, although the problem is a perennial one.

Both the United States and the Soviet Union have a continuing interest in restraining the initiative of their friends and allies with respect to issues which they do not view as of immediate vital concern. The common restraint exercised by the United States and the Soviet Union with respect to the interest of the two Chinas in the offshore islands is an example of such an issue. Soviet restraint of East Germany with respect to the issue of Berlin is an example of a great power exercising caution, because of its own views of the proper time for dealing with a particular issue. United States restraint of West Germany may be more difficult if a Soviet–East German Treaty is signed or if de Gaulle's view of Europe should prevail. Laos is an example of a high-cost conflict which, taken by itself, was not of vital interest to either of the giants, and in which they have exercised a restraining influence.

Great-power restraint of third states may be exercised with respect to their capacities, their intentions and actions, or in their efforts to play one great power off against another. In many situations unacknowledged as well as explicit cooperation between the United States and the Soviet Union is necessary in today's world. In handling these potential conflicts, the great powers may act in accord, but unilaterally, in restraining their client states; they may exercise their restraint jointly; or they may seek to use multilateral means. Unilateral action is most effective when the states which are parties to the conflict are heavily dependent on one or the other great power. Unilateral action is less effective in cases where one side is largely dependent on a great power and the other side is only marginally dependent. In these instances a degree of direct great-power coordination, perhaps opening the possibility of limited "field experience," may be essential to the control of conflict. There may also be many cases in which it is in the interest of both the great powers to avoid intervention entirely because of the danger it might bring of intervention by the other. In these instances United Nations action and a more highly developed world police force is a possibility that must not be neglected.

CONTROL OF NUCLEAR CAPABILITIES OF OTHER STATES

Since the Soviet Union and the United States are the principal sources of military equipment and know-how for the third powers, they have initially a significant opportunity to control the capabilities for conflict of third nations. But this opportunity may be dissipated in the absence of timely joint understanding and action. For many years their control over the spread of nuclear weapons, for example, was nearly complete. The common interest of the two powers in preventing the spread of such weapons to Nth countries gave rise to a continuing interest in the possibility of reaching an agreement on the test ban. Unfortunately, for a variety of reasons, no agreement was possible until 1963. Even then the Test Ban Treaty in no way reduced the nuclear capabilities of the signatories. While the test ban represented a step of great potential symbolic importance in the improvement of relations between the two powers, many other measures will continue to be required to modify in any conclusive way their dangerous adversary posture. Moreover, other actions of equal import will be required to dissuade France and China and possibly other countries from continuing to seek to develop their own nuclear capabilities. Should this not be possible it will still remain in the interests of the two great powers to seek to limit the nuclear capabilities of these countries or to bring the capacities under control in other ways.

CONTROL OF CONVENTIONAL CAPABILITIES OF OTHER STATES

The control of conventional capabilities is a problem of quite a different character. After World War II the aggressive intentions of the Soviet Union around its entire periphery led to the American program of strengthening indigenous forces all the way from Europe to the Far East. This program of military assistance has spread in varying degree to parts of Latin America. Within the program, it is possible to limit national capabilities by emphasizing the maintenance of internal order rather than the ability to counter and, therefore, in some degree, to conduct external invasions. The Soviet program of seeking to extend its political influence in some of these countries has been seriously hindered by the buildup of national forces. In order to counter this in certain areas the Soviet government has launched its own program of military assistance. Meanwhile its emphasis on peaceful coexistence has increased while its use of military assistance to support its political gains in some areas seems to have grown. The United States program of military assistance was necessarily launched without any serious consideration of the consequences for the security of the great powers if the Soviet Union should choose to follow suit. The present need is for both the United States and the Soviet Union to reconsider their programs of military assistance and to examine, to the extent required by their own national interests, the possibilities for a further modification of the programs in light of the developing competition and their own interest in stability.

CODE OF RESTRAINT ON CONFLICT IN THIRD AREAS

While it is useful for each of the great powers to be concerned with the need for a restraint in the actions of third states, the steady growth of this attitude probably requires the development of a code of semiviolent, nonmonopoly politics for the conduct of competition in these areas. Such a code must assume that the competition and conflict will continue and that some of it will be violent. On the other hand, it can also assume that both of the great powers will retain an interest in controlling the conflict and will be obliged to take a long view of the importance of any specific gain or loss.

The difficulty in capitalizing on the two powers' mutual interest in restraint arises, first, from their tendency when seeking to negotiate concrete agreements to place the negotiation within the framework of the total antagonism as professed in their long-run goals. Every formal agreement must thus meet the dual test of resolving the issue in conflict and if not advancing at least not giving any ground in their world-wide competition. In addition, explicit agreements inevitably have implications for the allies of each. In the case of the Soviet Union, for example, any hint of the growth of amicable relationships with the United States may serve to exacerbate Soviet relations with Communist China. Similarly, any indication that the United States may be ready to reach a settlement on Berlin gives rise to fears and raises a series of imponderable questions in West Germany. Second, each antagonist is today maintaining a whole array of pressures on the other. Removal of any one of these pressure points from the field of contention, even for a time, gives rise to changes in the significance of the others.

Since the conflict is to continue as before even after the settlement of specific issues, the decision to agree to their settlement involves the solution of a complex multiple equation which statesmen find almost impossible to solve. Thus the risk of settling a particular issue is subject to inflation as a result of the hypothetical influence it may have on the whole system of pressure which makes up so large a part of the relationships of the two great powers. The result is that, as opportunities for *détente* or other mutual actions change with shifts in leadership, public attitudes, or military technology, they frequently pass by before they can be consummated.

On the other hand, the world-wide conflict tends to persist and to develop certain uniformities in behavior with respect to similar situations. The very persistence of the conflict gives rise to the possibility of developing a tacit code of semiviolent, nonmonopoly politics which would help to control the conflict. However, it will be difficult to extend restraint if both sides pursue a policy of an eye for an eye and a tooth for a tooth, and it will not be possible if one believes that the behavior of the opponent is immutable and not subject to change by outside influence. In fact, however, the whole history of the postwar relationship suggests that the influence of the two powers on each other is a most significant long-term factor both in their external behavior and in their internal evolution.

The development of a code of conflict should begin with a careful elaboration of present patterns of behavior and then seek for ways to make the interaction less violent and less prone to escalate into war. An essential element of a code of restraint is the development of the concept of nonmonopoly politics in the world-wide competition for influence.[8] Indeed, an examination of past behavior suggests that this is the direction in which the two powers have been moving, in part from necessity and perhaps in part from choice. There are today very few areas of the world in which either power has excluded or could totally exclude the influence of the other.

There is an urgent need to attempt to generalize and elaborate the steps by which something in the nature of a semiviolent, two-party, nonmonopoly politics could become the norm in world affairs. What is suggested is akin to both the complex rules of warfare established in the Middle Ages and the tacit rules of political conflict which govern established societies. Initially, such a code would certainly have to recognize acts of violence such as the jailing of members of a minority, riots, and perhaps even the occasional political murder. In some areas of the world, it would have to deal with the politics of guerrilla and counterguerrilla activities and the rules of accommodation when violence had mounted to these heights. In other areas where the domestic military forces supported by the West are dominant, the minuet of violence and accommodation by which dissident views are taken into account would need to be developed.

Finally, there is an urgent requirement to elaborate the limits on the style and scope of intervention by the great powers which

[8] See Talcott Parsons, "Polarization and the Problem of International Order," unpublished paper, 1961.

will be permitted in the variety of circumstances that may arise. In some cases, of course, the interest in intervention to maintain the *status quo* may be mutual, and in others it may be very one-sided. The role of dissident nationals, of volunteers, and of organized national forces in such intervention needs to be investigated. In the development of a code, careful consideration should be given to the role of multilateral intervention as contrasted with the unilateral intervention of one side or the other. Just as in the case of economic assistance, the multilateral agencies of the United Nations and other institutions represent a significant alternative to military bilateral action.

In summary, the United States and the Soviet Union have common interests in limiting the military capabilities of third areas, in controlling the conflict which may be generated by the aspirations of these third areas, and in avoiding being exploited or having to engage in economic or military assistance on a competitive basis which might be costly and dangerous to both.

5 Science and World Enterprises—Space, the Atmosphere, and the Oceans

TWENTIETH-CENTURY man seems to have set himself six main tasks of particular interest to our theme. First, he seeks to understand the world around him. Second, he seeks to penetrate outer space. Third, he seeks to predict and ultimately to control the physical environment of his own planet. Fourth, he seeks to attain an advanced level of technology and production. Fifth, while planning enterprises for the future, he seeks to enjoy life more fully in a secure present. Sixth, he desires, in some degree, to assist the world-wide spread of technology and foster the social and political development of all peoples.

In this and subsequent chapters the nature of these tasks will be described and the possibilities for common action by the United States and the Soviet Union discussed. In this chapter the tasks of understanding the world, penetrating outer space, and controlling the environment of earth are dealt with. Chapter 6 discusses the interplay of production and patterns of use between the United States and the Soviet Union. Chapter 7 deals with the problem of communication and common approaches to the enjoyment of life. Chapter 8 is concerned with the economic and political development of third areas.

Our purpose is not to argue that particular lines of action must be followed, but to display a significant part of the front on which common Soviet-American activities could be undertaken. Our intention is to stimulate discussion and thought leading to action, not to attempt to specify the exact nature of the actions which will be found feasible and desirable in the end.

Each of these tasks raises issues between the United States and the Soviet Union, between the two states and the rest of the world, and between each state and its own citizens. Each task also opens possibilities for the development of instrumental interdependence of interests between the two societies. For all, new means and techniques of communication will be required if power is to be manifested by persuasion. No single individual may hope to survey this range of human endeavor with the eyes of an expert. No statesman, whatever the resources now at his command, can hope to say accurately just what is to be done. Nevertheless, it may be useful to scan the various tasks in the hope of identifying the medium-range possibilities for progress and of indicating some of the obstacles. The attempt may serve to suggest lines of appropriate action for the United States if it is to sustain a leading role in shaping the world environment in the second half of the twentieth century.

Understanding the Environment

Science is the search for a true understanding of the human condition—in its physical and social aspects. The search for understanding is personal and individual. The work of the individual scientist finds its meaning, however, in the work of his predecessors, contemporaries, and successors throughout the world. The language, methods, and values of the scientific search for understanding are universal.[1] Scientists share a common vision of the unity of the environment, however much their specializations may at times appear to divide them.

In the past half century the world-wide community of science has increased immensely in significance. While it as yet nowhere directs the affairs of a nation-state, its influence on the actions of states is widespread and growing. The culture of science with its universal values appears to be steadily advancing amid the clash of national interests, however one may wish it.

No comprehensive account of the spreading influence of the culture of science in the present period is yet available. The potential of science is suggested by the fact that in this generation there are more scientists alive than have lived in all previous history. Whereas a hundred years ago there were less than one thousand scientific and technical journals published in the world, and at the turn of the century the number was ten thousand, now there are one hundred thousand.

Science—because it is the work of talented individuals found in all countries—requires world-wide relationships if it is to be most fruitful in gaining an understanding of the environment. Moreover, not only is the progress of science heavily dependent upon a global framework of relationships, but the growth in all nations of a true understanding of the world environment is intimately linked with a science which is universally viewed as valid.

[1] Roger Revelle, former Science Advisor to the Secretary, Department of the Interior, in "International Cooperation and the Two Faces of Science," unpublished paper, 1962. He deals extensively with the role of science and scientist.

The world community of science requires easy and unimpeded communication between the scientists of different countries as they pursue their varied investigations. The forms of communication which the scientific community seems to require include the following: participation in international organizations and meetings; international scientific journals and information-retrieval services; exchange of scientists and students; exchange of data, instruments, and techniques; and, finally, the opportunity for the further development of the common languages of science.

Between the United States and the free world all these means of communication, although still inadequate, are growing. Between the Soviet Union and some parts of the world, they are, while seriously impeded, also growing. Between the United States and the Soviet Union, probably the two most advanced scientific nations in the world, they are limited, often impeded, and seldom adequately supported. The obstacles to the growth in scientific cooperation originate largely, but not wholly, with the Soviet Union.

In the postwar period, contacts between Soviet and American scientists were extremely limited until 1958. Subsequent to the signing of the first Cultural Exchange Agreement in 1958, the contacts have gradually increased but still remain at a very low level as compared with other areas of the world. In 1962, for example, less than one per cent of American university faculty members who spent extended time abroad for research or teaching did so in the Soviet Union. Only about two-tenths of one per cent of all American overseas students attended Soviet educational facilities. Soviet students and faculty in the United States were proportionately somewhat lower. The present agreement between the two National Academies of Science calls for an infinitesimal one hundred and sixty man-months of exchanges.

In terms of attendance at international conferences, the picture may be somewhat better, although no quantitative measures are available. The Soviet scientists appear to be participating in an increasing, though still selective, range of scientific meetings. The United States scientists have, for some time, to the limit of funds, participated in a wide range of international gatherings. The Soviet Union and the United States are now exchanging a large volume of scientific publications although there are continuing problems of effective utilization on the American side and perhaps in the Soviet Union as well.

For the natural scientists, the thirteen great international unions and their coordinating body, the International Council of Scientific Unions, are among the most active and effective means of fostering scientific communication. Both Soviet and American scientists are active participants in these bodies. There are also, of course, many intergovernmental organizations which contribute to effective scientific communications. The World Meteorological Association and UNESCO are examples of such organizations, some of which have a largely scientific orientation and others of which are charged with action responsibilities as well.

All governments have the power to either impede or support effective scientific communication and thus to block or advance man's growing understanding of his environment. Soviet and American doctrine on the world role of the scientist has been quite different. The Soviet government views the scientist first as a servant of the state. Within this doctrine, however, the opportunities for international communication and movement for selected Soviet scientists have been gradually widening. The American attitude is that the scientist is, in principle, free to travel and to talk to whomever he may wish. In fact, however, a variety of subtle practices and attitudes have grown up which in concrete cases may inhibit effective and timely communication. Laying aside communication of decisive importance to military strength, one may ask whether the American restraints on scientific freedom are now in the national interest of the United States. Clearly, answers will differ depending on the value individuals place on the international scientific community as compared with the national political community. But among those who place primary emphasis on the values of the state, there also may be differences.

As we have seen earlier, statesmen as well as scientists have before them a vision of a world community. For the statesman the foundation has been the class or the nation-state. For the scientist, it is the community of individuals seeking to understand their environment. For both, control of the environment remains an ultimate goal.

Scientists of many nations view themselves as colleagues, not competitors, in the search for knowledge of value to all mankind. From the steady, piece-by-piece accumulation of scientific knowledge, they see the possibilities unfold for man to gain control over nature, and ultimately over himself, and over the conflicts which divide him from his fellow men. Statesmen, viewing the achievements of science through a darkened but demanding glass, see it as their task to direct the fruits of science and technology to serve the security and welfare of their nation. They also sense the role of science in providing the foundations for the world community.

But since statesmen are, in the main, the managers of "what is" rather than of "what might be," they await the initiative of science and technology for the identification and crystallization of new tasks.

If the attention of science and technology is too largely focused on the nation, the tasks it helps to identify will strengthen the state, while the strength of the larger community will remain latent and its needs unmet. At the pace that science is now moving, this imbalance promises conflict, not peace; catastrophe, not progress. It is now possible for science to place the weight of its influence behind the devising of new methodology, new goals which represent a challenge and an opportunity for the larger community and which can be achieved, if at all, less well by the nation-state, whether it be the United States or the Soviet Union. At the Pugwash Conference at Stowe, Vermont, in 1961, a start was made in this direction, but much more remains to be done. Science is instrumental as well as objective. Statesmen stand in need of ideas and programs by which they may move toward the goal of the larger community they share with the scientists, but know no sure way to achieve.

At the same time science will do well to remain aware of the large element of uncertainty in the affairs of men. Public opinion, even more than statesmen, lags in appreciation of the constructive possibilities opened by modern science. Moreover, man's behavior is influenced not only by his belief in the prospects of the future but by the sentiments he carries forward from the past. Because of his history, man seems always to be ignoring some of his brightest present possibilities. The state has played a notable part in that history. Science needs to understand the state and learn to cope with it. Understanding is necessary not only because the individual scientist owes allegiance to a state, but because at present it is the main institution both for the maintenance of order and for the allocation of resources to the tasks of world science. Most of all, however, it must be understood because the functions of the state will need modification if peace is to be possible and science is to fulfill its promise.

Scientists, who are pursuing on a world-wide basis their efforts to understand all aspects of the environment, may play a critical role in laying the basis for a relationship of constructive interdependence between the United States and the Soviet Union.

Further advances in science and technology will be needed and may be expected. Equally important is the way these advances are perceived and used by the adversaries. Science and scholarship, technology and economic growth, at an accelerating rate, are increasing the basis for interdependence and peaceful relations among the nations and people of the world. Science is a common enterprise of men of many nations. Scientists, irrespective of the society to which they belong, are working on a common task— to give man a better understanding of nature and mastery over its forces.[2] It is not only command over nature that science promises but a more adequate understanding of man himself. The life sciences and the behavioral sciences are on the threshold of new insights which permit the hope that man may learn to live with himself, but the spread of new knowledge as it becomes available will take time and effort. While it is yet too soon to believe that

[2] Eugene Rabinowitch, "The Role of the Scientist in the Community," unpublished paper prepared for the Tenth Pugwash Conference in London, 1962. Rabinowitch presents a bold statement of the role and responsibilities of the scientist in the modern world.

man may not again seek to turn his power over nature and knowledge of man to the conquest of other men, an alternative use of his new-found powers in the interests of mankind now lies visible on the horizon. The answer will come in the tasks he sets for himself and the institutions he creates for their achievement.

SCIENCE AND THE WEB OF DECISION

The principal question for governments is whether it is in the interest of society not only to allow the scientist full freedom in pursuing his investigations of man's environment, but whether it is also in its interest to provide substantial material support for the effort, whatever direction it may take. For example, should American scientists be encouraged and supported in their efforts to develop working relations with their Soviet opposite numbers? If the answer is Yes, it well may be because statesmen and the public have come to understand how antithetical to dogmatic Communism, without being injurious to Soviet society, is the culture and outlook of science. Again, if the answer is Yes, it may also be because we in the United States have come to see more clearly that the allegiance of science to truth and understanding is not, as presently appears to some, a conflict of allegiance with the state. While inevitably the style of allegiance of the scientist to his state will be modified by his preoccupation with truth and knowledge of value or interest to all men, this is not a contradiction. The purpose of the state, in the view of the West, is also its service to man. This is not to suggest that, in the working out of the scientist's allegiance to truth and to his particular proportion of mankind, acute practical problems may not from time to time arise.

But as we in the United States seek to shape the environment in ways compatible with our emphasis on the rights and freedom of the individual, will it not be prudent to give our scientists the run of terrestrial space and help them by all feasible means to enlarge their relationships with the scientific community of the Soviet Union?

Will it not be wise to grant them the prerogative of the ant in the old fable? In the fable, a festival of the animals was being held from which the ant had been excluded. But as the lion, king of beasts, was reviewing his subjects, an evil worm crawled into his ear, causing great pain. After all efforts to remove the worm had failed, the ant was called. He crawled into the lion's ear and removed the worm. As a reward for this service, ants, unlike any other animal, were granted the freedom to live and move anywhere on earth, which they do to this day. Would not a comparable freedom for the scientist be in the interests of the West? After all, what is so subversive of dogma, so upsetting to the doctrinaire, as the patient pursuit of truth and understanding?

In expanding the freedom of science, it is arguable that the United States must take the initiative because it is more powerful, more advanced, and more free. The first two reasons may also be used to assert that the United States should seek to deny the Soviet Union any advantage that we may have. Yet, since each nation is vulnerable to destruction by the other, wisdom suggests that the danger be recognized and common pursuits be cultivated which will help to bridge the present gap between "we" and "they." The future of "we"—both sides—is about equally in the hands of both. Understanding his environment is, of course, only one of the tasks man has set himself. Other fronts must be considered simultaneously. For these, quiet conversation and scholarly exchange are not enough; substantial resources and numbers of talented men must be devoted to the task. Unless this also is done, time is as likely to aggravate the conflict as to reduce it. What is needed as much as the knowledge of what to do—for that exists in increasing degree—is the faith in the value of constructive efforts, the will to undertake them, the resources to support them, and the wit to involve the adversary in their doing. While these are not always at the disposal of democratic governments, they will be made available when the purpose is clear and challenging.

The case for seeking to increase scientific cooperation by a factor of one hundred or even one thousand over present levels does not rest alone on the general convergence of values and goals which might be affected, but also upon its contribution to the political matrix within which political leaders make their decisions. Many stories have been told which illustrate the scope of the mutual suspicion existing at present.[3] They suggest the complexity of

[3] One such story is told by a leading American about an incident during a recent visit to Moscow. "In the evening," said the American, "I attended a small dinner party given by a great man in Soviet science in his apartment near the Academy. The dinner, prepared by his wife, was excellent. In the course of the dinner the host and each of the guests, as sometimes happens in these affairs, proposed a toast. Toward the end of the dinner the host's wife said she would like to propose a toast to the youth of the world but would preface it with a story: Last summer the twenty-year-old son of 'someone' of great significance in the United States visited Moscow and was invited to their *dacha*. During that evening the youth said he 'voted for Kennedy because he felt he would spend more on arms.' " The implications were clear. Afterward, the American responded to the effect that if he had come to Moscow at twenty he probably would have made equally inept remarks, but at twice the age he came as a friend. At this point, "But how do we know?" came from the Soviet lady. On leaving, the host held the American back to apologize. The hostess confided the name of the lad, whose father is known throughout America for his interests in disarmament. But in the end the latent suspicion stood out starkly as stated: "How do we know?"

establishing communication which will significantly contribute to tipping the balance toward mutual respect and trust and away from suspicion, hostility, and conflict. Yet there are many illustrations of the ease with which Americans and Russians develop friendly and rewarding personal relationships. Against this can be set many statements and actions of the Soviet Union and, unavoidably, in response, of the United States, which reinforce the feelings of suspicion, anxiety, and hostility of individuals on both sides. Overcoming personal suspicion is not sufficient to eliminate the conflict of systems, but it may be an essential step in controlling it.

Even face-to-face dialogue is not a simple matter when each participant has a different frame of reference. Yet the basic requirement for effective communication is neither so hard to grasp nor so difficult to execute that it need escape an American in a dialogue with his Soviet opposite number. First, a context must be provided by making salient the areas of agreement or, rather, series of points of agreement or similarity. Once this has been achieved, it is possible to imbed in this context a small number of points of disagreement with reasonable confidence that a modification of view will occur. The process must be repeated many times before a significant shift in outlook may be expected to occur. Small wonder the convergence of values of citizens of the two sides is not swiftly apparent after a two-week or thirty-day visit. Yet, since the change is bound to be slow, states need fear mutual contacts less than they usually do.

Moreover, as compared with the modification of the views of individuals, the change in outlook of a society or even of its influential elites is unavoidably glacial. A moment's reflection will suggest why this may be true. Just as the communications between two sides must be located in a context of agreement, so also must the communications between the men at the margin and those within their own society. Those within the society are almost wholly intent on its progress and well-being. The context is fixed by the society. The area for successful introduction of dissonance is restricted in many ways. Not the least of these is the marginal man's knowledge that his acceptance, his career, and the meaning of his life are bound up with close adherence to the norms his society presently lays down. When both sides view the other as the opponent or enemy the limitations are especially great. These restraints help to account for the fact that it is sometimes the old, whose work is nearly finished, who seem to feel most free to communicate with the "enemy" and to seek to modify the outlook of their own society.

The complexity of change in the decision-context helps to explain why the position of a state may remain unaltered even after the negotiators have come to understand each other's views. Others may or may not perceive the consequences of unresolved conflicts of interest. Behind each negotiator stands not only the head of state but a vast organization largely untouched by the face-to-face transaction. The head of state cannot listen only to his negotiator. He must take account of the views flowing in on many other lines of communication from other parts of the state organization and, in the West at least, the views of the society at large.

In this whole process, the negotiator and those who are linked with him must always make sure that the communication of differences which arise from their contact with the other side is placed in a context of agreement throughout their own hierarchy. On both sides negotiators sometimes find this condition impossible to achieve fully. Thousands on both sides are on occasion able to throw their weight on the scales. On the other hand, many are separated from the negotiator by institutional gatekeepers, who control and limit the flow of communication, as well as by formal lines of communication and physical distance which also impede understanding. Scientist and engineer, strategist and economist, all have their role to play in the complicated decision-process of the modern state. Moreover, entwined in every formal organization structure are scores of informal channels of communication and influence along which messages may move to finally tip the balance against the negotiator on any given day.

How dissonant the communications of a negotiator with his own society may be, and thus the map of the possible which he brings with him to the table, depends in some incalculable degree on the condition of this matrix of elite opinion at any given time.

The complexity and breadth of the context from which agreement or disagreement emerges help to account for the importance of deeds as contrasted with conversation in international affairs. Action has greater visibility, as well as being more undeniable proof of purpose. Yet most action is subject to the same hazards as conversation. Unless the intention of action is indisputable—and action rarely is—interpretation of meaning and intention occurs within the context of the dominant belief system of the organization or influence structure. Thus, action intended to reassure or to indicate a convergence of interest may be almost useless if after a long period of conflict no way can be found to locate it within a new common context.

The demanding conditions for influencing another society in reasonably predictable ways by either negotiation or action lead to the efforts of statesmen and diplomats to give the maximum saliency to their primary purposes. The situation also argues for a wide range of channels of communication and exposure to common experience which will help to shape the context out of which the policies of the states emerge.

ASYMMETRY

The United States and the Soviet Union appear to be at present highly asymmetrical with respect to the extent to which their influential elites are exposed to communication from the opposing society. The United States, with its tradition of free press and free speech and with influential elites outside the governmental structure, is more accessible to Soviet efforts to influence the decision-making context. The Soviet Union continues to place many impediments in the path of its influential elites in their contact with the West and almost insurmountable obstacles to the development of work or other relationships providing a common experience. It has long been recognized as being in the United States interest to attempt to expand the transactions between Soviet and American citizens in many areas, but the funds and talent devoted to the task are minimal. The present inflated Soviet version of security which looks forward to an all-Communist world is an obvious obstacle. But, in the longer run, if the United States were to devote sufficient resources to the task, the possibility exists that the Soviet Union might come increasingly to see that in a nuclear world open communication best serves its security interests. As a lever of internal control, imperfect secrecy, which is the only kind possible for a modern society, may come to be seen as inadequate to preserve a dogmatic image of the world and thus more dangerous than useful.

Opening up the lines of scientific communication would seem to be a logical step in the process. Soviet scientists are familiar with Western publications. High-level contacts between United States and Soviet scientists have been going on for some time. A substantial body of scientific tourism—two-week and one-month travels—has been taking place on each side. The time would seem ripe to try to expand these relationships by an initial factor of ten or twenty. For this purpose, added funds and a good deal more managerial imagination and freedom will be required. As a first step, each natural and social science discipline, perhaps through the appropriate national organizations and using all available knowledge about the present state of Soviet-American relations in their fields of specialty, might be asked to develop a five-year pro-gram which would be operated on an autonomous basis by the academic organizations themselves. Either foundation or govern-ment funds would also be required to provide a center to advise on and facilitate cross-communication for the entire program. Discussions and negotiations would be undertaken on an inde-pendent basis with the Soviet opposite numbers, who may be far from independent but are not wholly fettered. The Federal gov-ernment's role would be limited to facilitation and watchfulness.

Whenever the specialized academic organization felt it to be desirable, collaboration with the Soviet Union could be set within a multinational framework. Indeed, in some cases, this might be found necessary to elicit Soviet cooperation.

Penetration of Outer Space

The second and third tasks of twentieth-century man are scien-tifically interrelated and present common problems of cross-national action. Ability to understand, predict, and control the terrestrial environment can make a contribution to space exploration. Penetration of space will provide information of value in controlling the terrestrial environment. Scientific investigation in space and on the total terrestrial environment requires large-scale funding and organization. Enterprises for exploration and control will require still more.

The United States has an interest in a more balanced allocation of Soviet scientific and technical investments to the entire range of the problems facing mankind, rather than overwhelmingly—as is the present case—to weaponry. Even on an uncoordinated basis, balanced Soviet investment in all fields of man's interest would be preferable to Soviet emphasis on weapons. But in order further to safeguard itself against scientific advances being turned to aggressive purposes, the United States may find it in its interest to seek to gain Soviet participation in joint undertakings. The geographical bias of the nations must be diffused by their peoples' participation in world-wide functional programs in which all play their appropriate parts.

SPACE EXPLORATION

The opening of outer space to human exploration may prove to be a discontinuity in the history of human development comparable to the discovery of the new world in the fifteenth century and surpassing in importance the advent of nuclear weapons. A new vision of what is possible and what is necessary is needed.

The time may already have passed when the landing on the moon could be converted to a joint enterprise as proposed by the United States. But there will be requirements for space laboratories and the exploration of the other planets in our solar system. In the context of the present struggle, these will inevitably be attempted in a costly and possibly more risky way by both sides. Alternatively, the United States may have the option to begin now to allocate substantial research and development funds for the specific purpose of devising and designing future efforts which could be accomplished more effectively by the two powers jointly than by either side alone. At the appropriate time the Soviets could then be invited to join in the planning and development of these efforts as well as in their execution if this were deemed in the nation's interest. In this way the United States could influence Soviet allocation of its resources toward a preferred use, as contrasted with military power, and begin to provide the structure within which the use of the resources will gradually draw the two sides together in a common enterprise.

While space capabilities represent an opportunity for common action, since they are possessed by both the United States and the Soviet Union, space is not apolitical. Cooperation between the United States and the Soviet Union, if it is possible, will have to be developed on earth just as is the case with other man-made programs. Space represents a special opportunity at this time because current efforts must be largely concerned with acquiring an understanding of the new environment and the ability to perform in it. The problems are thus, for the moment, primarily scientific, and the participants on both sides are more than normally influenced by the universal values of science. While cooperation in space, by itself, is unlikely to eliminate the political conflict on earth, it could provide common experience and interests which would work to offset the earthly conflicts. Conversely, the national conflicts will impede and delay the development of cooperation in space.

UNITED STATES GOVERNMENT AND SPACE

If successful Soviet-American collaboration in space is to be attempted, it is desirable to be as clear as possible on the various points of view within the United States government. Different parts of the government stress different primary purposes for the space effort. The different purposes lead to a different emphasis both with respect to the character of our own space activities and with respect to the extent of our cooperation with other countries, particularly the Soviet Union. The space programs and attempts at cooperation which emerge are the result of the play of forces within the United States government, the receptivity of the Soviet Union, and the technical requirements which must be met to conduct any program successfully in outer space.

DEPARTMENT OF STATE

The Department of State looks upon space and space programs as one of a number of means to strengthen the world order. In this view, the peace and stability of the world that was maintained for almost a hundred years prior to World War I was shattered by that war. It is essential to find ways to fit together the splintered pieces of the world and to re-establish a stable order. In this light, space programs provide a tool which may be used to weave together the fragmented nations into a community which is not dominated by the Soviet Union or Communist China.

International space activity provides an opportunity to contribute to this end because countries which become committed to space programs are required to make substantial investments of their resources and to develop common interests in the use of space for such things as weather control and communications. Moreover, in certain specific cases, countries may be able through space activities to get out from under certain international institutional arrangements which are viewed as outmoded.

Those in charge of United Nations affairs within the Department of State both in Washington and in New York, as might be expected from their more specialized responsibilities, emphasize a somewhat different purpose of space activities. They are inclined to accept the proposition that, because space is a new environment requiring scientific skills which are largely apolitical, it provides a unique opportunity which calls for bold new ventures in the creation of new forms of political power to manage affairs in outer space. They would feel that outer space represents the best opportunity for creating a world community. They are concerned with strengthening the executive role of the United Nations and would visualize outer space as an area in which the United Nations might well be given executive responsibilities. Thus, they see outer-space programs as a means of strengthening the United Nations organization and, through that means, of strengthening the bonds of the world community. Conversely, they would argue that the nature of space is such that this is an inevitable development and that the United States should move with the tide.

In specialized parts of the Department of State, space tends to be seen in terms of its contribution to particular objectives. The African Bureau may, for example, feel that the space programs can serve as one means, among many others, of increasing African consciousness of the unity of world affairs and offsetting their highly particularistic present interests.

From a functional point of view, lawyers both within and outside the Department of State are interested in outer space for a variety of reasons. From a practical point of view, there are a number of legal problems which have arisen or are likely to arise in the future. Of immediate practical interest are the laws which will govern the indemnities to be paid for damages done by objects falling from space. There are also a variety of new questions, such as how the rights to minerals on the moon are to be determined.

Thus lawyers see space as the new environment for which the ground rules must be laid through the normal legal processes. For this purpose, one may visualize international law on earth as applying, with suitable adaptations, to outer space. In this new environment, they seem to feel that lawyers can somehow improve on previous international law. Thus, while outer space will undoubtedly be an area of litigation, it is also viewed as an opportunity for the improvement of the application of international law to human affairs, whether it be legislative law, common law, or simply the development of precedents.

NATIONAL AERONAUTICS AND SPACE ADMINISTRATION

Within the National Aeronautics and Space Administration (NASA), which is charged with the primary responsibility for developing United States programs for the peaceful exploitation of outer space, there appear to be two main purposes that determine the character of the effort. First, and most important, there are a large number of people in NASA whose interest in outer space is purely scientific and technical. They are responding to the proposition that the challenge of space is immense. They find that working in the field of outer space is exciting and they are deeply interested in the knowledge to be gained. NASA and this large group of individuals within it are closely linked with the scientific groups throughout the country and, in significant degree, they are representative of American scientists. Second, there is a group within NASA for which the management of outer-space programs is essentially thought of as a challenge to their ability as executives and managers. The task, as they see it, is to create enterprises which succeed and which are managed efficiently and effectively. International collaboration tends to be seen, at times, as simply an additional complication in achieving efficiency.

DEPARTMENT OF DEFENSE

Next there is the Pentagon purpose. As might be expected, the Pentagon views the military purposes of programs in outer space as both primary and paramount. The Pentagon view, voiced mainly by the Air Force (which has the primary responsibility for military outer-space programs), is that "he who controls outer space controls the world." Thus, the military imagination sees outer space as the high ground from which the victory will be won. The military establishment, and particularly the Air Force, is committed to mastering the new environment and to developing the techniques and tactics required to give the United States control of outer space, and thus of our little world below.

The main institutional actors in the arena of outer space within the United States government are the Department of State, NASA, and the Pentagon. In addition, there is the very important role played by the President and his immediate staff, about which more will be said later. From the interplay of the differing purposes of these actors and their varying capabilities emerges the American outer-space policy. This policy is conditioned by the United States views of the Soviet space effort.

The judgment with respect to the Soviet program varies more with the agency from which the judgment originates than with the specialized knowledge which may be available. However, seers on the Soviet Union are regularly consulted as programs are launched or as cooperative activities are attempted. Generally speaking, to avoid Cassandra's fate, American experts on the Soviet Union have applied to the problems of outer space the same earth-bound views they hold of other Soviet-American affairs.

SPACE PROGRAMS

Space accomplishments constitute an element of national power and are used to bolster competitive positions in international politics. They may also have, in the longer run, a significant military potential. At the same time, efforts are being made to achieve cooperation between the United States and the Soviet Union in space science and applications.

American space efforts are a product of early military initiative in space. Space emerged as an area of international competition with the launching of the first Sputnik by the Soviet Union in October, 1957. The military implications, which were already understood by experts, suddenly became clear to all who were willing to see. The psychological impact of this accomplishment, however, which for many validated the achievements of Soviet society, was startling to nearly everyone. The United States swiftly turned to the task, as it saw it, of recouping its fallen prestige. It has now launched more than three times as many satellites and deep-space probes as the Soviet Union.

The United States space efforts, therefore, which began with military developments and, indeed, conflict between the services, have now been divided into two great space programs, one under the aegis of the Pentagon, and the other, of growing significance, under the responsibility of NASA.[4]

The United States, handicapped by lack of engines having the powerful thrust of the Soviet competitor, sought quite successfully to make up for the deficiency in its boosters by the variety and scientific relevance of its efforts. Before long a manned flight to the moon and back became the immediate target of the competition.

It seems unlikely that the effort of either the United States or the Soviet Union would be financed on the present scale were it not for the competition of the other. For this view indisputable proof is not available. What does seem clear, however, is that the objectives of both programs might have been quite different if either had concentrated entirely on the military uses of close-in space.

It is of great significance to note that so far as is known, the Soviet emphasis to date has been on scientific and prestige accomplishments and that this, in turn, has elicited a comparable response from the United States. This is not to suggest that either has neglected the earthly military utility of ICBMs hurtled through space.

---

[4] Attempts to link these two efforts led to the announcement of Department of Defense participation in the Gemini program.

While both may gain national prestige from landing a man on the moon and bringing him back, the prestige is likely to be both ephemeral and less significant than presently estimated, so long as both accomplish the objective in roughly the same time span.

In the long run, unless other events intervene, both the United States and the Soviet Union will no doubt seek to develop military capacity in space. But for the moment the informed opinion appears to be that neither has a specific weapons program under way, although programs for use of space for military support in communications, navigation and other fields are well advanced.[5]

At present the United States space program has widespread support. The reasons for the support vary. They include the high esteem in which science is held, expectation of practical applications, the drama of conquering the unknown, the desire to achieve national prestige and leadership and, perhaps most important, the potential contribution to national defense.

From a funding point of view, the space program is, in the longer perspective, just getting under way. Informed scientists expect expenditures to continue to rise until the end of the decade.[6]

Despite the widespread present support and the growing magnitude of the space program, it represents for a significant proportion of the population a subject of indifference, anxiety, or dissatisfaction. Sources of dissatisfaction are diverse. They include both fears that the space program will increase the probability of war and

[5] For a review of the United States military space effort, see the speech given by John H. Rubel, Assistant Secretary of Defense, at the Aerospace Luncheon Club, *Department of Defense News Release,* No. 1642-62, Oct. 9, 1962.

[6] Space Science Board of the National Academy of Sciences, Report of the Summer Study, *A Review of Space Research* (Washington, D.C.: National Academy of Sciences, 1962), 16-28.

fears that it may not be sufficiently militarily oriented. We do know that concern about the possibility of war is a salient attitude in the United States.[7]

Thus on the grounds that no specific weapons for use in outer space are presently contemplated, on the grounds that gains in prestige to be derived from two more or less comparable space efforts are probably overestimated, on the grounds that the projected space effort will be extremely costly, and on the grounds that wholehearted continuing public support cannot be taken for granted, it seems prudent to examine more thoroughly the possibilities and contributions of more widely based cooperation with the Soviet Union.

SPACE COOPERATION

To get an adequate perspective from which to view such cooperation, it is useful to step away from the specific narrow focus of the two programs which have been heavily oriented to achieving feats in space. Space must be seen as a new dimension of man's environment, which is unlimited in scope. Of equal significance for the years ahead, man's knowledge of this environment, through which he ultimately intends to move, is extremely fragmentary and incomplete.

There remain today not only a myriad of technical problems to be overcome in moving even the relatively short distances to the moon, but many unanswered scientific questions as well. National pride at our success is a proper attitude, but national humility at the unknown hazards and tasks ahead is equally necessary.

[7] Hadley Cantril and Lloyd A. Free, "Hopes and Fears for Self and Country," *American Behavioral Scientist,* Vol. VI, Supplement (Oct., 1962), No. 2.

It may well be that the talents of the entire community of man, not merely separate segments under a particular flag, will be required for the endeavor. The task of gaining such control as now can be exercised over man's terrestrial environment has been the work of many generations and of men of many nations. Is it more likely that the conquest of an environment for which, so far as is known, man is not particularly adapted will be the prerogative of men of a single nation working apart and walled off from their colleagues on other parts of the globe? Moreover, if the conquest of space can be achieved at all, how much greater will be the cost in time, men, and resources drained away from other more mundane but equally urgent tasks?

For all great changes in human affairs, some times are more propitious than others. Once space is armed, the chance of collaboration seems surely to be lost for the present era. In the meantime, an opportunity exists in logic, if not in earthly politics, to broaden and deepen cooperative efforts with other nations—particularly the Soviet Union—to understand and to explore the strange and alien environment of space.

Thus far, efforts at significant cooperation in space have been frustrated because the ideas advanced have been those which either side could implement, more or less well, alone. What are needed are ideas leading to projects which could be done far more effectively and at less cost together than they could be done separately, if in fact they could be accomplished at all without collaboration. The International Geophysical Year, 1957–58, is an example of one such common undertaking. The IGY was carried through by the cooperative endeavor of thousands of scientists of many nations, frequently with the substantial support of governments.

It illustrates the possibilities of scientific collaboration. However, cooperative data collection and analysis while important do not ensure the cumulative involvement of increasing numbers of men of all nations. Scientific collaboration will not be enough; it must lead to the involvement of thousands of talented men in constructive common enterprises, of whom scientists will be a minority.

The United States can exert pressure for increased Soviet allocations to space by increasing its own allocations for a competitive program of space exploration as it has done over the past few years. But as long as these programs are conducted on a unilateral basis, they do not reduce the long-run military threat to both sides. In time, space advances may be turned to military advantage. Thus, while space competition may be less deadly than direct military competition in the short run, the development of common interests in space is needed to channel the competition into constructive purposes in the long run. For this, common enterprises are necessary in which the tasks and the goals are shared.

Symbolically important, but materially insignificant, Soviet-American cooperation has already been agreed upon in certain space activities such as weather, information, communications, and magnetic mapping. These areas of cooperation are carefully delimited so as not to affect the pattern of resource-use on either side. They are highly valuable as beginnings. They demonstrate the profound dedication of the men who shaped them. Only as their scope is expanded can they play a significant role in linking the two societies. A series of world space enterprises utilizing substantial resources and involving significant numbers of people from both sides is required not only to influence Soviet resource allocations toward constructive scientific and technical purposes but also as a basis for a rational and comprehensive scientific and engineering effort to understand and explore outer space.

The time may already have passed when the Apollo program and its Soviet counterpart could be converted to a joint enterprise. The Apollo program for landing a man on the moon may be related to man's innate desire to explore unknown regions; it has been implemented, however, for reasons of national prestige. A space race is on to see whether a national of the United States or of the Soviet Union will be first to land on the moon. In this endeavor, and even in later efforts to reach other parts of the solar system, there may be a "winner." But if the winner is to be "man," to use a much abused term, then the feats funded by political leaders from the wealth of the nations must serve to advance our understanding of the new environment and to make our present situation more acceptable, more livable.

If the Soviet-American competition for prestige makes unavoidable a dual effort to reach the moon, it does not follow that all preliminary scientific preparations must be dual. Space is not just a larger ocean; the moon and other planets are not simply another West Indies. Space is a new environment. There remain many unanswered or imperfectly answered questions before the possibilities of travel, and return, through this new environment are assured. When the trip is accomplished, some questions will have more adequate answers but many new questions will arise. The space environment for a long time will present a physical, not a social, challenge; knowledge acquired by all nations will be of value to those who seek to understand and explore space. Intermittent scientific conferences are valuable but would hardly seem to be sufficient; the data becoming available is overwhelming, the interconnection of disciplines is too pervasive, and the skills of a national group are too dependent, for timely progress, on the knowledge of another. Surely, it would be wise to consider and to agree on such cross-national institutes or the common use of national facilities which would enhance the safety and fruitfulness of so momentous a journey.

Once the scientific and technological problems of landing a man on the moon have been solved, a whole range of scientific questions arises. The presence of man will open up significant opportunities for scientific observation which can never be accomplished by instruments alone. After so much effort and having traveled so far it would be ironic if both the Soviet cosmonauts and the American astronauts had been trained to make the same limited range of observations and, as a result, many other important aspects of the total situation went unobserved. Is it impossible to conceive of a Moon Science Collaboration Center in which the Soviet and American programs would be carefully examined stage by stage, under controlled conditions, of course, to ensure that man as well as the nation-state received optimum gains from the undertakings?

But, should this prove to be unfeasible, are there not other ways in which the Soviet, American, and other scientists could work together to advance our understanding of space, and ways in which technicians and engineers could collaborate in improving the reliability and performance of our means of exploring it? A reading of *A Review of Space Research,* issued by the National

Research Council of the National Academy of Sciences, leaves no doubt that there are many aspects of space to which there are no answers or where present answers are unsatisfactory.

Beyond the immediate problems of interplanetary exploration, the question of life in space remains one of the most fascinating to mankind. But a more immediate life-and-death issue is how the life of astronauts can best be preserved and protected as they live and work in space. A great deal of effort went into providing suitable life environment for the orbital flights, but much work remains to be done in this area. Joint large-scale Soviet and American efforts in space biology and medicine would seem unobjectionable, and possibly highly useful in improving the chances of survival of our own as well as the "enemy's" astronauts.

The possibility of finding life in extraterrestrial space, while less urgent, may be more intriguing. It is now said to be a serious objective of the international space race. There is, of course, no absolute reason why Soviets and Americans should not compete in seeking to find extraterrestrial life, but neither are there truly compelling reasons why they should. If the question is important, why not a joint effort rather than resting everything on the desire for prestige, or what for a movie star would be termed publicity?

One problem related to life out there is very practical. If human beings foul up the terrain of the moon or Mars, it may be difficult, if not impossible, to determine whether life existed before their arrival and if it did to be wholly clear in drawing inferences about it. Thus, the unsolved question of "sterilization" of space operations on the moon or Mars arises. Of course, either side could foul the planet; yet, in competition, it might be deemed unavoidable in order to score a first. Sterilization, if it is as important as scientists suggest, ought to be tackled cooperatively beforehand, both in order to ensure that adequate techniques are developed and to increase the possibility of restraint as M-for-moon-day approaches.

The foregoing suggestions and many others that could be brought forward are too limited, it may be argued. They would involve at the most a few hundred scientists and engineers in joint efforts. While this may be true, they appear worth attempting, since the momentum the collaboration might gather cannot be wholly foreseen.

Nevertheless, collaboration on projects which involve the design and construction of complex space hardware over a long time and on a large scale is more likely to involve and modify the interests of the nations. To find such projects, one must look well ahead so that the lead time required to devise the forms of cooperation falls within the period prior to the time when massive national resources have been committed on a unilateral basis.

Designing and placing a large and complex laboratory on the moon to conduct on-the-spot experiments, investigations, and explorations which require man's presence may be such a project. The Space Science Board has stated that it can "definitely foresee a need for such a laboratory." [8] It is far off. It will be costly and difficult to create and put in place. No great psychological triumph may be expected from its achievement. At present the relevance of such a laboratory to hard military requirements is remote.

But, it may be said, the Russians will not agree to collaboration. Let us try. When the time is ripe, let the United States announce

[8] *A Review of Space Research,* 1-23.

a first major allocation of, say, a half-billion dollars for research and development of a moon laboratory. Let us invite and encourage our European allies and others to contribute funds and talent, within their capability, to the project, leaving open the door to the Soviet Union—indeed, inviting their participation. Periodically, until they join, let us repeat the invitation. In the end they may come in, if past behavior is a guide. When they do, the first major world enterprise in space will be under way.

CONCLUSION

Man's program in space is an important phenomenon in the mainstream of interstate relations on earth. The requirements for its conduct may be so extensive and its implementation so dangerous that states will be compelled to explore and even to engage in cooperative efforts. The states which may make a contribution in this field will be limited, for some time, to the United States, the Soviet Union, and Europe taken as a whole. There may be some motivation within these political entities to seek to spread the risks and the costs. There are signs that this viewpoint is developing.

If cooperation is to be achieved by United States initiative, then the United States must develop proposals which seem likely to lead to short-run and long-run gains for both sides and which are sufficiently safeguarded so as not to threaten unduly the secrecy on which the Soviet Union believes its security rests. American proposals will not be acceptable if they are seen by the Soviets to be adverse at any stage, or if the total disadvantages outweigh the possible advantages. On the other hand, such activities, if they can be properly designed to safeguard the activities of both sides, may provide significant opportunities for collaboration with the Soviet Union. Thinking somewhat analogous to this may be occurring in the Soviet Union, since Premier Khrushchev took the public initiative, following Colonel John Glenn's flight, to propose cooperation in outer space. The origins of these proposals may be traced back to the latter half of the 1950s. Cooperation has been agreed upon and implementation is proceeding.

From the modest beginnings now under way, more substantial collaboration could in time develop; but there will be many obstacles. The diverse views within the United States government as to the role of space in shaping the world environment is one such obstacle. The continuing reliance of the Soviet Union on secrecy is another. In addition, there is the Soviet resistance to close collaboration. Perhaps the most significant factor, however, is that the office of the President, concentrating as it has on short-range problems, has not had an opportunity to review the long-run possibilities of space in shaping both the American-Soviet relationship and the world environment. Funding and implementation of any of the major collaborative efforts suggested earlier will require an American, and thus a Presidential, initiative. For this to occur the President will have to become more involved with the space program in a world context. The program will have to be his, not the State Department's, the Pentagon's, or even the Vice-President's.

Opportunities for collaboration do not emerge out of thin air; while the objective is a long-range one, day-to-day decisions are required to put in place the elements which will provide the basis for substantial collaboration in the future. It is important to understand the scope of the contact and close working-relations which are required for even a relatively simple joint effort. A steadily widening experience in collaboration in small programs is essential to lay the groundwork for larger efforts. The scope of cooperation required is suggested by the intimacy of working relations demanded for a single cooperative launching by the United States and the United Kingdom.

The launching required a United States booster and a United Kingdom payload. For this single effort it was necessary for a team of United Kingdom scientists to work with the American group for a year and a half. This was necessary even though the British group had had available and had assimilated a great deal of American technical and scientific knowledge with respect to the problem with which they were dealing. Such collaboration in the case of the Soviet Union, or any other national group for that matter, may be complicated still further by differences in language as well as in technology.

The practical difficulties of collaboration make those who will be responsible for implementing a joint effort extremely cautious. Indeed, to the operator responsible for the success of United States programs, there often appears to be a conflict between unilateral and collaborative programs. In these instances, in the absence of strong Presidential leadership, the tendency of an agency is to give priority to what it visualizes as its "own work," the United States unilateral effort. A call for Presidential leadership is of course the frequent resort of the partisans of a particular program. Space may in the future, as it has in the past, require a new and systematic review by the President as part of a general realignment of United States policies toward the Soviet Union.

Predicting and Controlling the Terrestrial Environment

The characteristics of the atmosphere and the world ocean are such as to suggest and, ultimately, demand broad areas of common action by the United States and the Soviet Union as well as by other nations. Large-scale weather control without international collaboration seems likely to be not only troublesome but perhaps dangerous. At some point it might be like having two thermostats for the same house, each controlled by a different person. The world's ocean is the world's largest communal property. As its exploitation and control becomes increasingly feasible, significant problems will arise in the absence of collaboration. For example, a unilateral Russian decision to proceed with the damming of the Bering Strait or other actions to modify Arctic weather—projects long discussed in Soviet literature as important to their economy— would raise a host of new possibilities and problems.

THE ATMOSPHERE AND THE WEATHER

The atmosphere is so often taken for granted that a brief description of how it is viewed by modern science may be useful. The atmosphere is a gaseous wrapper surrounding the earth. It interacts with earth and oceans at the bottom and with solar phenomena at the top. Scientists now view the atmosphere as a single system in which changes in one part of the system may affect many other parts. Meteorology and aeronomy are the sciences which seek to describe, understand, and predict future states of the atmosphere. Meteorology is concerned with the lower reaches of the atmosphere, and aeronomy with the upper reaches. Meteorology is also commonly used to refer to the services provided by the weatherman, who until recently relied mainly on experience rather than on valid scientific knowledge. Indeed, this is still largely the case although the advance of the science of meteorology is swift.

The foundations for the science are being rapidly put in place.[9] In the past three decades, capacity has been developed to lay the groundwork for exploration of the motion of the air up to 100,000 feet. Relatively inaccessible parts of the globe are now being covered by automatic weather-reporting stations. Radar and airborne probes are opening up new opportunities. Exploration of the upper reaches of the atmosphere have been advanced in the last few years. New light is being shed on the link between solar activity and earthly phenomena. In sum, an adequate description of the atmosphere is within reach.

As the vast array of new data is acquired, understanding of the operation of the atmospheric system is being advanced. A blend of mathematical and physical insight, aided by high-speed computers and other devices, is beginning to provide a systematic knowledge of the circulation system of the world's atmosphere as well as specific processes such as condensation and precipitation. Rational numerical methods are replacing traditional methods of empiricism in prediction. Today it is justifiable to hope that a scientific basis for weather prediction may be established in the not-too-distant future.

The atmosphere is an international resource of fundamental im-

[9] For a survey of the present state of meteorology and aeronomy, see *The Atmospheric Sciences—1961–1971*, Vols. I, II, III, National Academy of Sciences, National Research Council, Pub. 946.

portance for human activities. By its very nature it is a world-encircling system which disregards national boundaries. Today's weather in one nation is, as often as not, tomorrow's weather in another. At many stages the problems and potential of the atmosphere require international collaboration if they are to be handled most effectively.

In order to describe the atmosphere, observations are needed on a global basis and at many heights above the earth's surface. A world-wide system of weather-observing facilities are necessary to obtain the data. In turn a high level of competence is necessary throughout if data are to be adequate and comparable. To handle the vast mass of information, modern data-processing and communications systems have become necessary. These systems must serve both long-term scientific and current forecasting requirements. International collaboration on a greatly increased scale is necessary in order to advance both the sciences and the services of meteorology. The cooperation of many nations is involved but especially that of the Soviet Union and the United States, whose satellite launching and data-processing capabilities are an essential part of the new prospects for meteorology. Fortunately, and perhaps inevitably in the nature of the problem, meteorology is one of the areas in which the two powers have reached agreement on parallel if not common action.

But developments of far greater import may be just over the horizon. As the world-wide collection of data is accomplished, as understanding of the entire atmospheric system improves, as prediction of the future state of the weather is put on a solid scientific basis, the prospects for weather control may swiftly emerge. Already it has been demonstrated that certain kinds of clouds and fog can be artificially altered and precipitation possibly affected, that electrical properties of cumulus clouds can be changed and evaporation processes controlled to an extent. The possibility of triggering energy stored in the upper atmosphere has been recognized. Plans are under way to attempt to alter the energies of hurricanes and tornadoes. Finally, new tools which did not exist fifteen years ago are at hand for studying and testing hypotheses of either small- or large-scale weather control. In short, weather control is no longer a dream. "Progress in physics, for example, points toward new possibilities of modifying atmospheric systems on relatively large scales." [10]

The global aspect of the atmosphere, the disrespect of the weather for national boundaries, the geographic relationship of the United States and the Soviet Union to each other and to the Arctic—all these factors suggest that collaboration on weather control ought to be particularly compelling to the two superpowers as well as to other nations. Both nations are now devoting increased resources to advancing the date when weather control will be possible. There is much speculation on the possibilities and consequences of such projects as filling or deepening the Strait of Gibraltar, damming the Bering Strait, pumping water from the Arctic region, or opening up passes in the Sierra Nevada to permit the intrusion of moist air in the Nevada desert. Other proposals have been to spread carbon black over the snow cover or to create ice-crystal fog over the Arctic to interfere with radiation balance and thereby influence the dynamics of air at high altitudes. The new theoretical tools developed within the past decade make it in-

[10] *Ibid.*

creasingly possible to analyze the physical consequences of such actions and to design meaningful experiments to be conducted in nature.[11]

Undoubtedly, on the part of both the United States and the Soviet Union there is a tendency to think in cold-war terms, to see weather control as a potential instrument of conflict. The use of weather for conflict might be feasible if only one side made the attempt, although the advent of scientific weather control might be delayed. But the history of the scientific contest suggests that when one side makes a breakthrough it will not be long before it is also made by the other.

Weather control brings prospects of great benefit to mankind. It may also, for the first time in the present period, raise fundamental conflicts of economic interest. A weather war is conceivable. Yet the same knowledge, the same skills, could work to the benefit of all men—since all are dependent on the behavior of the atmosphere. It would seem undesirable to leave the control of weather entirely to individual nations, however continental their reach. The question is thus posed whether we should not now conceive and initiate, however modestly, the joint enterprise essential for the achievement of the goal and for the management of its consequences.

Today, weather control poses a series of scientific problems. As these are solved political problems of great complexity will arise. If the political problems are to be worked out in their time, a prerequisite may be the collaborative solution of the problems of re-

[11] Thomas F. Malone, "Tomorrow's Weather," *International Science and Technology* (May, 1962), No. 5, pp. 39–45.

search and development which precede them. Fully effective collaborative effort even at the research and development level will involve difficult international political issues. But these may be less acute and easier to cope with than the consequences of scientific advance in the absence of prior experience. Now is the time, in the interests of national security and development, for the United States to apply resources and talent to the task of developing the precedents and the structure within which the growing powers of man over the world's weather will be exercised in the future. World-wide cooperation in weather research and experimentation may be essential, but the close collaboration of the two leading scientific nations—the United States and the Soviet Union—would appear to be equally necessary. The United Nations and its specialized agencies no doubt have an important role to play, but as is the case in all the highly specialized and scientific fields the initial endeavor must rest with those who have the capabilities. For this the leadership of the United States and the Soviet Union together with the other industrialized nations is essential. Now is the time for them to be laying out a five- or ten-year program of collaborative effort from which all may benefit in the future. The preparation for weather control requires, perhaps in even more substantial degree, long-range planning and investment similar to that which now goes into the development and design of the longest lead-time modern weapons systems.

THE WORLD'S OCEAN

The initial common enterprise with respect to the sea is to understand it. "The Seas present a challenge to man which in magnitude approaches that of space. . . . We know less about many

regions of the oceans today than we know about the lunar surface." [12]

In order to understand the world's ocean, basic research and
systematic data collection on a substantial scale are required. In
1959 American oceanographers set as their ultimate goal a survey
of the world ocean. The survey was estimated to require forty
ships over a ten-year period to make bathymetric, magnetic, and
gravity measurements along lines five miles apart. Still other ships
were needed to measure physical and chemical properties and
biological contents of the water. Since the United States had
neither the ships nor the scientists to undertake the survey, two
courses of action were suggested. First, capabilities—in terms of
ships, shore facilities (such as laboratories), and manpower—were
to be increased so that the United States could shoulder its fair
share of the task. Second, planned cooperation among the maritime powers was to be sought.

Earlier, in 1957, a program for a cooperative expedition to survey the Indian Ocean had been conceived, and in 1959 it was
agreed that the Special Committee on Ocean Research (scor) of
the International Scientific Unions would sponsor the enterprises.
As a result, the Indian Ocean Expedition became in effect the
first step in a larger collaborative effort. In 1960 unesco agreed to
co-sponsor the expedition with scor.

Thus, at the present time, a fleet of ships from many nations
carrying highly specialized equipment and scientists is sailing
the Indian Ocean on new voyages of discovery. The Indian Ocean
covers one-seventh of the surface of the earth. In the countries

[12] Harrison Brown, *Oceanography—1960 to 1970* (Washington, D.C.: National
Academy of Sciences, National Research Council, 1959), p. 3.

bordering on it live twenty-five per cent of the world's population. Although less is known about the Indian Ocean than any other, fragmentary evidence indicates that biologically it may be the most productive of all the oceans.[13]

The International Plan was developed under the chairmanship of an Englishman, Dr. George E. R. Deacon, assisted by Vice-Chairman, Professor U. G. Kort, a citizen of the Soviet Union, plus a number of American representatives. This plan calls for a study of the entire Indian Ocean system from below the bottom of the sea, through the water itself with its biological contents and its physical and chemical characteristics, through the boundary between the sea and the atmosphere, and on upward to the upper atmosphere. Investigations will be carried out in marine geology, geophysics, and bathymetry; physical and chemical oceanography; biological oceanography and marine biology; and marine meteorology and large-scale atmospheric circulation.

Vessels from Australia, South Africa, the United States, and the Soviet Union are carrying out extensive exploratory cruises. Ship operations for the expedition are scheduled to continue through 1964. Representatives from twenty-eight countries participated in the planning of the expedition. Planning has included the ship schedules and ship tracks and identification of the scientific personnel to be involved, equipment requirements to carry out the program, descriptions of the scientific problem to be investigated, and the detailing of various responsibilities—including the interrelated activities of the several nations. In a number of countries,

[13] See "The Indian Ocean Expedition—An International Venture," by R. G. Snider, Coordinator, International Indian Ocean Expedition, 30 East 40th Street, New York, N.Y. Reprinted from *Transactions American Geophysical Union,* Vol. 42 (Sept., 1961), No. 3.

among them the United States, working groups have been established to coordinate the national effort and to link it with that of other countries. International working groups have also been created which provide an opportunity for direct comparison of field techniques, especially among the Australian, Japanese, Russian, and American ships expected to participate.

Plans have also been worked out for the establishment of logistic and analytical centers around the Indian Ocean area and for the provision of laboratory space at various institutions for local work with research material. A major center for biological research and classification is being established in India. Centers are also being provided for the training of technicians, and the plan calls for advanced training of at least sixty scientists a year from lands of the Indian Ocean area in institutions outside the area.

To achieve the maximum results during the life of the expedition, rapid data processing and analysis were essential. For conventional oceanographic observations the IGY World Data Centers A and B (Oceanography) in the United States and the Soviet Union will be used. The Moscow Center continues, and a new Oceanographic Data Center in Washington supported by five government agencies under the U.S. Navy Hydrographic Office will provide American facilities. Individual institutions and scientists will work up their own data and exchange it directly with others as well as through the centers.

The expedition is the first full-scale effort to coordinate oceanographic and meteorological observations in a single oceanic system. The fundamental science developed during the expedition in all phases will serve as a basis for understanding the processes of this vast oceanic system on which applied sciences can build for the direct benefit of the large population of the Indian Ocean area.

The Indian Ocean expedition has been dealt with at length since it may serve as a prototype of more extended work in other parts of the world's oceans. At a recent meeting of the Intergovernmental Oceanographic Commission, the Soviet Union proposed a detailed plan for similar investigation of the North Atlantic and North Pacific Oceans and the United States proposed an international oceanographic investigation of the Tropical Atlantic Ocean. Both proposals were favorably received and in the end it was unanimously agreed that the American proposal should receive priority. At the same meeting the project for a comprehensive program for world ocean study was further advanced by a resolution requesting scor to prepare the scientific framework for the effort, which would require the free exchange of information collected by all participating nations.

The decision taken in 1960 to expand the United States oceanographic capabilities represents an important step in the direction of giving the United States the means of either competing or collaborating in the task of understanding and the opportunity of using the world's ocean. The program drawn up at that time is gradually being implemented but at a very modest rate. In terms of Soviet-American collaboration some additional dramatic move could now serve a useful purpose. One suggestion, which has merit, is that the United States should announce that it is willing to build four nuclear-powered oceanographic vessels which can operate the year around in the Arctic and Antarctic, providing the Soviets will in some sense match and collaborate in the effort. A commitment of this kind would indicate in a striking way the American desire to use nuclear power for understanding man's environment and would be valuable whether or not matched by the Soviet Union.

Scientific efforts such as the World Ocean Survey together with basic research are designed to give man a better understanding of his ocean environment. When this is accomplished, the next stage is to predict its behavior so that man's activities may be carried on without disruption, and finally to manipulate it for his own purposes.

In addition to questions of navigation, which have historically been most significant, the oceans are of practical interest because they are a source of food, because they may be a more significant source of minerals, and because they are, as in the past, a medium for the operation of offensive and defensive military forces.

Sea fisheries are by far the most important extractive ocean industry at present. Fish provide a major source of protein food for the world's population. Fish, of course, exist both on the high seas where they are common property and in the coastal waters where there are certain national property rights. The fact that fish are not respecters of national boundaries and the tendency of the harvest to decline as a result of overfishing have long made necessary international collaboration in the regulation of the take of certain commercial species. The International Whaling Commission, to which the United States and the Soviet Union belong, is one of the oldest collaborative bodies in this field. There are also several others. As knowledge of the oceans including its biological environment grows, significant expansion of the fishing industry may occur as one means of feeding the earth's growing population. Management problems will spread from the few presently preferred species to many others. The complexity of the problem will also increase as fishing technology continues to shift from older methods to modern mass-production methods involving fleets of vessels employing the latest devices for locating, harvesting, and handling the catch. The Soviet Union seems already to have made substantial progress in this direction.

Since the United States and the Soviet Union share with the other nations the world's largest common property—the ocean and the life that inhabits it—the increasing range and complexity of their activity will require new organizations and arrangements for managing and using it equitably. The problem seems likely to be severely aggravated, in time, as the overpopulated areas of the world become more competent and active in the ocean fishing industry. Moreover, as its population increases and if its dependence on imports grows, the United States may become increasingly interested in the control of this element of its food supply. In the meantime, the United States has a stake in playing a constructive and significant role in helping the underdeveloped countries to increase their sources of fish protein.

Mineral resources of the ocean presently being exploited lie entirely on the continental shelf. About one-third of the earth's remaining reserves of oil, it has been estimated, lie below the continental shelf.

In addition to these resources, the deep sea is known to be covered in many places with low-grade deposits of cobalt, copper, nickel, and rare earths associated with iron and manganese in nodules. Preliminary studies of the economics of development indicate that it may be possible in time to mine the deep-sea floor profitably if a few technical problems can be solved. When and if these sources of material become economically attractive, difficult problems of exploitation and ownership may arise. Should the Soviet Union show an interest, it might be to American advantage to suggest a collaborative effort for an undertaking which might prove long and costly but highly productive in the end.

For the Navy, the ocean is the principal environment. World War II revealed that the other services also have a vital interest in the ocean. In recent years as military systems have become more dependent on detailed knowledge of the environment in which they must operate, the interest has increased. By and large, however, the knowledge is sought for purposes of conflict, and its preclusive possession is viewed as an advantage.

In the context of an arms control and inspection agreement, or even in its absence, if nuclear arms should proliferate in the hands of other maritime nations, common research and development efforts by the United States and the Soviet Union might prove interesting. The ocean, at present, provides the best means of ensuring secrecy as to the exact location of weapons. At some point the United States and the Soviet Union may find that they would like to have means of making the ocean as transparent as the air to ensure surveillance of submarines and other vessels moving in the ocean depths. While both might prefer to have a preclusive power in this regard, joint collaboration may be necessary to devise and put in place an effective system.

The world's ocean is the common property of mankind; the world's ocean exerts a significant influence on man's total environment; the ocean areas are a major source of food and a potential source of minerals. They are avenues of commerce and arenas of possible conflict. They divided continents but wash the shores of most nations. They are world-wide in scope. A world community will require that many problems of the ocean be tackled in common. At present, the United States lacks a comprehensive program not so much for understanding the oceans as for coping with the tasks that the increase in understanding will bring to the fore. We are likely to be confronted with the task of dealing with the problems of the world's ocean created by the advance of science before an adequate framework and structure has been devised for dealing with the new tasks. Is it not time to reassess the American outlook on a comprehensive basis? In this reassessment the possibility of collaboration with the Soviet Union should be an important element.

6 The Spread of Technology—Levels of Production and Patterns of Use

Two FACTORS of fundamental importance shape the resource relationship between the United States and the Soviet Union. First, American economic resources are at present more than double those of the Soviet Union. Second, the Soviet Union is seeking to catch up with the United States in total output. Together, the two factors provide the United States with an unusual opportunity to influence the composition and balance of Soviet use of resources. Measures of economic resources are of course only approximation.[1]

[1] Any definition of economic resources is open to challenge. As used in this chapter, economic resources is roughly synonymous with Gross National Product (GNP) calculations. The main weakness of the GNP comparison is, first, that there is a considerable "froth" in the United States calculation and, second, there are serious problems of comparative pricing because the systems are different and because of the differences in the major sector—personal consumption.

What is needed but not available are comparisons of "transferable resources" from one general end-use to another, those already in existence and those producible within some period of time. Thus, there may be fewer people transferable from Soviet agriculture to something else than from American agriculture (despite the fact that they outnumber us in rural population—which is not the same as farmers—by 2 to 1), simply because the bulk of the Soviet rural people are "unurbanizable" in less than a generation, while a rather large percentage of ours are capable of becoming urbanites in that period. Against that, a lot more of our produced capital—existing plant—in percentage terms is undoubtedly less transferable than their more basic capital. Automatic popcorn-making machines are not really much use if you want to change your product—and a lot of our capital in existence falls into the general class of specialized consumer-goods machinery and distribution facilities.

Today the United States still possesses predominant strength. Eventually, however, the capacities of the Soviet Union may reach those of the United States. In the meantime, the Soviet Union may achieve certain triumphs at the sufferance of the West. The long-run relationship of the two will depend in important ways on the pattern of competition and cooperation established while the West has an advantage in strength. Thus, if the West is prudent, it will utilize its advantage to lay the foundation of a relationship of responsible interdependence.

To foresee the possibilities inherent in the present relationship of the two economies, it is useful to think of them in dynamic rather than static terms—both on the consumption as well as on the production side. Catching up merely in terms of over-all material production with a society which has achieved abundance is an increasingly meaningless concept. But there is a second sense in which the Soviet Union might seek to catch up with the United States. This is in the value attached to consumption—to meeting the needs and desires of the individual—as the primary goal of the economic system.

Catching up involves not only matching the production of the United States but a convergence of cultural-economic values which would result in more identity of the pattern of economic life. It is in the United States interest that the Soviet concept of catching up include, not only the idea of matching the quantity of production, but some reasonable approximation of the quality of life —one measure of which is the quantity of resources devoted to consumption. The objective does not appear impossible of attainment since there are already enough recognizable similarities to place the two societies on the same side of any sensible dividing line that can be drawn through the conglomerate total world culture or economy.

The Soviet Union is at present placing primary emphasis on matching us in the production sense. The American interest is in shifting the stress to an emphasis on equaling us in the cultural-economic convergence sense. The aim of the United States ought to be to foster changes which at some time in the future will bring about a condition in which the two societies find an approximate identity on many points. Both would be materially rich, both spending their riches in nearly the same way—giving overwhelming emphasis to consumption—and both standing well over on the conservative side of whatever happens to be international radicalism of the time. The task for the United States is to so conduct itself and use its resources as to foster an increasing convergence of the pattern of life before the near identity of the level or quantity of material output has been achieved.

What the United States should in effect be seeking is, by analogy with a single nation, a situation in which those who are catching up try, without resorting to murder and robbery, to emulate the pattern if not the level of life lived by the leaders. Ultimately, the followers can catch up with respect to level as well. For this to be achieved without violence a belief system must be brought about in which those who seek to catch up do not feel that the advanced want to keep them eternally at a disadvantage. Rather, they must come to believe that the advanced want to help them improve their status as rapidly as this can be done without demolishing the unity of the social structure which the advanced have managed to build. Those seeking to catch up must believe the advanced when they say, "We are with you and we will help you to advance; but don't jeopardize the whole business by burning down the shop." While this is a difficult idea to put across, it has been accepted in every reasonably stable society.

Today, American efforts are overwhelmingly devoted to deterring the Soviet Union from burning down the shop. The United States has largely avoided in word or deed saying, "We are with you, we will help you to catch up." In the absence of American efforts to direct the catching up toward a nonthreatening pattern of life with an emphasis on consumption, the catching up continues in terms of production with its emphasis on military expenditures and heavy industry.

In the economic relationships of the United States and the Soviet Union, it is useful to distinguish three different modes of action. First are the actions which may affect the total output and thus the rate of growth of the two societies. Second are the actions which may influence the pattern or composition of resource use by each nation. Third are actions which influence the style and scope of resource transactions between the two countries and others—questions of trade, aid, and common enterprises.

Total Output

The gross national output of the United States is at present roughly twice that of the Soviet Union. In contrast, the annual rate of growth of the Soviet economy has been twice as rapid as that for the United States. This is not accidental.

Despite the fact that Soviet output is half that of the United States, the investment in growth in the Soviet economy may be almost as much as in the United States. The effect of the investment is to expand the total output of the Soviet Union more rapidly than would otherwise take place. As a consequence the Soviet Union has been able to maintain a growth rate of five to six per cent per annum.[2] In effect the Soviet Union has been applying to its nonwar economy a variation of the wartime rule of "seeking to increase total output to the maximum extent obtainable." [3] The modifications of wartime practices and allocation criteria have been only those necessary to take account of the need for a sustained long-term effort to achieve the objective of catching up with the United States.

Two points can be made about the interaction of Soviet-American economic policy. First, short of hot war, the United States has few means at its disposal for impeding the rapid over-all growth of the Soviet economy, and seems unlikely to increase its own growth rate to a level comparable with that of the Soviet Union. Second, the smaller size of the Soviet economy, coupled with its drive both to compete and to catch up with the United States, continually forces it to make hard choices of alternative uses of resources which may be influenced by the manner in which the United States uses its more abundant resources.

The United States, some recommend, should seek to slow Soviet growth by attempting, for example, to reduce or eliminate Western trade with the Soviet bloc. This would force the Soviet Union to replace lower-cost imports with high-cost domestic production. Since American trade with the Soviet Union has already been virtually eliminated, the task would be one of convincing our Eu-

[2] Western estimates of Soviet growth vary considerably due to the deficiencies of the data and the differences in method used. Some are, of course, higher than the rate used here.

[3] W. K. Hancock, *War and Peace in This Century* (Cambridge, England: Cambridge University Press, 1961), p. 21.

ropean allies of the soundness of a parallel policy. In present circumstances this does not appear to be politically feasible. The European allies of the United States have long been restive over the East-West trade controls and policies. They do not see the problem in the same light as the United States does. Recently, for example, the Europeans were willing to sell wide-diameter pipe to the Soviet Union, while the United States was vigorously opposed.

But even if it were feasible to reduce Soviet-bloc imports from the West, such imports are not of overwhelming importance. In 1960 they amounted to about $4.4 billion.[4] This volume is not so great that its elimination would inflict a crippling blow, although it could delay certain developments in the Soviet Union.

Others have sometimes argued that, when the Soviet Union devotes a significantly larger proportion of its resources to meeting consumer requirements, its growth may be expected to level off. In the very long run when services become a large proportion of these requirements a leveling off may occur. But even then as the product mix changes there will be a need for different types of capital goods. In the intermediate range, when the requirements of consumption goods are being met, a continued and rapid increase in production appears more likely.

Conceivably, the United States rate of growth might be increased to the level of that of the Soviet Union. To do so, however, would seem to require a range of control or direction of the economy by the Federal government which would be unacceptable to

[4] Samuel Pisar, *A New Look at Trade Policy toward the Communist Bloc,* materials prepared for the Subcommittee on Foreign Economic Policy of the Joint Economic Committee, U.S. Congress (Washington, D.C., 1961), p. 77.

the American people except under the most dire circumstances. A radical reversal of the economic policies of the past decade would be required. At present the United States relies on its substantially greater resources to meet its security and other needs. Economic policy has been primarily concerned with avoiding fluctuations in the economy and controlling inflationary pressures. A high level of employment and steady growth has been the goal of the United States. While some have argued that the growth rate has been less than the feasible optimum, few reputable economists have suggested that it would be either possible or desirable to seek to increase it to the level of the Soviet Union. While increasing the rate of growth in the United States somewhat may be economically feasible, the effort would face substantial political obstacles. The most likely course of events seems to be the continuation of the policies of the past decade with perhaps minor improvements, largely of a technical nature.

The long-range outlook, in the absence of war, is thus for the Soviet economy gradually to approach the scale of the United States economy. This does not preclude American influence on the nature of Soviet economic developments in the intervening years, but it casts them in a somewhat different light. Since it is not reasonable to expect two mature continental economies to exist wholly independent of each other in the modern world, attention must be focused on the composition and pattern of resource use in each, and the interaction between them. The United States, at present the stronger, must use its advantage to try and create a viable relationship of interdependence for the two roughly equivalent economies which will in the course of time result from present trends.

Pattern of Use

Today, the desire of Soviet authorities both to compete and to catch up confronts them with a series of choices in the use of their relatively limited resources. While the initiative in making these choices lies in Soviet hands, the choices may be influenced in the future as they have been in the past by the way in which the United States uses its own resources. Examples of American influence abound. For instance, in the 1950s the American economic aid program was followed in due course by a smaller but substantial Soviet program of long-term economic loans to selected third areas. Similarly, the increases in United States military expenditures have found a response in the Soviet Union. The United States space program, which originally received its impetus from Soviet successes, has now been enlarged to the point where it poses a challenge to the Soviet Union which, if it is to be met, may require additional resources. Other examples of this two-way interaction could be cited.

The United States has been slow to seize the opportunity to influence Soviet resource use toward constructive goals. Throughout the postwar period, the United States has not infrequently found itself responding to Soviet competitive initiatives. Even though the Soviet economy is smaller than that of the United States, Soviet initiatives were possible because of the tight control exercised over the allocation of their resources. It was thus possible for the Soviets to direct nearly as many resources to national-power purposes as the United States was. Moreover, the United States has been concerned with the protection and development of a much larger and diversified area. The consequence has frequently been that the United States has had to respond to Soviet initiatives by quickly bringing to bear resources in new areas in which Soviet ingenuity or aggressiveness had given them an advantage. American resource allocations were thus frequently determined by a fixation on the short-term requirements of countering the Soviet Union. The nature of the American political system, which makes it more difficult to arouse and organize support for positive action than to meet an obvious threat, reinforced the tendency to concentrate action on short-run specific interests.

The weakness of this kind of countervailing action, from the American viewpoint, is that it leaves the initiative largely in the hands of the Soviet Union, while doing little to modify the Soviet vision of the future or their pattern of resource use. It stems from a kind of historical determinism that ultimately the Soviet Union will change its ways and modify its interests. It may be true that, as the Soviet Union becomes an affluent society, it will have a greater stake in the Communist *status quo*. Yet countervailing action mainly in the military field is unlikely to ensure that the outcome will be either peace or stability. The Soviet economy will continue to grow and, in the presence of widespread and continuing apparent conflict of interests and difference in values, could with equal likelihood be devoted to a more aggressive policy. While the growth of the European Common Market and the latent strength of the United States make the more pessimistic consequences of a policy of countervailing action unlikely, the possibility that the United States would have to curtail individual freedom and control the economy in order to compete in the long run are not beyond the bounds of imagination.

The limitations of countervailing competition seem to have led, beginning in the late 1950s or early 1960s, to a new element in United States policy. No systematic exposition of this new element appears to be publicly available if, indeed, it exists. Perhaps it represents more a frame of mind, an attitude, than a coherent program. The new element may be characterized as "keeping the pressure on" the Soviet Union. Examples of the application of this new viewpoint were reflected in the military field in the emphasis on United States military "superiority"; however, efforts to keep the pressure on may be made in any field. Some may contribute to the control of conflict. Others may aggravate it. Keeping the pressure on is a kind of imperfect preclusive competition by which the United States seeks to hold its position of political and military predominance over the Soviet Union. The purpose of such competition must be to lead the Soviet Union to believe that it cannot afford to compete with the United States. Yet such competition aggravates the competitive task for the Soviet Union without bringing it to change its behavior in any significant way.

The logic of preclusive competition as a means of keeping the pressure on leads in time to a further expansion in United States military expenditures to which the Soviets would be forced to respond. Indeed, versions of the preclusive policy, in the military field, have, as P. M. S. Blackett has pointed out, "no obvious limit to the number of weapons required." [5] Additional expenditures in conventional armaments, space, and economic programs designed for predominance will also be needed before the Soviet Union will even be forced to consider whether a settlement is necessary. The aggregate program must be large enough virtually to freeze or

[5] P. M. S. Blackett, "The Way Ahead," unpublished paper for the Ninth Pugwash Conference on Science and World Affairs, Cambridge, England, 1962.

force the Soviet Union out of all or most of the third areas of the world.

While such a program would clearly increase the pressure on Soviet resources and force the Soviet Union to make hard choices, including, undoubtedly, cutbacks in consumption and investment, a prediction that the outcome would be a greater willingness to live peacefully in the world would be hazardous. When and how the Soviets would be forced to capitulate is uncertain. Moreover, the policy if carried to its logical conclusion would seem to require the cooperation of both United States allies and neutrals. From their vantage point, however, American actions might look both dangerous and belligerent. Moreover, it might strengthen their belief that their interests would be better served by a world in which neither the United States nor the Soviet Union was predominant.

Thus striving for predominance may weaken United States leadership of the free world while eliciting a militant counterresponse from the Soviet Union. To increased arms, the Soviet Union seems likely to respond with increases in its own arms. Within the bloc, pressure on resources is apt to result in a reversal of the liberalizing developments of recent years. The obvious external threat would make increased control measures more palatable. In short, the alternative of keeping the pressure on by preclusive competition appears to be risky in the short run and unlikely in the long run to produce the desired political changes in the Soviet bloc required for the control of conflict. Meanwhile, the Soviet economy continues to grow and its potential for resisting pressure continues to increase.

The limitation of countervailing competition is that it accepts the long-run growth of the Soviet economy, without a positive effort to use United States economic superiority to influence the pattern of use of Soviet resources in the interim. Preclusive competition, on the other hand, while it seeks to use American economic superiority to keep the pressure on the Soviet Union in order to force it to modify its outlook, underestimates the costs of an effort with a chance of success and understates the consequences of failure. Instead of the Soviet Union being drawn toward the United States pattern of resource use, the United States in effect moves toward that of the Soviet Union. Both approaches suffer from the lack of a coherent picture of the changes the United States desires and believes are feasible in Soviet society.

Interdependent competition represents an alternative to the previous policies. It may be defined as a course of action which seeks to divert Soviet use of resources into areas conducive to the exercise of restraint and the development of a common pattern of constructive resource use. The premises of interdependent competition are three:

First, the Soviet economy is growing at a rate approximately double that of the United States. The instruments available to the United States for impeding the long-run growth of the Soviet Union are extremely limited. Thus, in the course of the next decade or two, the production of *the Soviet economy may draw abreast of the United States in all material respects* (providing of course, the large remaining body of rural people can be assimilated into the industrial society).[6] This projection should be a significant factor in the calculation of United States interests.

[6] The projection of present trends which would lead to the Soviet Union catching up with the United States is, like all projections, open to argument. The Soviet society, for example, continues to carry a heavy burden of rural people who

Second, the Soviet economy at present and in all likelihood throughout the intervening period will be operating at capacity. This means that a *demand for increased resources in one sector of the Soviet economy must be met by reduction of the resources available to another sector.*[7] Broadly speaking, from the point of view of the interest of the United States, Soviet resources are allocated to one of four major purposes. These are: (1) weapons systems and related capital investment; (2) development of science and technology, including space exploration; (3) foreign investment and external assistance; (4) civilian consumption, including the necessary investment in agriculture, light industry, and surface transport.

Third, the United States has the opportunity of using its resources in a manner which will influence in some degree the allocation of Soviet resources among the major purposes listed above. It can do so because of the greater size of the United States economy. Moreover, the American economy is not operating at the highest feasible level and could if necessary increase output without harmful effect.

---

may not be easy to assimilate into a modern industrial society. Recent rates of change suggest that progress in this sector is slow. Note, for example, the following figures of the urban-rural split in the Soviet Union in which the decline in the rural population is negligible.

U.S.S.R. Population
(in millions)

	Total	Urban	Rural
July 1962	221.5	113.4	108.1
Jan. 1959	208.8	100.0	108.8

[7] It should, of course, be noted that since the Soviet economy is growing at the rate of five and six per cent a year, this additional output is available for distribution among the various purposes.

United States actions will differ radically, depending on the direction of the shift in Soviet resource use one believes is in the American interest. Views of the American interest will depend upon the relative emphasis on short-run gains as compared with a stable relationship with a mature Soviet society. Moreover, each shift results in both gains and losses for the United States position. Some losses have come to be more accepted in conventional wisdom than others. There are, in addition, different types or processes of interaction between the two societies, some of which are more preferred than others.

In order to illustrate the range of choice open to the United States, two different sets of preferred resource shifts will be compared. The first represents an approximation of the present course, and the second, possible preferences if a policy of interdependent competition were being followed.

Up until the middle of 1963 United States action suggested that the preferred Soviet resource use in order of priority was as follows:

1. Weapons systems and related developments.
2. Science and technology but particularly space exploration.
3. Foreign aid and investment.
4. Civilian consumption.

On the whole, American actions till mid-year in 1963 may have been rather successful in achieving a modest trend toward the higher priority element in this program. United States increases in military expenditures and increased emphasis on American superiority have been complemented by cancellation of planned Soviet cutbacks in military strength in some fields and increases in expenditures in others. To a lesser extent, the steadily mounting United States investments in space research and development, and the announcement of the intention of the United States to seek a first in space, can surely be counted on to lead to proportionately larger allocations to competitive Soviet efforts. While United States allocations to foreign assistance, for domestic political reasons, have remained more or less on an even keel, modest effort has been devoted to making Soviet assistance efforts as costly as possible. Thus the result of the recent United States policy of "pressure" is to tip the allocation of resources away from civilian consumption and toward investments in military power and space competition.

In the short run the United States may gain an advantage in that the Soviets may not be able or willing fully to match American allocations. But temporary military advantages are of dubious value unless war is expected, while the psychological gains in space can hardly do more than counter earlier Soviet gains. The longer-run effect is to expand the arms race, intensify competition in space, and force the Soviet authorities to maintain or tighten control over civilian consumption, and to intensify their efforts to place the blame on the "foreign enemy." Continued long enough the policy will find two nearly equal antagonists engaged in an insidiously spreading conflict, each side being capable of playing the game to the hilt.

Interdependent competition has a different arrangement of priorities for the Soviet economy from the point of view of United States interest. These are as follows:

1. Civilian consumption.
2. Balanced scientific and technical development.

3. Foreign investment and assistance.
4. Weapons systems and related developments.

The means for achieving a shift in Soviet resources toward this set of priorities are primarily trade and technology, mutual scientific and technical enterprises, and multilateral assistance programs designed to induce Soviet participation. They also include actions designed to reduce the degree of interaction and dependence in the military area and thus to permit Soviet diversion of resources from military to other purposes.

The extent to which United States allocations of resources may influence Soviet resource use must, of course, be carefully tested over time. Radical shifts in Soviet resource use as a result of most American action are not to be expected, but acceleration and modification of present trends may become apparent. Moreover, patterns of resource use are by no means the only factors in the situation; political purpose may also disrupt or inhibit the interrelationships.

Transactions between the United States and the Soviet Union

The success of any strategy depends on the synchronization of all its parts as much as on any one element, no matter how important. The success of a strategy of interdependence depends not only on the achievement of desirable shifts in the use of Soviet resources but on the part played by the United States in those shifts. The aim is not an affluent Soviet society for its own sake, but a mature Soviet society with which a web of interdependence has been created that will enhance stability.

When a nation lacks a reasonable standard of living, many activities may be limited or precluded which would contribute to the growth of a common outlook. The Soviet Union is surely the next likely candidate for full modernization; yet there are significant ways in which the United States may contribute to the transition. At present the principal remaining area of American superiority is exactly in the field of consumption—the standard of living of the people.[8] The conventional ways in which a contribution to a developing society is made is by the transfer of technology and by trade. In the case of the Soviet-American relationship there are, as we shall see, a number of obstacles to be overcome. Action in the field of technology and trade must be accompanied by action in other areas to form a coherent strategy for linking the efforts of the two societies.

TECHNOLOGY

Acquisition of Western technology has been widely viewed in the twentieth century as the essential means for achieving independence from the West. The Russian leaders from Lenin to Khrushchev are no exception. For them industrialization, the fruit of the acquisition of technology, was designed to enhance the power of the state. A powerful state was required to speed industrialization.

The Soviet development was achieved without the aid of substantial long-term capital assistance from the West. Significant commercial credits were obtained from time to time, but the basic source of capital was a high level of forced savings within the Soviet society itself. However, during and after World War II

[8] Agriculture was discussed in more detail in Chapter 5.

significant assets were obtained, first through the United States lend-lease program and second as a result of reparations and extractions from Manchuria, Germany, and the East European satellites.

Engineering and technical know-how acquired from the West seems to have been a more significant factor in Soviet development. In the twenties and thirties, foreign technicians and engineers were employed to help create the foundations of Soviet industrial society. Throughout its history, on an increasingly systematic basis, the Soviet Union has collected and disseminated to its growing technical elite, information on Western technical progress for adaptation and application to Soviet problems. A steady investment has also been made in acquiring prototypes of the latest Western equipment which were then presumably broken down, analyzed, and produced in the Soviet Union. Efforts to acquire Western know-how in the past seem to have been concentrated in areas directly related to heavy industry and defense. In recent times, with the broadening of the Soviet goals, efforts have extended into the fields of consumer goods and agriculture.

The Western response has been a belated effort to restrict in some degree the Soviet effort to acquire Western technology. In part, American-created obstacles are an effort to deny the Soviet Union technology of value to their military program and, in part, an attempt to impede the progress of Soviet industrialization. Further, they are a response to the unwillingness of the Soviet Union to recognize the patent rights system of the West.[9] On the whole, however, Western technology in due course seems to have

[9] A group of Soviet scientists have recently applied for U.S. patents on their inventions.

become available to the Soviet Union by one means or another. In recent years, Soviet progress in some fields has aroused a moderate interest in the West, and some attempts have been undertaken to ensure an improved level of reverse flow. So far results of these efforts have been useful but not dramatic. Progress to date has been modest, partly because of a lack of intense interest or requirements for Soviet technology, and partly because of the difficulty of doing business with the Soviet Union.

Soviet interest in United States technology, if the composition of their delegations is an indication, has been an important element in their support of the cultural exchange program. The bulk of Soviet visitors under this program have been in technical and engineering fields, whereas the United States has been more interested in other aspects of Soviet society.

Russian scientific capability was well known before the Revolution. Since that time it has continued to develop. Soviet leadership in mathematics and certain areas of pure science is acknowledged. At this level of abstraction, the West in a growing number of areas may have as much to learn from the Soviet scientists as they have to learn from the West. The Soviet Union has been effective in mobilizing its scientific talent around certain major national goals. In recent years, with the creation and gradual increase in scope of the role of the Science Advisor to the President, the United States has in certain fields such as space, oceanography, and the atmospheric sciences been reasonably successful in laying out and getting financing for long-range efforts which in time will pay practical dividends.

On the whole, the interplay between Soviet and American science has probably been more symmetrical and pervasive than either the flow of capital or technical know-how between East and West. This is partly due to the nature of the subject matter—politicians and others on both sides become aware of the practical implications only after a time lag—and also because of the universal value system of science which was discussed earlier.

The interplay of institutional arrangements is more difficult to summarize. Obviously, basic property arrangements for the management of capital investment remain quite different in East and West. In the Soviet Union, means of production remain communal property, the economy is centrally planned, a large proportion of output is saved and invested, individual talents are more closely directed to national purposes, and deviation is punished.[10] Yet, despite the continuing differences, a certain tendency for the economies to converge may be noted. The Soviet Union has in practice, though not necessarily as doctrine, given up many earlier ideas. Workers do not manage industrial units. Income is, as in the West, more or less geared to productivity. Interest has gradually come to be accepted as a cost element. Even the value of international exchange seems to have become better understood. Decentralization in decision-making has been introduced, and price as a regulator of economic activity has been discussed if not yet given a greatly enlarged role in Soviet development.

In the West, while private property remains central, a much larger role has been given to economic planning, especially in Western Europe. In the United States planning remains diffused, but the amount of such forward thinking in industry has increased immensely. Forward planning by advisory groups which influence

[10] Jan Tinbergen, *Shaping the World Economy* (New York: The Twentieth Century Fund, 1962), p. 32.

government action has also greatly increased not only in such fields as science but in investment and financial management generally.

In terms of the spread of technology and industrialization the Soviet Union and the United States, to an impartial but Western-oriented observer, do not present black-and-white alternatives.[11] The present Western economies are a mixture of nineteenth-century capitalism and socialism. The Soviet economic system is a product of its Russian environment and Western ideas and technology. In the Soviet system there remain certain quantitative gaps, as in agriculture and consumer industries. As attempts are made to overcome these deficiences, the tendency may be to move the entire system closer to those of the West. In the West there remains great room for qualitative improvement, and perhaps—in the United States at least—a need for additional acceptable means for achieving the growth of the system as a whole. In summary, the interplay between the Soviet and Western systems, fostering the advance of technology, has been substantial. The transactions have on the whole, but not entirely, been in the direction of the Soviet Union. Interaction leading to a further convergence of technological competence may be expected and seems likely to be somewhat more symmetrical than it has been in the past.

TRADE

The United States, to increase its influence on the pattern of use resulting from the convergence of competence, would have to open up trade with the Soviet Union in order to assist it in raising

[11] *Ibid.*, p. 39.

the level of civilian consumption—the standard of living of its people—no more, no less. Whatever actions are required to open up and expand such trade should be taken in the American interest. Action in the field of trade should be balanced by continuing shifts in Soviet resources toward consumption and by commitments to world enterprises and multilateral aid. They should be accompanied by actions to reduce military expenditures and to restrain the use of force as the positive aspects of the strategy are developed. It will not be easy for the United States to change its trading policy, but neither will it be as difficult as is sometimes believed. At the same time, it will not be easy for the Soviet Union to accept a trading relationship with the United States designed specifically to influence a shift of Soviet resources to civilian consumption.

On the one hand, there will be many in the United States ready to interpret any trade with the Soviet Union as strengthening its war potential and, on the other, Soviet planners will be reluctant to modify their goals in ways that permit a growing American participation in an improving Soviet standard of living. The answer to Americans is, first, that in the slightly longer run the Soviets will be able to do for themselves whatever they can do more quickly with American participation; and, second, that there are finite limits within which the trade will take place. Trade which strengthens consumption will be permitted; that which makes a direct contribution to military capabilities will continue to be prohibited. Moreover, Russian planners will also have hard choices, as new techniques may be insufficient without the diversion of numbers of technicians. To produce consumer goods American plants will require Soviet raw materials which must be created

or diverted from other uses. Moreover, in the longer run further resources will be required for export. Designing a pattern of trade
which will enhance the trend to consumption and further limit
the possibility of increased allocation to war industry should on
the whole prove feasible.

A major obstacle to a significant development of economic interdependence between the United States and the Soviet Union
is believed by many to lie in the basic differences of the respective
economic systems. It may be argued that United States firms will
be at a disadvantage in trading with the state institutions of the
Soviet Union. Without doubt this difference in structure will
present a problem to both sides. New forms of cooperation between United States business and the United States government
in order to guard the national interest will be needed. Similarly, on
the Soviet side greater independent power of decision for the individual "firm" or industrial complex in its dealings with the
West will be necessary if trade is to grow to the mutual advantage
of both sides.

The United States follows a multilateral system of trade with
the rest of the free world and permits relatively free movements
of commodities, services, and capital. The amount of trade is
determined by its economic advantages as decided by individual
buyers and sellers. On the other hand, the Soviet system tends to
emphasize autarchic self-sufficiency. The volume of trade depends,
therefore, to a major extent on the political decisions of the government. While this system of trading is contrary to the free-world
approach, it should be noted that an increasing amount of trade
between the Soviet bloc and the rest of the world, even though it
is mainly conducted on a bilateral basis, does increase the inter-

dependence between the East and West. Moreover, the fact is that multilateralism appears to be increasing in trade between the East and West.[12]

Trade between the bloc and the rest of the world has been expanding over the past decade. The dollar value of the bloc's trade turnover (imports and exports) with the West rose from $1.0 billion to $4.5 billion between 1950 and 1960. (More than seventy countries outside the bloc carry on some trade with it.) However, trade between the United States and the bloc is very small.

The pattern of trade between the bloc and the free world varies as between the industrial West and the third-area countries. From the industrial countries, the bloc has received machinery, equipment, and other manufactured goods. In return, it ships industrial raw materials, fuel, and food. With respect to the third-area countries the pattern is reversed. The bloc ships machinery, equipment, and other manufactured goods, and receives in return raw materials and food.

Trade of this magnitude does indicate already a limited degree of interdependence between East and West. Moreover, as the Soviet Union and the bloc as a whole continue to develop, the volume of trade can be expected to grow also. Mikoyan, for example, at a recent Communist Congress, spoke of expanding exports vigorously.

The problem for the United States is how it shall proceed in

[12] Bilateralism, while facilitating the system of controls of a centrally organized system of production, is not essential. Before World War II, most of Soviet trade was on a multilateral basis. Today, particularly with West European countries, there is a substantial amount of multilateral trade. See Robert Loring Allen, "An Interpretation of East-West Trade," *Comparisons of the United States and Soviet Economies,* Joint Economic Committee, U.S. Congress, Part II (Washington, D.C.: U.S. Government Printing Office, 1959), pp. 405–412.

the face of these developments. American policy, at least up to the time of the proposal for the sale of wheat, was to restrict such trade so as to minimize as far as possible any increase in the strategic economic strength of the Soviet bloc. This policy was carried out with the reluctant assent of our NATO allies and Japan.

So far as the United States is concerned, the policy has been successful in keeping trade to negligible proportions. In 1960 the trade picture was as follows: United States imports from the Sino-Soviet bloc amounted to $81 million, of which about $23 million was from the Soviet Union; United States exports to the bloc come to $193 million, of which $39 million was to the Soviet Union. Indeed, the exports overstate the true situation, since we exported substantial quantities of food to Poland under Public Law 480 to be paid for by local currencies. American policy has not, however, prevented a large expansion in the trade between the bloc and the rest of the world.[13] Nor is it likely that over the long run it will hinder the growth of Soviet strategic power. Indeed, it may help to pinpoint deficiencies and set the Soviets to work to overcome them.

Even if the United States were willing to expand trade with the Soviet Union, the question of how the Soviets would pay for the additional imports is a difficult one. The Soviet Union could perhaps pay in part with exports of gold. Some increase in Soviet exports to the United States might be possible, but in general the range of exports that the Soviets can offer in exchange does not match United States requirements and, even where it does, might create "excessive" United States dependence or raise dif-

[13] Pisar, *op. cit.*, pp. 70ff., for a discussion of the difficulties experienced in enforcing the embargo on strategic items and the consequent dualism which has developed between the United States and the European countries.

ficulties with the trade of third countries already supplying such goods. Finally, the Soviets might seek to achieve a surplus of exports over imports to other countries. While this latter method would contribute to multilateralism, it might be objectionable to United States allies and impede the improvement in Soviet consumption levels. Thus if a substantial increase in Soviet-American trade were found to be in the United States interest, a favorable view of Soviet attempts to obtain credit would be required. Credit might be obtained indirectly from investment banks in Europe or from the United States. If the loans were obtained in the United States, a more direct opportunity would be provided to ensure that the funds were utilized for civilian purposes. Moreover, the loans could be made dependent upon Soviet plans for shifting resources.

The area of possible United States exports to the Soviet is substantial. However, the Soviet Union is primarily interested in the latest developments of American technology, for example, textile spindle mills for worsteds, cottons, and synthetics, polyethylene plants, transistors, pumps and compressors for the petroleum industry.[14] There also appears to be considerable interest in machinery to meet the need for agricultural requisites. While some Soviet requirements appear to fall within the framework of civilian consumption credits, others may be outside. Continuing discussions and negotiations are necessary to explore the volume of possible trade.

It may be argued that, if the Soviet Union were to be granted credits to purchase the latest industrial products even though they had no direct bearing on arms capability, there might be the

14 Pisar, *op. cit.,* p. 52.

prospect that these machines and others would only accelerate the ability of the Soviet Union and the bloc to export commodities which would increase competition in those markets with Western goods or would compel it to increase such exports to pay for these goods. It is frequently said that the Soviets seek to disrupt free markets and that anything which helps them to expand their ability to export *a fortiori* helps them to exercise political pressure via exports.

The trend in the free world is toward expanding the area of competition as, for example, in the Common Market and the announced policy of the United States government to negotiate greater access to this market.[15] Increased competition always tends to hurt some and benefit others, and those who may be hurt bring political pressure to lessen the pain. But the presumption guiding the West, even though it is not always honored fully, is that competition or greater trade produces more benefits than disadvantages.[16]

The comment may, however, be made that, while this principle may be true for increased competition from countries with the same basic system of private enterprise, it does not follow for trade with the Sino-Soviet bloc with its system of government trading corporations and its method of pricing.

On this point, the evidence, while not conclusive, does not sup-

[15] The Common Market, while it increases the degree of competition within its area, does carry the danger that it may reduce the degree of competition between it and other countries where competing goods are produced. This will depend on the tariff policy finally adopted.

[16] The problem of the gains or losses from trade is, of course, much more complicated than the summary above. However, while a more complete statement would require qualifications, the essence is approximately as above.

port the charge that the Soviet Union's prime objective is to disrupt markets. It has been well put by Pisar:

> On the question of Soviet machinations to disrupt world trade the case is still moot. There is no doubt that Soviet trading organizations are hard competitors, who pressure sale prospects with great zeal. But the only clear charge that can be made so far is that the Soviets have shaded prices in commodity markets which were otherwise characterized by regularized if not administered prices. This is a not-unheard-of technique in the case of capitalist countries which are interested in entering an established market.[17]

The Soviets have a basic interest in getting the best terms for their products. As new sellers, they have to make concessions, but in the long run it does not pay them to follow uneconomic tactics. Such political capital as they have been able to make from trade has been in small countries that were having difficulties in selling their products, such as Iceland with its herring, Egypt with its long-staple cotton, Uruguay with its wool. Unless the West is prepared to provide markets for these products, the small countries are likely to continue to sell them wherever there is a buyer.

There are risks involved in greater trade with the Soviet Union but there is also the possibility of influencing the direction of shifts in the use of Soviet resources. Moreover, such trade could increase Soviet contacts with the United States, give the Soviet Union an increasing stake in its trade with the free world, and gradually widen the area of true economic interdependence with the United States. All these possibilities are foreclosed by policies followed during the past decade.

[17] Pisar, *op. cit.*, p. 34.

If the United States wished a growing trade between itself and the Soviet Union, it would probably require modification of certain existing legislation. Settlement of the legacy of disputes from past financial relationships would also be necessary. The granting of credits would permit the United States to control the rate at which such trade was expanding. If it appeared that shifts of Soviet resources toward civilian consumption and progress toward political stability were being made, trade could be allowed to expand. The United States could cut off the trade at any time it appeared that the Soviet Union was behaving more, rather than less, intransigently.

While the short-run advantages and disadvantages of trade with the Soviet Union must be carefully weighed, the long-run effect of United States policies which influence the Soviet pattern of resource use and relationships between the two societies can be of far greater significance. The short-run hypothetical gains of a policy of pressure which force diversion of Soviet resources to weapons and instruments of war must be weighed against the longer advantage of encouraging shifts to consumption. A few years from now the difference may be decisive. As a mature economy the Soviet Union will find it possible to match in every important way the United States efforts to achieve military superiority. The pattern of resource use in the interim and the relationships which have been cultivated will have much to do with whether Soviet strength is directed toward war or peace.

7 *Communication and the Enjoyment of Life*

Communication and Understanding

Good communication is not sufficient for the control of conflict but it is a necessary condition. The prerequisites of effective communication are to be heard and understood. Effective communication is essential for influence, for persuasion. The growth of a number of specialized elites and the increase in mass participation in social if not political action enlarge the ranks of those who must hear, if a stable world environment is to be achieved. In the relationships between the United States and the Soviet Union, the need for effective and expanded channels of communication is particularly acute. As one historian has remarked, "Russian-American relations since that time [the end of World War I] in addition to all the real differences between the two powers have displayed the peculiar quality of two people talking past one another."[1]

If understanding and correct perception of each other's behavior are to be improved by contact and "exchanges," the development of interdependence between a large number of elements in the two societies will be required. There must be opportunity for specialized groups to meet and to gain an understanding of

[1] Henry L. Roberts, "Russia and America," in Ivo J. Lederer (ed.), *Russian Foreign Policy* (New Haven: Yale University Press, 1962), p. 591.

the perspective and points of view of their opposite numbers. Moreover, situations must be provided in which there can be the kind of argument and transactions that work to modify the perceptions on both sides. Ultimately, these should result in the development of common projects both in research and in action.

To suggest that other lines of communication are essential for the control of conflict is not to derogate the important role that diplomacy must continue to play. It will remain a primary instrument for the communication of the views of the heads of state and for the development of a full understanding of the position being taken by each side. Diplomacy will also have a continuing role to play in inducing restraint on both sides and in working to achieve the settlement of outstanding conflicts. Before diplomatic negotiation can play its full role, however, it will need to avail itself more fully of the new knowledge presently being generated in certain of the social sciences and in the new techniques for investigating and improving the prospects of settling outstanding disputes.

The collection and analysis of intelligence with respect to the capabilities and intensions of a prospective opponent developed along parallel lines with diplomacy. In the twentieth century, and particularly with the development of intercontinental weapons systems, intelligence collection has come to play a steadily more vital part in the relationships of states. Prevention of accidental war as well as surprise attack is of great importance in today's world. Intelligence has a positive as well as an analytical role to play in the actions of states. The lack of reliable information in the past has been one of the single most important stumbling blocks in the development of arms control and disarmament agreements. But the absence of adequate information on the life of the two societies is a more general impediment. What one side does depends more than ever before on its evaluation of its opponent's intentions and capabilities.

There is today a large degree of interdependence in the intelligence systems of the Soviet Union and the United States. The interplay of these two systems has a powerful potential for contributing to the aggravation of conflict or to its alleviation. A clearer understanding on both sides is needed of the role intelligence is playing in their understanding or misperception of their adversary's behavior and the goals of each society. Secrecy, for example, which is so highly valued by the Soviet Union, is a double-edged sword in that, while it may conceal a weakness, it may also contribute to the exaggeration of existing strength and the obscuring of common purposes. Until recently, both sides have been largely dependent on either diplomacy or intelligence for their knowledge of the other. These two channels of communication while vital are anything but sufficient if conflict is to be controlled and the people are to find enjoyment in life over the longer run.

The rise in literacy and the improvement of means of communication have brought to the fore the importance of public information in the relationships of states. Western newsmen have been used frequently to communicate a correct understanding of Soviet positions within the American society. The Voice of America and other foreign broadcasts play a similar role in the Soviet Union. As yet, this two-way communication to the informed public on both sides is severely limited. Beginnings have been made in the past two or three years to improve the flow of information. Much remains to be done not only to increase the quantity but to give it the character of a true dialogue. Nothing would be as helpful in correcting public impressions on both sides and in moderating the position of both governments as the simultaneous and balanced transmission of news and views in parallel columns or the equivalent. The possibilities of expanding the flow of information, while they have been explored by dedicated public servants, have been neither investigated nor attempted on the scale which the importance of this channel of communication warrants.

In recent years the conventional means of communication have been broadened somewhat as a result of the contacts of a limited number of scientists. Scientific exchange and discussion can provide a strong thread in the web of interdependence which is necessary for the maintenance of peace.

Technology, while inevitably closely linked with national aspirations in the present period, is also an essential communications pathway between the two societies. Technical information is now flowing between the two societies in the form of books and periodicals. Limited technical exchanges have been arranged in areas of particular interest to one of the adversaries. The more rapidly Soviet society acquires a technological base comparable with the West, the more swiftly will it have to take account of the value of the individual to an advanced technological society. Even as the Soviet Union acquires Western technology, it is becoming increasingly apparent that it must soon expand its interest in the human values without which it will remain barren. Not only are diplomatic, scientific and technical communication as well as accurate intelligence required for the control of conflict, but also in our day a vast variety of human communication and on a large scale.

Many men and women on both sides must know from experience that the adversary is human—and that the human values applied in daily life are applicable to those in another state as well as in their own. Communication by action as well as word will be required. Action which demonstrates a concern for the enjoyment of life of both peoples will prove most fruitful.

Enjoyment of Life

The enjoyment of life is something both Russians and Americans have a tendency to postpone, yet neither can truly be said to be an unhappy or morose people. Both societies live, more than many others, for their children, and this is rewarding.[2] Both nations tend to postpone the enjoyment of material well-being, the Soviet Union because other goals have received priority, the Americans because the pleasure of present possessions is displaced by the desire for further acquisition. The Soviet Union is bent on catching up and the United States on keeping up.

Enjoyment of life is also eroded by anxiety about security in the nuclear age. Not alone nuclear weapons but an inability to see clearly what may be done to bring them under control and keep them under control feeds the anxiety. On both sides there seems to be a widespread belief that nobody wants war, nobody really expects war, and that not many could survive a great war. Yet the world continues to spend $100 billion a year preparing for the war that nobody wants. The unreasonableness of this behavior aggravates the anxiety of thoughtful people.

[2] Raymond A. Bauer (ed.), *Some Views on Soviet Psychology* (Washington, D.C.: American Psychological Association, 1962).

If the Russians and Americans are to enjoy life and be less a threat to each other, they must learn to work together. They must also learn to play together (just as within the nation games like baseball and golf make a significant contribution to community solidarity). Art, music, and games bring their own rewards in the excitement of accomplishment. They also serve as guides and images of the manner in which the more demanding tasks of life may be dealt with. Work, as in science and the arts, may also take on the attributes of play once basic needs are met. Work may be enjoyable for itself.

There remain in the Soviet-American confrontation many problems requiring hard work for their solution. Yet if they could be tackled in some degree jointly, their solution would help to lay the foundations for the enjoyment of life.

Of all the internal tasks remaining, the provision of an adequate level and variety of food and consumption for the Soviet citizens is the most immediate. In the West, it is often said that if only the Soviet regime would turn the resources of the Soviet Union to this purpose all would be well. But such an outlook is utopian, as long as the East-West conflict calls for sustained and even increased armament. Reduction in armaments would, of course, permit diversion of resources to other purposes. But reduction seems less likely in the absence of increased interest on both sides in the mutual enjoyment of life.

Is it possible that working together on a common problem—Soviet agricultural production and marketing, for example—might contribute to a reduction in anxiety, and thus in time to an acceptance of reductions in armaments? If so, the solution of what is presently viewed as mainly a problem for the Soviet regime might contribute to the enjoyment of life in both the Soviet Union and the United States—in the one for urgent material reasons and in the other for intangible but no less valid reasons. Those who help no less than those who are helped, it is well to recall, often receive satisfaction from the deed.

The enjoyment of life is not usually listed among the foremost national interests by statesmen and strategists. In part, the failure to mention it occurs because it is taken for granted, but in large part, the reason lies in the necessity of leaders in times past to urge their people on to greater endeavor merely to survive. Enjoyment of life in those days could at most be an incidental benefit of survival. Among all the changes of our time the widening opportunity for all people to enjoy life is the most profound and, curiously, among the most difficult for men fully to take into account. Our approach to the age of plenty bears a heavy burden of attitudes carried forward from the era of scarcity. In all past times the central task has been to divide the grossly insufficient. Today, science and technology confront us with the task of managing a growing abundance in which all may have more without of necessity taking from those who have already acquired plenty. The world, it must be admitted, is such a short distance down this path that it is difficult as yet for most men to sight the destination.

Food and Fiber

But let us turn now to view the resolution of the Soviet agricultural problem as a next major step along the road. Three elements are cited by students of Soviet agriculture to explain the officially acknowledged stagnation as contrasted with the continuing high level of production in the United States. The three are (1) natural environment, (2) institutional factors, and (3) insufficient capital investment.[3]

Before considering the three elements, it may be useful to clarify the dimensions of the problem. The Soviet people are not starving, nor are they likely to lack a basic diet. The problem of Soviet agriculture arises in part because of the annual population growth of three and one-half to four million a year, but its present character is determined as much by the growing urbanization and industrialization of Soviet life and the desire for improvement in the variety and composition of the presently predominantly starchy diet. The task then is not so much to obtain basic ingredients as to provide the new components required by a rapidly growing urban population which desires an improved standard of living, of which food is an important part.

Whatever the approach, the task would not be as easy in the Soviet Union as it has proved to be in the United States. While the soils are comparable, the climate is not. Both the northern location and the continental harshness of the Soviet Union result in the work and growing season being considerably shorter than in the United States. Unless and until rather large-scale weather modification becomes possible, Soviet agriculture must continue to labor under this handicap. Much of Khrushchev's expansion of sown land, estimated at approximately one hundred million acres, has taken place in climatically unfavorable areas even for the Soviet Union, it should be noted. In the United States, in contrast, while total cultivated acreage is smaller than in the Soviet Union,

[3] Lazar Volin, *The Agricultural Picture in the U.S.S.R. and U.S.A.* (Washington, D.C.: U.S. Dept. of Agriculture, July 27, 1962), p. 3.

three hundred and thirty million as compared with five hundred million acres, it is confined on the whole to the more suitable agricultural areas.

Institutional inadequacies have compounded the climatic problems of Soviet agriculture. Soviet agriculture is predominantly organized into collective and state farms. Collective farms in 1960 averaged over fifteen thousand acres with an average sown area of close to seven thousand acres. State farms were even larger and their average sown area exceeded twenty-two thousand acres.[4] This compared with an average of a little over four hundred acres for United States commercial farms.

The size of the units within the Soviet Union would tax the capacity of the ablest manager with a wide freedom of decision. In the Soviet Union the tenure, initiative, and power of decision of Soviet managers have been limited by the party-state bureaucracy. While Khrushchev has taken steps to correct some of the structural weakness by decentralization, liquidation of machine-tractor stations, and other measures, they have by no means been overcome. Moreover, the central government has tended to support nationwide agricultural practices which, in the absence of local power of decision, could not but be unsuitable in many areas. In addition, under the system the farm manager had to rely on labor which, while hard working with respect to the private plots, lacked adequate incentives to work efficiently on the collective and state farms. Thus, it seems true that the Soviet Union is perpetuating the agricultural problem, in part, because of obsession with impractical dogma.

But even if the farm managers were to attain the right of un-

4 *Ibid.*, p. 6.

hampered decision-making, many deficiencies would remain. Among the most apparent is an insufficient information-research structure to help guide decisions and an inadequate farm requisite supply system which limits the choice of seeds, materials, and equipment. The Soviet Union has not developed to a comparable degree the immense and effective management consulting and supporting services represented in the U.S. Department of Agriculture, the Extension Service, the State Experiment Stations, the Rural Electrification Administration, the Farm Credit Administration, and many other agencies. Ironically, the role of government in the success of agricultural production may actually be more significant in the United States than in the Soviet Union but the means by which the influence is achieved are quite different. The task of the government in the United States is to help improve the decisions of the individual farm manager, whereas in the Soviet Union it has been to control his decisions. But inflated control serves the longer-run interests of neither the state nor the society. The nature of the agricultural problem with its wide range of variables favors flexibility over rigidity, decentralized but coordinated decisions over centralized action.

However, even within the present structure of Soviet agriculture, substantial increases in productivity are possible as a result of increased capital investment. For example, the gap between Soviet and American capital investment in agricultural machinery, and between the present level and what Khrushchev has estimated to be the requirements, is shown in Table I (p. 266).

In addition to the machinery deficiency illustrated by the Table, use of electricity on Soviet farms is probably no more than a third of that in the United States. Moreover, such machinery as

TABLE I

Selected Agricultural Machinery Inventories for
U.S.A. and U.S.S.R.[5]
(in thousands)

	U.S.A.	U.S.S.R.	
Implements	*Jan. 1, 1960*	*Jan. 1, 1962*	*Requirements* *
Tractors	4,770	1,168	2,696
Grain combines	1,065	503	845
Silage harvesters	285	121	257
Trucks	3,110	790	1,650
Tractor trailers	**4,400	292	820
Tractor drawn ploughs	**2,750	784	1,180

* For performance of farm operations during optimum periods.
** Jan. 1, 1957.

is available in the Soviet Union seems to be less well cared for than in the United States. Shortage of spare parts seems to be chronic. The result is that many of the available machines cannot be fully or efficiently utilized. Since timing of farm operations is of even greater significance when the growing season is short, this is more crucial for the Soviet Union than it would be for the United States. Nor are fertilizers, herbicides, and other requisites of production used as extensively in the Soviet Union, although efforts are being made to increase the supply.

In order for Soviet agricultural production to begin to approach the efficiency and variety of the United States, it has been estimated that a capital investment of about $20 billion would be required.

[5] Nikita Khrushchev's Report, *Pravda* and *Izvestiya*, March 5, 1962, and U.S. Dept. of Agriculture.

In addition, of course, significant institutional changes, designed to place a much greater proportion of decision-making at the farm level and at the same time enrich and expand the research and information system to improve the scientific basis of the decisions, would be necessary. Paralleling these efforts there would need to be improved incentives for farm labor. This, of course, has implications for the production of consumer goods and services. To cap the entire effort, agricultural production and civilian consumption would have to be accorded a significantly greater priority in the planning of the Soviet regime. Measures such as these which would lead to greater agricultural productivity in the Soviet Union cannot be termed perpetuation of the present system—they call for its continuous modification.

The consequences of such a shift have large implications for the Soviet-American confrontation. Concentration on agriculture and consumption would mean that, for the time at least, the Soviet regime was focusing on providing the material basis for the enjoyment of life by the Soviet people. There would be less resources and time to devote to foreign adventures and to military preparations. Dogma about driving out individualist "capitalist" attitudes may inhibit the shift, but concrete success will impel it. What can the United States do to contribute to a shift in priorities toward agriculture and, similarly, toward other consumption areas? What should it do?

The Soviet Union, while steadily gaining on the United States in the industrial sectors most closely related to military power, remains an underdeveloped country in the area of civilian consumption. Living standards of the population, while improving, remain extremely low for a modern industrial state. The output of agriculture and light industry, as well as other sectors, is inadequate to meet the needs of the Soviet people. The United States has both resources and technicians which could provide valuable assistance to the Soviet Union in raising the living standards of the people. The Soviet Union is already obtaining some of the benefits of Western technology through its purchase of technical publications, its carefully selected exchange missions, and its trade with Western Europe.

Capital contributions whether by normal trade or as the result of long-term loans as has been suggested might be most effective in influencing increased emphasis on agricultural production. Capital equipment accompanied by technical assistance might well have an influence on the institutional structure of Soviet agriculture toward patterns favored by the West since the underlying economic factors seem to be pushing in that direction. Problematical but worth exploring is to what extent the Soviet regime would permit, let alone welcome, United States assistance in improving the material basis for the enjoyment of life by its people. On the American side gains for trade and production as a result of supplying the Soviet Union with farm machinery and other agricultural requisites would be welcome. But the long-run benefits while intangible may be more significant. Increased contact between the Soviet and American citizens may enhance confidence and dampen anxiety. The enjoyment of life for Americans may be much more interdependent with that of the Soviet people than is at present accepted.

The possible effect of United States collaboration with the Soviet Union in the development of the consumption side of its economy have never been fully explored on a sector-by-sector basis. It is a task that deserves more attention, both in terms of the increased restraint it might exercise on Soviet short-run policies and in terms of the creation of one element of the long-run interdependence which is required for the control of conflict.

Children and Education

Persuasion had best begin with the identification and understanding of areas of similarity.[6] The quest for similarity ought to be pursued across the whole of society, not as an end in itself but as a moral and psychological preparation for discussing differences and how they may be resolved.

While there are differences in the way American and Soviet children are raised, on both sides they receive a great deal of love and affection. There is on the part of parents and others throughout both societies a continuing interest in, and attention to, their development as individuals and as members of society.

It would be useful if both sides knew much more about the care and attention each side lavishes on its children, not so much to make them better competitors but out of parental love. It would be well if each side appreciated the extent that affection permeates the relation of society with its children not only in the home but in the schools and other organizations as well.

The description of an eminent American psychologist provides one insight into the attitude of Soviet society toward its children. He wrote:

[6] Anatol Rapoport, *Fights, Games and Debates* (Ann Arbor: The University of Michigan Press, 1960), p. 287.

We were graciously led by the arm by mid-adolescent girls to the room in which band practice was going on (anybody with a musical skill can play, so that there were eleven accordions in a group of forty pieces, but they played with spirit and vigor and reasonable competence) on into a very charming show of five-year-olds learning the first ballet steps —Russian children mixed with Uzbek children, that is, white with brown—and that great grace which one thinks of in terms of Russian dancing.

Then on into the children's parks. We saw everywhere health and agricultural slogans and posters, a statue of Lenin and a quotation to the effect that the strength of government is based on the people's understanding: "A government is strong only insofar as the people are free to know everything about everything."

In one area there was a place for quiet play at large tables, with games and toys from a "lending library" of toys, operated as we would operate a lending library. That is, a child signs out a doll or toy which he ordinarily could not afford and plays with it for a period and then turns it back for some other child to use. Elsewhere in the playground we saw children playing group games and we joined in one of the simple dances. We also watched a delightful blind-man's-buff game in which a tiger boy and a bear boy (with appropriate masks) chase a girl who has castanets, which she must keep sounding to help them chase; of course, they stumble and bump into one another many times before they succeed in touching her.

In another part of the playground we saw children between the years of five and mid-adolescence playing chess, including a young Korean, apparently not more than five or six years of age (reputed to be quite a master for his age level), playing a Russian child. A few hundred yards away we saw another open space in which peace exhibits, flags of many nations and pictures of white doves were prominently displayed. The whole feeling was one of pride, confidence, sense of social participation; much planning for the children, and joyful response of the children to it. . . .

We certainly didn't see much evidence that children were growing up in a militaristic world, in a world where they were being poisoned against enemies, where they were being taught to hate, or where they learned to fear.

On the contrary, the children are being given the best. By and large their clothes seem nicer than those of grownups. The children, at least those that one sees on the streets, are healthy and vigorous. They are loved, are given many opportunities, and are in turn growing up to love their country, to be proud of it, to try to help to make it still better. . . .

When I asked in Leningrad how they chose the staff for the children's hospital, the answer was simple, "When we need new people, we try them out and if they are good to children, we keep them." It is assumed that being good to children is good for the children.[7]

From an appreciation of our common devotion to our children may come many ideas and opportunities for common action. At first, such opportunities might develop in specific fields of educational development and research. Later, broader studies of the entire approach to education and development may become possible.

[7] Gardner Murphy and Lois Murphy, "Soviet Life and Soviet Psychology," in Bauer, *op. cit.*, pp. 253–254, 265.

Research on the development of normal children is important, but inquiries into the problems of the handicapped may be particularly poignant. A single example of the kinds of possibilities that may exist will have to suffice.

Cooperative research by psychologists of the two countries, particularly in areas where marked disagreement prevails, might prove mutually beneficial. Thus in the U.S.A., low I.Q.'s are apt to be treated as justifying an unfavorable educational prognosis for children (particularly so if there is no evidence indicating that the apparent intellectual retardation is a result of emotion problems), in which case psychotherapy tends to be recommended. In the U.S.S.R., psychologists express more favorable attitudes towards the potential efficacy of instructional procedures with educationally retarded children, provided that the children do not have damaged brains, and that the missing components of the complex educational skills are located by appropriate experimentation. There is the possibility that a Russian psychologist working in an American institution for the feeble-minded, using Russian non-test experimental techniques, may be able to find the educationally neglected children who can be rehabilitated by the instructional methods which have been developed by Russian educational psychologists. On the other hand, an American psychologist using psychometric tests may be able to identify the children in a Russian remedial school who are not likely to benefit from remedial instruction; or he may use projective tests and interviews in order to identify the children who need counseling or play therapy. There are undoubtedly many additional research problems, the solution of which may be advanced by cooperation between American and Russian psychologists. One such research problem, for example, could stem from the many Russian reports of successful applications of Makarenko's techniques of work with collectives of children and young people. An attempt at utilization of these techniques in the problem schools of our own large cities, or in community work with delinquent youth, in collaboration with a Russian consultant who is an expert on these techniques, may prove fruitful.[8]

As each side comes to appreciate the bond of affection for the children, as each side understands the specific common contributions which may be made toward their development, larger enterprises for the study of the entire educational process will become easier to launch. Education in a modern society is an amalgam of its social history which links the present with the past, of its art which provides a vision of its future, and of the state of its technology whose needs must be met if its progress is to continue. As Sir Julian Huxley said in presenting his proposal for cross-national discussions of education at the Tenth Pugwash Conference, "One of the tasks in education is to identify the needs and wishes of the individual and the needs of society and to reconcile them." This is the universal task of education in all societies.

It is of utmost importance for the future that the way in which the needs of the individual and the society are conceived and the manner in which their reconciliation is being attempted by means of education should be thoroughly understood and compared across national boundaries. This is of particular significance for two great powers such as the United States and the Soviet Union

[8] Alexander Mintz, "Introduction to Contemporary Soviet Psychology," Bauer, *op. cit.,* pp. 24–25.

at the present stage of world history. The suggestions that Julian Huxley made for discussions of the relationship of education and human ecology and the relationship of education to society and to world development provide the seed for the beginning of a dialogue which could be of immense importance for mitigating the conflict over the longer run. At the level of individual development at which education must deal, some of the global terms of conflict may turn out either to be irrelevant or to have quite different meanings.

Social and Behavioral Sciences

Closely related to child rearing and education but also concerned with the problems of adult society are a whole series of disciplines which have grown up in the West and which until the last few years had no counterpart in the Soviet Union. While at the present time parallel lines of investigation can be found, the difference in perspectives from which they are approached remains significant. Among these are cultural anthropology, psychiatry, and social psychology, and the study of international political systems. A beginning has been made at initiating a dialogue with Soviet "social scientists." In light of the present Soviet tendency to rely excessively on outmoded Marxist doctrines, it is of great importance that a continuous stream of transactions between Western social scientists and their Soviet counterparts be developed as rapidly as possible. On both sides there may be a certain reluctance among statesmen and diplomats to foster such an interchange. Impediments must be patiently overcome and the ability of Western social scientists to step outside their own culture to examine the common characteristics of societies must be mirrored in comparable states of development among Soviet social scientists.

Games as Models of Interdependence

Another element in the enjoyment of life which should not be lost sight of is the ability to play together. In a sense, the ability to play together may be a kind of prerequisite to effective collaboration in many other fields. Play provides a simple environment for shared pleasure, excitement, and accomplishment in which the psychic costs of nonachievement are drastically reduced.

Too often in Soviet-American contacts the element of play has been lost sight of by the audience if not by the participants. Athletic contests have for some become not a pleasure but merely another expression of intense national competition. While this cannot wholly be avoided, it should not be aggravated. Although newspapers cannot be prevented from adding up team scores no matter how illogical this may be, cultivation of a regard for individual performance, of whatever nationality, would seem more fitting for a society which emphasizes the uniqueness of the individual. In organizing cross-national competition, the element of enjoyment as well as individual and team competence could be brought out if the team on occasion were drawn from regions or states rather than from the nation as a whole. It really is not necessary that Americans or Russians win every time; the point is to play the game respectably and with courage and pleasure.

Games represent an important activity of the young which may serve as a model for their adult behavior. Sportsmanship, regard for rules and officials, courtesy, acceptance of the good qualities in the other player, are qualities to be cultivated quite as much as concern for the final score. The essence of a game is that it can be repeated. When one side loses, there is always the presupposition that another time it may come back to win.

Since games provide a model for adult behavior, it would seem that in the Soviet-American relationship new forms of games are urgently needed which would help to provide alternative models to the present ones. One particular requirement would seem to be new forms of gaming activities in which high achievement is rewarded but with a minimum emphasis on national wins and losses. International music festivals, international mathematics and science fairs, and many other forums where young people can display their talents and be recognized—without their achievement being wholly distorted as a victory for their nation—are needed. A system by which several performers are given the "highest award" is to be recommended.

Applied social science now has the ability to develop new forms of play, games, and competition which would satisfy the need for excitement and at the same time contribute to an appreciation of the growing interdependence of the international environment. Modest funding of research and development of modern games seem likely to pay important long-run dividends. Games of war and crisis are heavily financed by the government. It may not be too bold to suggest that a foundation put a small amount of money into integrative games which would serve as models for controlling conflict. It would be useful if the Soviet Union and the United States could cultivate a more detached view of the achievements of their citizens on the field of play.

History and Art

The study and reading of history and the production and appreciation of art are additional areas of great significance in achieving understanding between the Soviet Union and the United States. Unfortunately, the Soviet Union has sought to make them instruments of current policy. This is a dangerous and impossible task when tackled directly, and earlier controls are giving way to caution.

Obviously, if history is rewritten as each new premier takes office, the study of history will be undermined. Self-understanding suffers, and the outsider's understanding of a nation is made much more difficult—a dangerous condition in the nuclear age.

History is not conventionally thought of as vital means of communication and understanding between two nations. Yet, in the present confrontation between the United States and the Soviet Union, it may have a critical part to play. A considerable part of the confused perceptions and lack of understanding on both sides may arise from an inadequate appreciation of the important strains of historical memory that influence the behavior of each. Much of the interpretation of the adversary's behavior is made without adequate appreciation of its historical antecedents. Moreover, a common understanding of each other's history may enable the two peoples to find that they have much more in common than is at present generally believed.

Art, while contributing to the understanding of the past, may play a dynamic role in opening new paths to the future. An appreciation of the art of an adversary provides a basis, however circumscribed, for common perception of the present. Equally important, art in many forms may play the role of critic of society, heightening awareness of the imperfect justice and humanity of one's own society as well as that of the adversary. Popular art, the movies under the exchange program, for example, by dwelling on the universal concerns of man may also communicate a sense of common human aspirations and limitations. Moreover, art provides a source of entertainment and pleasure without regard to the invisible boundaries of the nation-state. In short, art is found in search of the eternal verities of human existence, and these may turn out to be not so much different in Russia and America! The verities when expressed in a new form may, of course, be rejected for a time by groups within a society. As the Senator from Idaho is reported to have said, "There is one thing Khrushchev and my constituents in Moscow [Idaho] agree on. They don't like modern art." [9]

Tourism

The list of activities which contribute to the common enjoyment of life and thus to good communication would not be complete without some mention of tourism. The freedom to be a tourist is one of the important facets of an advanced state. Tourism plays a special role in permitting a wide variety of citizens to gain, however superficially, a view of the "whole society" of the adversary as a developing system. It helps, as nothing else can, to correct stereotypes and to bring up to date the always lagging vision of what the adversary is really like. It is useful to have people

[9] *New York Times,* April 21, 1962.

scattered through each society who can say, "I was there and it is not exactly that way."

The number of tourists moving between the Soviet Union and the United States has been quite unbalanced. While in some years as many as fifteen thousand American tourists have visited the Soviet Union, only a few hundred Soviet citizens have reached the United States. Moreover, those who have come have normally traveled in groups under some form of supervision. Increased attention on the United States side seems warranted to attempt to help the Soviet citizen gain the freedom of movement presently enjoyed by the West.

Interdependence requires a concerted action along the entire front of Soviet-American relations, on those sectors that seem less significant as well as on those conventionally accepted as important. Because of the stimulus provided to man's imagination and desire for new goals, interdependence can be as challenging as modern war, which in a sense may be waged too easily any longer to represent a challenge. Where, after all, is the excitement of war when you no longer have to go to war—it will come to you.

8 *The Common Problem of the Developing Areas*

Nuclear war is not the only path to world chaos; there is, as has been recently pointed out, the possibility of creeping catastrophe eroding world stability.

> While our thoughts are occupied with the possibilities of catastrophe through nuclear war, another catastrophe is taking place before our eyes—the slow starvation of two out of three of our fellow human beings. This is not a sudden, shocking disaster. But it is dramatic enough; as dramatic as watching a man slowly sink to his death in a quicksand.
>
> We could not turn our backs on these people, even if we were callous enough to do so. Too many of them have seen or heard of the changes that are possible through science and technology, and through social progress.[1]

The idea that "poverty breeds Communism" is largely an accident of history. Poverty—and an attempt to overcome it through the mechanism of the state—breeds authoritarianism, and Communism happens to be the most popular form of authoritarian system at the moment. As the Soviet Union begins to look like us in most respects, Soviet Communism ceases to be the preferred form of authoritarianism. There is some evidence this is already happening. China apart, Presidents Nkrumah of Ghana and Touré

[1] A. Salam, "The Creeping Catastrophe," unpublished paper, London, 1962.

280

of Guinea and others are substantially disenchanted with Soviet Communism and are now engaged in developing their own brand of authoritarianism.

The United States and the Soviet Union will gradually find themselves in a similar relationship to the creeping catastrophe of hunger and the population explosion in third areas. In the future, they will find themselves compelled to deal with it in two ways or a combination of both. They can seek to contain it, very much as the United States has sought to contain the Soviet Union in the period through which we have been passing. Or they can try to overcome it, much as we have tried to do with our better aid programs. The point is that before many years it will be clear that the United States and the Soviet Union face a common problem because they both have a wide range of mutually conservative interests to protect. In many areas, both may be dealing with poor and authoritarian states and the authoritarianism will be less and less Soviet-led because the Soviet experience will be seen as less and less applicable to the problems of the poor states. The Soviets seem bound to appear less heroic as they become more apparently a conservative force.

The proper role for the United States, at this point, is to seek to hasten the process of the evolution of the Soviet role in relation to developing nations. Once again, the United States should seek to push the pattern and instrumentalities of Soviet action in the direction compatible with the American style before the Soviet Union reaches the American level of economic output. A few may continue to dream of excluding the Soviet Union from the free world, but this is not possible at a price the free world can pay and remain free. Thus, the United States must seek to induce the

Soviet to act both toward its own bloc and toward the rest of the world in ways that are compatible with the free-world pattern of behavior.

The free-world pattern is essentially one of diversity, of pluralism which is moved forward by a judicious admixture of competition and coordination or cooperation. The United States must strive to create the conditions in which the Soviet Union can be permitted to compete and will be impelled to cooperate.

The spread of technology takes on a special significance as the Soviet Union and the United States confront each other in third areas of the world. Widely distributed in the world are men with strong motivations to move their nations along the path of industrialization. It would be hard to find an underdeveloped country today without its band of dedicated men intent on acquiring for their nation the skills and productivity of modern technology. Equally hard to identify is any developing nation which has in abundance all the elements required for technological advance. Capital, both domestic and foreign, is usually hard to obtain. Adequately trained engineering and technical manpower is insufficient. The scientific backup—even the most essential kind of applied science—hardly exists anywhere. Finally, the institutional arrangements necessary to open the way for an instrumental regrouping of the society without wholly alienating or eliminating traditional groupings are seldom seen clearly as a problem, let alone dealt with effectively.

In this environment the West and more recently the Soviet Union have been contributing in some degree to the spread throughout the world of all four elements which contribute to the effective transmission of technology.

Capital

In the last half of the 1950s total capital outflow to the developing countries is estimated to have been on the order of $5 to $6 billion a year or just under $30 billion for the period 1955 to 1959. Of this amount, just over $16 billion was in the form of governmental grants and loans. Table II shows the main sources of aid funds.

TABLE II [2]

Government Aid to Newly Developing Countries:
A Comparison of the West and the Soviet Area, 1956–1959
(in billions)

	Total	*Grants*	*Loans*
United States	$ 8.42	$ 5.57	$2.85
France	3.36	2.73	0.63
United Kingdom	1.03	0.72	0.31
Germany (F.R.)	0.48	0.13	0.35
Other West	1.35	1.01	0.34
Total	$14.64	$10.16	$4.48
U.S.S.R.	0.60	0.03	0.57
Grand Total	$15.24	$10.19	$5.05

Two points of interest here emerge from the Table. First the United Kingdom and France, contrary to the popular impression, have been engaged in continuing large-scale aid—principally, of

[2] Jan Tinbergen, *Shaping the World Economy* (New York: The Twentieth Century Fund, 1962), p. 38.

course, with their former colonial areas. Second, the Soviet Union which was very active in the 1950s in entering into commitments, actually was making expenditures at a very modest level.

At present, the United States and the Soviet Union are engaged in continuing competition in providing bilateral aid to third-area countries. The United States assistance, which amounts to approximately $4 billion a year, far outstrips that provided by the Soviet Union.[3] However, the Soviet bloc has continued its activities in the aid field. The bloc has extended credits for economic aid and military assistance of approximately $6.0 billion to the less developed countries.[4] Bloc aid has been granted to twenty-five countries spread all over the world. Approximately ten thousand technicians from the Soviet bloc have served in third countries. However, actual Soviet expenditures have continued to run well behind the total aid which they have agreed to provide. The actual volume of deliveries by the bloc may be running at about $½ billion annually, compared with several times that amount delivered by the United States government alone. The total picture suggests that while the Soviet Union is a significant source of finance in the case of certain countries, on a world-wide basis its contribution does not yet approach that which might be expected of a great power.

[3] Foreign aid consists of economic aid, military assistance, and sales of surplus-fund commodities. In addition, the United States extends credits through the Export-Import Bank and private capital also makes investment. Furthermore, Western Europe, Canada, and others also provide capital in a variety of forms so that the free-world contribution is greater than the official $5 billion a year.

[4] Samuel Pisar, *A New Look at Trade Policy toward the Communist Bloc,* materials prepared for the Subcommittee on Foreign Economic Policy of the Joint Economic Committee, U.S. Congress (Washington, D.C., 1961), p. 28.

Technical Assistance

Engineering and technical assistance provided by the Soviet Union has in the past been closely tied to specific projects which it has agreed to undertake for the developing countries. This is in marked contrast to much of the United States technical assistance which has been independent of any specific American-financed capital project, although technicians supporting a particular undertaking have also been widely used. United States technicians have advised governments on their over-all economic plans, the development of statistical services, budgeting, highway construction and maintenance, communications systems, public administration, health, and many other fields. In only rare instances, such as in Afghanistan, has the Soviet engaged in general technical assistance in the Western sense.

Technical assistance tied to a particular capital project provides the least learning experience for the grantor. A specific industrial project may to a considerable degree be isolated from the more complex problems of a mixed economy. It is in the long-run interests of the West to have the Soviet become more knowledgeable on the problems and possibilities of mixed economies. Experience with these economies has had a significant effect on the role of planning in the West. In the case of the Soviet Union the impact could well be to encourage in a modest degree decentralization and diversity in the Soviet system. Opportunities to involve the Soviet Union in technical assistance, as distinct from capital projects, may be limited but should not be overlooked. Whether or not they are in the United States interest would depend in part on the strength of the local government and in part on the ability of United States advisors to avoid being excluded or layered by Soviet technicians.

The advantages of Soviet technicians without projects is that they must then relate to the local environment if they are to be at all effective. Soviet contributions to development in these circumstances cannot be isolated but must be modified to fit the total process of industrialization. Moreover, the individual technician in many areas would unavoidably be forced to rub shoulders not only with the local, largely Western-trained, government officials but in many cases with Western technicians as well. While the East-West competitive element would remain, the competition would be fragmented and tested in terms of the contribution to practical everyday problems of the developing economy.

This approach may prove interesting not only within the local government organizations proper but in regard to technical institutes, universities, and other training centers where the participation of advisors from a number of countries provides the opportunity of day-to-day comparison and testing of the applications of different approaches and styles to the immediate problems of training students. The longer-run objective, in carefully selected cases, might be to involve Soviet engineers and technicians in advising the private sector of mixed economies.

There are many other facets of the problem of the engineer-technician contributing to the spread of technology throughout the world. Improved preparation and assignment is needed on the American side. A better understanding of when a technician can be effective and when he cannot is needed. The independent role and limitation of technical assistance in developing areas has never been adequately explored. For example, among the growing literature on development, there is no objective and comprehensive book on the potential and limitations of technical assistance apart from basic capital inputs. Yet the Soviet and Chinese cases suggest that foreign technical know-how, however acquired, may be at least as significant a factor as foreign capital at certain stages and for specific countries. If true, the task is to devise means of transference and application of technical knowledge on a large scale without resort to excessive coercion.

Scientific Support

Scientific backup is perhaps the most neglected aspect of Western and Soviet assistance in developing areas. Reasons for this are not hard to find. Local education often does not provide people with the equipment to pursue a life of science. Institutions within which the indigenous scientists can work are few in number and often underfinanced. The task of creating scientific competence is long and demanding. Western scientists are on the whole not eager to spend time in the developing areas. Yet the growth of a scientific outlook and of scientific competence in developing societies is essential to an effective approach to the innumerable problems of change. While growth of a scientific outlook is important, the emphasis in the immediate future in most areas should undoubtedly be on basic applied science.

Recently, the United States has shown a modest increase in interest in fostering scientific and research competence in the developing areas, but much remains to be done. As institutions develop for the conduct of research—mainly, in the first instance, applied research—the opportunity may open up for including members of Soviet science. The standards of universality and objectivity of science, as well as the unique environment of particular developing countries, provide a good setting for confrontation of representatives of the United States and the Soviet Union. The standards of achievement in science are exacting and nonideological. Scientific advance provides a form of competition from which all three sets of participants—local, Soviet, and Western—may profit. Set prescriptions for progress tend to dissolve in the face of objective research.

As Roger Revelle has pointed out:

> Much modern technology must be simplified to be useful to developing countries. New technologies suited to available energy sources, environment, and economic and social patterns must often be developed. To meet the specific needs of particular underdeveloped countries or regions, substantial efforts should also be devoted to devising adaptations from the vast store of modern scientific and technical knowledge. This adaptive research must usually be performed in the area or region concerned. At any rate, the problems must be identified and the proposed solutions must be tested there.[5]

The more that the Soviet Union can be drawn into competition to solve the local problems, the more the contest will be diffused, fragmented, and made constructive. Moreover, Soviet participation in such enterprises will inevitably involve Soviet citizens in face-to-face confrontations which will emphasize the complexity of progress and the limits of ideology.

[5] Roger Revelle, "International Cooperation and the Two Faces of Science," unpublished paper, 1962.

Institutional Arrangements

The institutions through which the United States advances the spread of technology throughout the world are and ought to be diverse. It is equally important that the recipient country have and employ a diversity of institutions for assimilating and using the technology.

An appreciation of the range and balance of the United States and, indeed, of the total Western impact is needed at the top level of the United States government. However, the gears and controls between this over-all comprehension, which must of course include longer-run objectives, and the many institutions through which they are effected need not be numerous. Planning in this sense is essential, but planning in a hierarchical sense will be detrimental. The environment is too varied, the creative application of technology too dynamic, and the burden of hierarchy too great for efficient central control.

In American efforts in recent years there has been a movement toward both centralization and diffusion. The drift toward centralization should be resisted. Top-level appreciation, general guidance, and affirmative action to maintain balance are needed to take the place of futile efforts at detailed control. To locate all aid operations in a single organization, for example, is to ensure that only a single operative point of view prevails, whereas a diversity of approaches is necessary. The United States Department of State could well increase the effectiveness of its effort by denying to itself any direct operating responsibilities for any of the facets of technological advance and by concentrating instead on seeking to appreciate and guide what is occurring in the world as a result of the spread of technology or the lack of it. In the endeavor to foster the world-wide spread of technology, the Communist bloc is not the only one that has lessons to learn with respect to decentralization.

Semi-autonomous governmental institutions, private industry, universities, and nonprofit organizations, as well as a variety of intergovernmental and nongovernmental international organizations, are all required to play an appropriate part. The first task of a government is to comprehend the total effort and its effect on the world environment. Its second task, because it is a primary source of resources, is to supplement and support these diverse activities.

Rational diversity of the Western effort will present a challenge to the Soviet Union to which it will be obliged to respond in kind, even though slowly and reluctantly. Such a response is in the interests of the United States and of the developing nations. The organizational arrangement it suggests is not as neat as a single streamlined operating agency tightly controlled by the Secretary of State in theory, yet, in practice, on a day-to-day basis, by the desk officer —if by anyone. The first requirement, of course, is for the Federal Government to give itself the tools to comprehend what is going on in the world with respect to the spread of technology—whether by capital transfer, technical assistance, training, or scientific advance. In more than a decade of assistance programs this has never been done. The result has been a growing concern for detail and an increasing lack of comprehension of the over-all impact.

In effect, one tendency has been to duplicate the hierarchical arrangements of the Soviet Union both at home and in the developing countries. Fortunately, the tendency has been somewhat checked in practice by certain independent factors at home and to a lesser extent abroad. American universities in certain areas have exerted a healthy influence toward diversity as they have become involved in foreign programs and training. Respected international agencies such as the International Bank for Reconstruction and Development, to which the United States has made available substantial capital, are also playing an important role. In many cases American private industry has also invested abroad. More and more industry is becoming aware of the need to shape its policies both to accord with the local environment and to help shape the advance of technology in areas in which it operates.

The character and variety of the institutions employed in the developing area are also of great importance. If all aid must go through the central government bureaucracy, not only is speed and effectiveness reduced but the tendency to centralization is aggravated. Most governments wish to have a say in the advance of technology within their borders, but the manner in which they exert their influence is significant for the outcome. So far as possible their voice should be limited to guidance, facilitation, and balance among the segments of society. A multitude of outside agencies encourages diffusion of power within the society, although this may be slow in developing. But even where centralization of control is judged essential for rapid development, the nature of the control will have an important impact on short-run efficiency and long-run diffusion of power.

From the point of view of this study, the purpose of diversity is to help induce a complementary diffusion of the Soviet efforts to demonstrate that their highly controlled approach is less effective in practice. As and if the Soviet Union accepts the challenge of diffusion, the competition is fragmented and made more amenable to restraint by those with an appreciation of the total effort. In addition, it leads to maximum exposure of Soviet technicians to the reality of the diverse environments of the developing countries as well as to the United States participants.

Up until the present time, the United States has relied primarily on bilateral aid to further its interests. The contribution of many of these bilateral aid programs has been not so much unimportant as insufficient. Population increases have continued to outpace or offset economic growth. Striking advances in governmental cohesion in third areas have been few and difficult to discern. Perhaps most significant, it has been impossible within the framework of bilateral aid to bring to bear on world problems the great strength of the United States industrial complex.

While the overwhelming proportion of United States assistance is given on a bilateral basis, a significant amount is channeled through various multilateral agencies. The percentage of public funds handled by international agencies has increased slightly over the past decade and the American share seems to have at least kept pace. Today, the percentage of United States assistance funds being handled multilaterally may be as high as ten to twelve per cent. The bulk of this is, of course, handled by agencies in which the Soviet Union does not participate.

On the Soviet side, the percentage flowing through international agencies is negligible, probably less than one per cent. Despite the much smaller volume of bilateral aid which the Soviet Union is making available, it has become a significant factor for some third areas to take into account. While it is unlikely that the Soviet Union will come close to the present United States level of aid in the foreseeable future, the Soviet Union, as its output grows, will have an expanding potential to grant aid. The shortcomings in the American bilateral aid efforts and the Soviet economic interest in third areas suggest the need for a hard look at the current pattern of United States aid.

The bilateral-multilateral dichotomy does not do justice to the varieties of American giving. For the present purposes, which are, first of all, concerned with United States actions that will influence the Soviet Union toward a pattern of behavior more compatible with the West, five categories will serve. In effect, the categories represent points on a continuous spectrum of assistance from the most restrictive to the most universal.

First are the monopoly bilateral arrangements in which a single country is virtually the sole source of assistance for a developing area. The beneficiaries of such monopoly assistance have been termed "client-states." Taiwan, South Korea, and South Vietnam are the leading examples. Despite their complete dependence on the United States for aid, these countries retain limited room for maneuver and a considerable capacity to aggravate the conflict between the East and the West. At the same time, their dependency leads them to accept many conditions which states otherwise situated may avoid. In such client-states an intensive though not wholly successful effort is made to eliminate Communist influence. This frequently requires authoritarian practices which help to maintain the *status quo* at the same time they may contribute to the disenchantment of the population. To offset popular unrest, additional external resources for the economy as well as for the military establishment represent a continuing problem. By and large, client-states are able to obtain larger amounts of assistance than they would receive if their status were modified. On the other hand, their stability remains in continuous jeopardy between the subversive efforts of the Communists, on the one hand, and the rigidity of authoritarian rule, on the other. While no other course may be open, political stability is precarious under these conditions.

Second, assistance may be granted on a competitive bilateral basis. Prominent among the countries receiving assistance in this fashion are the neutrals such as Burma, Egypt, and Yugoslavia. However, a large number of the developing nations are in one degree or another receiving assistance from more than one country on a competitive basis. The United States is active in most of them. In the recent past, efforts have been made by the Western developing nations to coordinate their efforts but, in practice, there continues to be a substantial competitive element—often fostered to the extent possible by the recipients. The result of competitive efforts whether within the West or between East and West is to somewhat increase the independence of action of the developing areas. Independence is limited, however, because funds remain short and no one state has a truly compelling bargaining position, though some find themselves better situated than others and some make more efficient use of their levers of influence.

Bilateral competitive assistance provides the developing nations with considerable experience in dealing with the industrial states. In contrast, the advanced nations acquire only limited and indirect experience in taking each other's objectives and style into account. Objective economic criteria tend to be abandoned in the competitive situation because of the erratic desires of the developing states and the search for influence of the advanced states. Thus, it was largely in response to the competitive opportunity provided by the objective standards of the West that the Soviet Union in the first years of its aid program undertook to support numerous marginal projects. Since then some of the United States efforts at "impact" have been in the nature of reciprocal abandonment of earlier standards.

Third, coordinated bilateral assistance began on a large scale, so far as is known, in India and is gradually spreading. This represents both an effort to assure a definite level of capital flow and understandings with respect to its rational use. Coordinated bilateral assistance in practice may involve both states and international agencies such as the International Bank for Reconstruction and Development (IBRD). It represents a useful step toward recognizing the interdependence among givers and recipients of assistance.

Fourth, functional multilateral assistance is the dominant form of international aid. A number of international agencies were created following World War II to provide capital, technical, and special assistance to the developing nations. Others have been added in the intervening years. The Soviet Union participates in a limited number. However, those handling the largest volume of funds, such as the IBRD, have only Western participation.

These institutions function predominantly as multilateral givers. While the developing nations participate on the governing boards, the institutions deal with the recipients of assistance essentially on a one-by-one basis. In their decision-making process, the views of the givers and the advice of the international staffs appear to be the most important ingredients. However, some multilateral logrolling may occur among the representatives of the recipients. The one issue on which the recipients from time to time find a common interest is the need for more funds for the international agencies individually and collectively. In this they are, however, forced to face the fact that there is an opposing common interest among the more advanced nations.

The interests of the great powers are diverse and the interests of the small states provincial. Thus, in many instances, arrangements other than world-wide international agencies will serve their objectives more directly and effectively. While the world on certain great issues is highly interdependent, on innumerable practical problems something less than a universal organization may be more suitable.

Fifth, regional organizations have been much discussed, occasionally organized, and sometimes used in connection with assistance. Regional organizations emerge because they are clearly essential to the performance of a particular function or because a value is attached to handling particular activities on a multilateral regional basis. The development of a river valley extending through two or more nations, such as the Mekong or Indus, are examples of the former emphasis. The Organization of American States (oas) and the Communist Council for Economic Mutual Assistance are variations of the latter interest. Regional arrangements for particular purposes may be viewed both as ends in themselves and as steps on the path to political and economic integration of an area.

By and large, while there has been discussion in the United States about the desirability of regional organizations, there has been considerable caution in fostering them and a good deal of day-to-day reluctance to strengthen them once they exist. Exceptions are those organized for a clear and specific objective such as a river valley development. The lack of interest of the states in a particular region is frequently given as the explanation for the halting progress of regional organizations. But this does not entirely explain great-power caution. There is support for the view that regional organizations if they develop momentum may make it more difficult for great powers to achieve their day-to-day objectives. In addition, there is the concern that once regional coherence is achieved, the entire region may shift to one side or the other in the East-West contest. Basically, in terms of assistance, regional organizations give the recipients certain advantages they otherwise might not have. At the same time, regional organizations may contribute to both political viability and economic progress in the area. Both the gains and losses are matters of probability and open to innumerable special influences. Thus, in the absence of strong initiatives from within a region, the United States, as others before it, has looked with mixed feelings on the development of regional coherence.

Returning now to the relationship of the United States and the Soviet Union, what is the relevance of these alternative forms of assistance? The United States and the Soviet Union, as well as the European nations, are furnishing capital and technical assistance to speed the modernization of the developing nations. From the point of view of the latter, all the industrialized states are potential contributors to the common task of modernization. The industrialized states have opposing political objectives. Yet, in the longer run, it will be seen to be in the interests of all the advanced states to expedite the task of modernization in order that sufficient stability will be achieved both to avoid their being drawn into conflicts not of their own choosing and to contain the creeping catastrophe of the population explosion.

The problem is one of finding ways to continue the political competition which at the same time permit the challenge of the creeping catastrophe to be dealt with most effectively. From the United States point of view, this should involve drawing the Soviet Union into a pattern of competition and assistance which is compatible with the American view of the manner in which the world community must function and might be organized.

Exclusive bilateral assistance arrangements, while they may be unavoidable in the present, surely are not satisfactory as goals for the future. The United States cannot accept them as a permanent feature of the bloc and should not be satisfied with them in the West. They are corrosive of democratic values or extremely costly or both. Moreover, they are likely to be more prone to instability in the long run than other arrangements which encourage year-to-year adjustments.

Competitive bilateral assistance represents an advance over single-source arrangements. Among Western nations this is accepted. The United States has been working for the last several years to encourage greater participation by the European nations in development activities. What has not been so clearly noted but has been accepted is that Soviet participation represents an advance over earlier forms of competition resting mainly on subversion with a tendency to violence. In Eastern Europe, United States aid to Poland must also be judged as preferable to dangerous efforts to incite the Poles to violence. In neither case is a reversion to earlier views precluded and in both the dominant power seems to be following the principle of seeking to prevent the third area from becoming excessively dependent on the other.

Despite the advantages of competitive bilateral assistance, it remains far from a wholly adequate basis on which to project the future development of the world. Competitive assistance makes it almost impossible to ensure that resources are used effectively. As Lord Hailsham has pointed out:

> New nations prize their independence more than any other asset. It follows that it is difficult to assume any other means for identifying projects worthy of priority than the wishes of the government concerned—which are quite frankly not always very sensible—and there are perhaps few methods open to a developing country to secure favorable treatment other than a rather squalid attempt to offer, in return for aid, some degree of qualified political support . . . in the struggles for superiority between East and West.[6]

Moreover, competitive assistance reduces the long-run value of aid as a means of getting and maintaining influence. In competitive bilateral relationships the interplay between donor and recipient tends to lead the former to be excessively responsive to the latter. When aid is provided on a competitive bilateral basis, the only real lever available to influence internal allocations is a threat to withdraw the aid. This may have limited value, however, in a situation in which the recipient then has the choice of turning to the adversary.

The use of aid by the great powers has not proved in the longer run to be particularly useful in the ideological struggle. This fact is noted with pleasure when the Soviet Union is the disillusioned

[6] *Congressional Record* (Washington, D.C., Saturday, Sept. 29, 1962).

victim, but is often de-emphasized when the United States is the target. Aid is unpopular in the United States, not with those groups who value its humanitarian purposes, but with those to whom it has been presented as a means of stopping the Communist threat. While bad administration is given as a reason, even good administration cannot prevent an independent state from leaning now to the West and now to the East in an attempt to maximize external assistance and retain independence of action.

Moreover, competitive bilateral aid has proved unable to link the primary interests of private enterprise in the United States with the needs of the developing areas abroad. Private enterprise has looked with skepticism on investment in third areas which are either actual or latent fields of East-West conflict. It seems unlikely that the great potential of American industrial strength can be directed outward to the development of third areas in the absence of some new framework for channeling resources and of some means of reducing the conflict in those areas. The advantages to the United States of being able to bring to bear its immense industrial strength on third-area problems would in considerable degree offset any tactical gains which might be expected for the Soviet Union through its participation in coordinated or multilateral assistance programs.

The Soviet Union is already engaged in aid programs in approximately twenty-five countries. At the present time, it has an entirely free hand as to how it will distribute its much more limited funds. The Soviet Union is concentrating most of its aid in certain key countries in which it is seeking to gain a major political advantage. Indonesia, Egypt, and India have received about half of the total grants which it has made. The bulk of these funds are in the form of long-term loans which are repaid by exports tied to bilateral agreements.

The United States has an interest in the political stability and economic growth of the emerging nations, an interest which, with different emphases and objectives, the Soviet Union must increasingly share. Thus, each has an interest in seeing that the total resources made available are used economically and that the power of third areas to play one off against the other is reduced. In addition, the United States will benefit by changes in the character of the East-West conflict which encourage a more active interest and greater investment by American private enterprise. These interests, as well as the general objective of seeking modifications in Soviet behavior and a world environment compatible with the American view of the shape of the world of tomorrow, argue for seeking to draw the Soviet Union into coordinated or multilateral aid relationships.

The move toward coordinated bilateral or multilateral assistance which provides a place for the Soviet Union when it is ready to participate can be taken in a number of ways. For example, under present conditions the United States and the free world undertake certain projects and the Soviet bloc others. Thus, in the case of India's steel expansion, the West Germans undertook one mill, the British a second, and the Soviets a third. In addition, the United States is investigating the possibility of a fourth. While this kind of operation, from the point of view of the West, may reflect competition with the East, from the point of view of India, it represents common contributions toward the building of her steel industry.

It would appear to be in the interests of both the East and the West if some kind of forum of coordination could be created in which all parties could discuss the common undertaking. Once such forums were created, it might be possible in the future to move to the point where the undertaking of a particular large-scale project could be divided between the United States and the Soviet Union or between the Western European countries and the Eastern European satellites, depending on the relative capabilities of each. Beyond that it is possible to envisage formal East-West consortiums on particular projects. Steps such as these should be envisaged as experimental efforts at finding the most suitable methods for leading the Soviet Union to more systematic participation in the world development.

After the possibilities of common action had been tested out in coordinated bilateral situations, the time would come when both sides could consider participation by the Soviet Union in functional multilateral organizations from which they presently exclude themselves. A Soviet initiative to join the IBRD would be a most significant move in this respect. While Soviet participation might create initial difficulties for the IBRD, the long-run benefits must be weighed. Application for membership, although it might be made with reservations and mixed motives, would mark an important step in Soviet acceptance of the United States pattern of world-development assistance.

The Soviet Union already participates selectively in the multilateral technical assistance agencies of the United Nations. The United States, while a member of all these agencies, has shown a preference for channels of multilateral assistance in which the Soviet Union is not a participant. While a dual policy is necessary to draw the Soviet Union out, greater resources and efforts ought to be directed to those in which the Soviet Union does participate in order to induce it to increase its contribution and commitment. The United States also has an interest in seeing increased resources made available to third areas, provided this does not unduly increase dependence on the Soviet bloc. The United States thus should seek continually to use the multilateral aid mechanism to argue for increased Soviet assistance as well as to point up the limitations of the present Soviet pattern of aid. Multilateral assistance provides an opportunity for the United States to bring limited pressure on the Soviet Union to increase its allocations to economic assistance, to diffuse such assistance more evenly among the developing states, and to diversify the methods used. Multilateral aid helps to avoid the more uneconomic aspects of the East-West struggle. While bargaining and logrolling are still possible, the possibilities of objective criteria for use of resources are enhanced.

Regional organizations for channeling or coordinating assistance have been one element of Western policy for some years. The OEEC in Europe, the Columbo Plan in South and Southeast Asia, the OAS in Latin America, as well as CENTO and SEATO, have all had one or another function with respect to either military or economic assistance. Their role has varied from nominal to substantive.

By and large, however, the difficulties engendered by an intermediate level have led to operations being carried on largely on a bilateral basis. In seeking to create the ties required for a stable and productive world community a renewed emphasis on regional organizations is needed. A policy of strengthening regional organizations requires considerable conviction and vigor on the part of the top officials since the operators inevitably prefer the direct route. Regional emphasis is, however, required for both stability and long-run growth. In regional organizations, as in the universal multilateral agencies, a place should be provided for the participation of the Soviet Union. Delays may result but the outcome is more likely to be the control of conflict. Not that the Soviet Union's participation will end conflict; on the contrary, conflict will continue but it will be fragmented and contained within a variety of structures which provide an increased opportunity for its control.

An additional long-run benefit is that Soviet participation in multilateral aid programs might provide the opportunity for countless Soviet technicians to work together with Western technicians on common problems. There is sufficient ignorance about economic development throughout the world to provide a challenge to both groups. While in the beginning such common efforts might be painful and filled with ideological nettles, the proof of the effectiveness of alternative ways of tackling concrete problems would be the success of the various development projects throughout the world. Ideology would inevitably have to take a back seat. There is no useful ideological explanation for cement that does not set, spindles that do not spin, or dredges that do not dig.

Finally, the United States has an interest in the strength and cohesion of the developing areas as a whole. In many cases, the present nation-states, even when fully developed, will hardly be viable entities in the modern world. There is a significant deficiency in the present cross-national organization structure for bringing nations together to work on their common problems at the regional level. In some areas structures could be created which for the time being would exclude the Soviet Union; yet it retains the choice of intervention in almost any area by simply increasing the attractiveness of its aid offers. Because of this fact, and because it is in the American interest to draw the Soviet Union toward its pattern of assistance, it seems prudent to seek to draw the Soviet Union into multilateral organizations for planning and allocating the assistance, whether regional or world-wide. This does not imply that all bilateral aid should be transferred to multilateral organizations, but it would suggest that the United States gradually channel a larger proportion of its assistance through such organizations.

While shifts in American assistance resources from bilateral to multilateral institutions and Soviet participation in these institutions raise difficult political problems, both must eventually be attempted if viable growth and development are to be achieved and stable governments capable of sharing the products of growth on an equitable basis are to be maintained. However, the proposal for overt collaboration in the aid field cannot be taken separately from the general approach to Soviet-American relationships in other fields. From the American point of view, the primary purpose, once again, is to induce the allocation of Soviet resources in a preferred direction and to engage the Soviets in common undertakings which will work to modify both present values and visions of the future toward a convergence with those of the West.

Social and Political Development

While society, like an individual, develops as a single system, it is useful to abstract certain characteristics in order to examine and understand them. Social and political development are such abstractions. Social development is an aspect of the total ongoing activity of society. It could be, and occasionally has been, defined to include political development. For our purposes, it is useful to distinguish the two.

Two things are new about the historical process of social and political development. First, since 1945 there has been a tremendous acceleration of the pace of change and greatly increased participation in the process. Second, the sciences of man and nature have taken as one of their tasks aiding and assisting in the acceleration of change and the integration of the participants.

Social development is the process by which the individual is provided the skills, knowledge, and attitudes which enable him to feel he is an integral part of society. Political development is the process by which individual participation in politics is vastly increased and by which the modernizing individual acquires a position in and an influence on the political life of a nation.

The expectations an individual acquires about the role, processes, and institutions of government help to orient him either toward a willingness to work within the existing structure or to seek to change the structure of government in ways more or less radical. The social development process may also provide a predisposition toward the intentions and political processes of other states. An Arab, for example, in the process of socialization acquires attitudes not only toward his own state but toward Nasser's Pan Arab nationalism, Israel, and perhaps the United States and the Soviet Union as well.

In societies in transition, governmental leaders may play an especially significant role in social development. In Cuba, for example, Fidel Castro's prolonged television appearances serve both social and political purposes. In all modern societies, of course, the state through its support of education and by other means plays a role in the social process, but the West, at least, permits considerable diversity with respect to the political overtones of social development.

By and large those leaders and states which are more or less satisfied with the *status quo* tend to concentrate their attention on influencing the process of political development. In contrast those more concerned with change in the society or in disrupting the present political order, initially at least will give greater attention to influencing the character of the socialization processes of the society. These processes present different problems and prospects for external groups seeking to influence them. On many occasions the two processes blend and are hardly distinguishable, but it is useful, especially for great powers such as the United States and the Soviet Union, to seek to view the two separately as they work in the underdeveloped lands. A great deal of Soviet propaganda and most of the effort of the United States Information Agency are directed at affecting the social development—that is, of influencing an individual's attitudes toward the values and forces of the world in which he is living. The launching of the first Sputnik had no immediate operational-political impact in the developing areas, but undoubtedly was of great importance in emphasizing the Soviet Union's growing competence in science and technology. The general effect was to push public and elite attitude in the direction of equating Soviet and American scientific capabilities. While viewed in the West as a gain in prestige for the Soviet Union, it may also be seen as contributing toward equating the Soviet Union and the United States as advanced nations and therefore as different from the developing ones.

So little seems to be known about the effect of competitive external influences on the process of social development of emerging areas that both great powers in their efforts in this field are operating in the dark and largely on faith. A great deal of the effect of external influence depends upon the opportunities provided the individual by the internal political-social structure once he comes of age. The United States, in the past, has provided training for thousands of individuals who later became members of the cadres of governments unfriendly to the United States. No one knows how many Western-educated Chinese now faithfully serve Peking, but the estimates are that they are numerous. Ex-Communists who now serve Western-oriented governments are less numerous but their numbers are not insignificant. The number of one-time fellow travelers who have been assimilated to Western-oriented national governments is probably much greater. In addition, there may be literally millions throughout the world who at one time or another had an interest in Marxist literature but who now direct, work within, and support the policies of mixed societies.

The United States, in response to Communist efforts, has had programs of grants for leaders, exchange programs, cultural exhibits, and almost every form of effort that could be devised to influence the social development process. All the major powers conduct a large variety of radio programs, establish libraries, or distribute printed material.

These efforts are influencing the process of social development in unpredictable ways. On the whole, however, the effect seems to be to increase the expectations of the elites and masses about what the society ought to be and, in some lesser degree, to stimulate the desire to acquire the skills to play a role in its forward movement. On occasion, external efforts have also had the effect of generating resistance to outside influence and of enhancing support for local leaders pledged to resist the impact of Western civilization on the local society, whether for cultural, economic, or political reasons.

The uncertainty of the effect of great-power influence on the social development process suggests that they might take a more relaxed view toward their competition in this area. It may well be that being associated with programs which provide modern knowledge and skills for developing peoples is about as far as their effective reach extends. If this is the case there is no reason in logic that the efforts need to be entirely separate. Why not, for example, accept mixed Soviet, American, and other faculty to staff technical institutes. Nor would collaborative efforts to design elements of a modern education system be excluded if the host country retained the right to accept or reject the specific proposals. From the third-area point of view there are certain advantages in this kind of collaboration, since neither great power is presently ideally equipped to make the necessary adaptations of its own system to a particular local environment. Not only technical schools but libraries and other facilities might turn out to be both more useful and less expensive if they were brought together within a common framework.

Within the common framework there would remain considerable room for the great powers to engage in indirect efforts at influencing political development, but these would for the first time be within a setting demanding minimum standards of objectivity and would provide a buffer against forms of competition which tend to rend the fabric of society. Health projects and other types of welfare activities from which each side seeks to gain an advantage appear to be likely candidates for common objective developmental enterprise.

The suggestions set forth above are, of course, highly tentative, and careful investigation of the possibilities and problems will be required. They are offered in the belief that they open meaningful opportunities in the American interest to influence Soviet technicians, if no more than by further complicating their view of the world—no mean gain. They also seem likely to contribute to more progress in the developing nations.

Public media of social development are in many respects as important as the educational system of a country. A continuing tendency exists for the Soviet Union and the United States to find themselves confronted with the need to get their message across through the same media.

The issue may be posed in more dramatic form than in the past as global communications satellite systems are developed and eventually move in the direction of world-wide television. While it may be too much to expect to achieve planned common use of media in the present stage of the conflict, technology and the requirements for really effective communication encourage the tendency. The local radio station remains the most credible radio outlet and the local television station is likely to be the most credible television outlet. It is not too early to consider the procedures and code of conduct for the contestants when they are obliged to share facilities. This may be left to the discretion of the various countries, but Soviet restraint in return for time on the air is a desirable objective. Again the possibilities appear to be worth investigating. In this field the United Nations is already playing an active part, and positive United States attention to the problems and possible gains from improved and coordinated communication systems is warranted. The alternative is likely to be competing American and Soviet systems in which the inducement to restraint is minimal.

Political development in the emerging areas is a problem so vast and complex that its exploration cannot now be attempted. The United States if it desires to reduce the use of violence in these nations in order to avoid dangerous involvement, while at the same time continuing the competition for the minds of men, should undertake to conceive a system of political competition compatible with its objectives. Simple reliance on the developing nation-state political structure is not an adequate answer. Some evolving form of regional structure seems essential. Small-state politics may be influenced by the great powers. Some form of two-party or multi-party system which permits competition but avoids chaos seems essential. An increasing requirement in the system is that it have a place for certain acceptable kinds of Communist political action. *De facto* acceptance of such action has existed under Republican and Democratic administrations alike. The time is coming and, as the social and political development continues to accelerate, coming rapidly when a more systematic view of the kinds of political competition we are willing to accept will be necessary, if for no other reason than to avoid stumbling into violent conflict.

9 The Political Feasibility of Initiating a Strategy of Interdependence

Of Time

HORROR has the intrinsic quality of precipitating at once a world-wide insight into the brutal nature of the times. The disclosure of Nazi concentration camps at the end of the war was such a moment. After that, the world could never again be the same. Of quite a different character, but sharing the same quality of instant visibility, was the launching of the first Sputnik which established in the mind of the world the Soviet Union's claim to scientific and technical competence.

Other critical points in time resemble the first movements of a turning tide, whose significance is not appreciated until the tide is at the flood. In these, the decisions of a small group make themselves manifest in later events. Such was the case with the initiation of the cold-war foreign policies of the United States, which demonstrated a renewed grasp by American policy-makers of the verities of the nation-state system. As the policies were hammered out in the period 1947–50 one event followed another to give visibility and meaning to the new insight. The Truman Doctrine, the Marshall Plan, and the NATO Alliance came in swift succession. But only with the Korean War were military expenditures lifted substantially above the postwar level. Only then did the world, East and West, take in the full implications of containment.

The thaw in the Soviet Union after the death of Stalin and the rise of Khrushchev is apparently felt by many Soviet citizens to mark another turning point after which their world can never be quite the same again. The full meaning of this development has yet to be revealed. Whether it was a discontinuity opening the way to the future or whether the path to a better world remains blocked has not been settled.

Time—at turning points in history—indeed "flies," just as in the long quiet years between it may "drag." This is not strictly an illusion. The clock so dominates our thinking about time that it normally escapes our notice that time is widely conceived not only in ways that are more or less consistent with clock time but in other ways that appear to be inconsistent with it.

Consistent time has been a dominant element in Western thought for centuries. Modern civilization moves to the tick of the clock. The coordinated action of millions of individuals in the great modern urban complexes depends on consistent time. Modern man moves among the forces of nature and the institutions of society, being buffeted by them or seeking to manipulate them, by consistent time.

Inconsistent time is evident in two different life situations. The first, popularly termed "the moment of truth," occurs when an event or experience dramatically changes the shape of the future. The second, less obvious, stems from the continuous inner experience of individuals. It is manifest as the unique propensity of human beings to think in terms of "the possible." De Gaulle's Europe and Mao's map of China are portentous examples of this attribute. This inward sense of time represents an expression of the living energy of the individual. The moment of truth has been designated by some psychologists an *Augenblick,* meaning literally the "blinking of an eye." [1] The inner time sense has been variously termed, "the stream of consciousness" (William James) and "the vital impetus" (Henri Bergson).

In considering the feasibility of a strategy, all three concepts are relevant—clock time, inner time, and *Augenblick.* The period required for the conversion of resources must be measured by the calendar. The inner time sense which limits or enlarges what is possible must be assessed. Finally, preparations must be made to take advantage of the opportunities presented by moments of discontinuity.

While preparations for the initiation of a new strategy for waging war or controlling conflict must conform to consistent time, they need not be put off until the old strategy is abandoned. Events occur simultaneously in consistent time, and conscious preparation of two different lines of action is realistic. The development of plans, the training of men, and the shaping of resources to new uses, all require time—the time that runs like a line through space from past to future. They will not be ready when their full-scale use is possible unless action has been started much earlier.

Existence for the healthy society, as for the normal individual, is marked by a sense of emergence, of transcending the past and present in terms of a future. Man has the capacity to orient himself beyond the immediate limits of the moment and to act in terms of a future. But he may also come to view the future as "empty" or "blocked" and thus ignore profoundly important events. Preparations for a new strategy are important in helping to maintain a view of a future which is open. They will also influence the prevail-

[1] As the source of this discussion of time, I am indebted to Rollo May's and Henri F. Ellenberger's analyses in Rollo May, *et al., Existence: A New Dimension in Psychiatry and Psychology* (New York: Basic Books, Inc., 1958).

ing view of past conflicts. The past is in a sense not past. Present activities involve a highly selective use of the past; one event is used and remembered while a thousand are forgotten. Preparations for a new strategy affect the outlook on both past and future and thus help to determine the reaction to intervening events.

The discontinuity in time marked by a moment of truth can affect the future course of events in decisive fashion. Yet, some apparently pregnant moments abort into a formless, chaotic, or contradictory era. Progress or confusion seem to depend upon the preparations for the discontinuity.

The more significant moments of truth, whether revealing a future of added promise or horror, can be seen to have been preceded by a period of preparation. This period may have been dominated by the unbridled march of events or by the conscious purposes of men, but a period of preparation there must have been. Great events may be at once decisive and ambiguous.

Hiroshima—symbolizing the opening of the age of nuclear irrationality—was such an event. The immediate consequences were suffering and death and the end of the war. But in ending a war, "the bomb" did not end war preparations. In presaging the end of the ability of the state to protect the nation, it did not end the claims of statesmen that they can best protect the society. While they may admit, as did Henry L. Stimson, that "war is death," they continue to imply that they can still save the society.

Yet, great leaders have, on occasion, pointed out that protection for the nation is no longer possible, as did President Dwight D. Eisenhower in his farewell address of 1961. He said:

> As one who has witnessed the horror and lingering sadness of war, as one who knows that *another war would utterly destroy this civilization* which has been so slowly and painfully

built over a thousand years, I wish I could say that lasting peace was in sight. . . . Much remains to be done. As a private citizen, I shall never cease to do what little I can to help the world advance along the road.[2]

President Eisenhower is not unique among the leadership of the great powers in understanding that if deterrence should fail, the state cannot protect the nation. Unfortunately, in office the knowledge of statesmen is tempered and confined by the absence of a view of the future in which reliance on nuclear force for security could decline. Statesmen may aspire to world unity, but their world is divided. The present is shaped by obsessive efforts to strengthen one or the other half of the divided world. The leader's moment of nuclear truth, while it has closed the road to future fulfillment by the rational use of unbridled force, has not yet brought forth new avenues of great promise.

In these circumstances the citizens, or such elite elements as count in the nation's decisions, might be willing to accept and support new kinds of initiatives designed to reduce their nuclear insecurity, if the leaders could fully share with the people their moment of truth. But this the leaders are unable to do. They are unable to share their insight because no alternative strategy has been devised and accepted. Preparations have not been made for the pursuit and justification of an alternative strategy. No strategy is accepted because the public perception of a common and interdependent future is obscure.

In times like the present, a radical shift in direction is not

---

[2] Dwight D. Eisenhower, "Farewell Radio and Television Address to the American People," Jan. 17, 1961, *Public Papers of the Presidents—1960–61* (Washington, D.C.: U.S. Government Printing Office), p. 1039.

feasible, nor is it likely to be desirable in a nuclear-armed world. The requirements for a new strategy should be put in place steadily, not precipitously. The implementation may be envisaged as falling into four relatively distinct periods: (1) the preparatory period, (2) the period of redefinition of national security interests and programs, (3) the period of development, and (4) the period of common commitment. What may be possible, initially, is an increase in the preparations, at first modest and later substantial. Beyond the first two periods, the direction of progress is open to conjecture. Clearly, a radical shift in public and leadership attitudes toward what is possible would be required. Perhaps some new moment of truth, visible throughout the world, will be demanded.

The main tasks of the preparatory period are the following. First, a relationship of mutual respect, limited but stable, between the leadership of the United States and the Soviet Union is required. A major element in the relationship is the recognition that a strategy must be pursued which serves the interests of both sides. Second, the leaders must identify and find the means of dealing with the initial obstacles which may be raised by their internal opposition and their allies. Third, a substantial commitment of resources, both to planning the interdependent strategy and to the implementation of enlarged experimental programs, must be made.

Relationship with Adversary

Evidence is strong that for some time the leaders of the United States and the Soviet Union have shared a common understanding that in the nuclear age the state can no longer protect the nation and therefore nuclear war is to be avoided. Within this limitation they have sought to advance the interests of their state. The constraint has unavoidably led in the direction of a redefinition of each state's security interests. In this process, which has been carried on with only limited success but with no catastrophic failure, the growth of a kind of respect for the adversary has arisen. That it exists is fortunate, both for the present precarious stability and for the initiation of a new strategy. Whether it is sufficient remains to be tested. Respect is not to be confused with trust in the usual sense of the term, an attitude which is hardly relevant to the present multistate system. By respect is meant the recognition that the adversary has the ability to perceive his nation's interest and act rationally and prudently in pursuing it.

Respect in this sense arises over time from the experience each adversary has with the other, not so much in face-to-face meetings, however important these may be on occasion in crystallizing the outlook of leaders of great powers, as in the day-to-day and year-to-year actions each takes in coping with crises and pursuing long-run goals.

The United States and the Soviet Union both during the Kennedy Administration and earlier had occasionally found it useful to cooperate in handling current problems and in laying a limited foundation of a longer-run relationship. While subject to a variety of interpretations by the propagandists of both sides, these actions surely must be judged of value by the leaders of the day. In the Suez crisis, for example, United States pressure on Great Britain was swiftly reinforced by Soviet threats. In the Taiwan Strait the United States and the Soviet Union each seem to have sought to restrain their ally while taking judicious action to deter the ally of their opponent. In the Cuban confrontation of 1962 the setback for the Soviet Union was followed in rapid succession by the reopening of bilateral talks on Berlin. And, of course, through the years the dynamite-packed issue of Berlin has been handled with an abundance of bold declaratory statements, but with force movements calculated with great caution. Across the world in Southeast Asia, the low strategic value of Laos to both sides has been recognized and an attempt made to neutralize the conflict.

In the field of nuclear weapons both sides have for more than a decade held fast to a common policy of no nuclear sharing. The desirability of maintaining the nuclear monopoly was accurately perceived by both and their actions have been in accord with a common understanding. Of late years the dangers of nuclear accidents have been recognized. A number of actions have been taken by each side to reduce the hazard. The agreement to create a system of direct communications between Washington and Moscow, popularly known as the "hot line," was one such action. The nuclear test ban may be seen from one perspective as a prolonged effort to find new means of adapting the no-nuclear-sharing principle to a period in which other countries are developing the capability for the production and delivery of nuclear weapons.

Common constructive undertakings are not numerous but those which have been initiated have tended to display a remarkable resistance to the day-to-day clash of interests on other fronts. Except for the withdrawal prior to the Korean conflict, the Soviet Union has displayed remarkable steadfastness in its participation in a substantial range of United Nations activities even though it has been cast in the role of permanent minority. The cultural exchange program, once initiated, has continued to serve the changing but common interests of the two sides. The program of space cooperation, recently initiated, represents a remarkable achievement of dedicated men who have managed to create a coral island of promise among the complex and often conflicting political, legal, military, and technical interests in space—an achievement concurred in by the leaders.

For two great powers supposedly engaged in a struggle on every front, the experience in common action should not appear wholly devoid of promise from the point of view of the leaders. At the same time great uncertainty remains as to how far the common interests can be developed, or should be permitted to develop, since there are citizens on both sides who might wish to go much further. Each leader may recognize that the other believes that there is a compelling need to strengthen and preserve the sense of unity and continuity of his own side. Each, perhaps, doubts that the efforts of the other need take quite the form that they do, in light of the common dangers posed by the nuclear age.

An American President may find it hard to accept as compatible with a strategy of interdependence the continuing Soviet assumption of total conflict in the ideological field. The assumption is hard to square with the essential acceptance by the Soviet leader of the permanence of the American system. Conversely, when the President is engaged in maintaining his leadership of American public opinion, certain of his pronouncements may be read in the Soviet Union as displaying an equally threatening lack of acceptance of the permanency of the Soviet system. The necessity of leaders to emphasize the either-or structure of the conflict may be regrettable, but appears unavoidable in the multistate system for the maintenance of their internal leadership. Yet, in that system, it must be remembered that kind words can have no intrinsic value, although they may be of great significance as symbols or symptoms. Thus, the standard of performance by which the leaders must necessarily measure each other's behavior in modifying the inner content of the conflict is likely to remain one which focuses on good works rather than on moderate words. Nevertheless, restraint in pronouncements and more scholarly formulation of the "ideological" or "way-of-life" issue can be useful in imparting a more civilized tone to the dialogue even on this threatening topic.

In considering the initiation of a strategy of interdependence, the President, in addition to reviewing the record of common action and taking into account the Soviet leader's respect for civilized usage in the conduct of polemics, will necessarily make a judgment of his adversary's reliability during the period of implementation. The most appropriate time for launching the strategy may be when both leaders are, and feel themselves to be, relatively secure in their own positions. Security of position increases the chances for sustained support of the strategy during the period required for it to prove itself.

On the other hand, if the strategy is initiated by the President, a certain feeling of frustration or insecurity may be necessary on the Soviet side if a response is to be forthcoming. Possibly the insecurity most likely to produce a response is a gnawing doubt about the rationality of other lines of United States policy if the interdependence initiative were spurned.

For both parties, protection against a radical change in the behavior of the other is of great importance. One of the principal weaknesses of formal disarmament, it may be imagined, is that if the opponent changes his mind or fails to carry out the agreement, the political consequences at home may be very severe whether or not the vital security of the nation has been seriously compromised. One of the advantages of the constructive programs envisaged by a strategy of interdependence is that for a considerable period they can be pursued simultaneously with military preparedness. They are and can be presented as programs whose potential payoff is high and whose intrinsic risk is low. In the early stages, the argument that the probability is low that they will decisively change the relationship of the great powers may be set against the costs if military deterrence were to fail. By contrast, if the preparatory programs of interdependence should fail to produce results, the initial cost will be no greater than the obsolescence of a single important weapons system. Of course, if the period of major commitment to the strategy should ever be approached a new equation would emerge.

Thus a feeling of respect, a tested belief that limited common actions are possible, and a sense of security are among the requirements of the leaders in the initiation of a strategy of interdependence. But a larger environment than just the relationship of the two must be taken into account. Both the internal opposition in each state and the relationship with allies are critical parts of the larger environment.

Relationships Internally and with Allies

A statesman may undertake a new line of action with the highest of motives—the belief that it will enhance the security or welfare of the people he serves or rules. Yet he does so at his peril unless he has carefully calculated in advance how he will deal with the opposition at home who will seek to turn his initiative to their advantage.

Despite radically different circumstances, the issues between the leaders in the Soviet Union and in the United States, and their respective oppositions, are framed by a common set of questions. First, who can best protect us or ensure the security of the nation? Second, who can best maintain and strengthen our relations with our allies and increase our influence or authority in other areas? Third, who can best direct or guide the nation's economy so as to foster its growth and increase its ability to meet our requirements? Fourth, who can best set forth the goals and show us the means whereby we may transcend the present and achieve progress in the future?

National Security Issue. Who best can protect us? Posed in this way, the issue is detrimental to the country and disadvantageous to the party in power. Those in power cannot avoid knowing that while they may hope to deter attack, if it comes, nothing that they can do will prevent catastrophe. Yet when the question is asked, they feel compelled to answer, "We can best protect you." The party out of power, being without immediate responsibility, will always assert that more should be done, that new initiatives are needed, or that some kind of a gap exists.

In this argument, the weight of the prestige of the military establishment and the interest of the industrial complex which it supports tends to drift toward the opposition. A military establishment never has all the resources it would like to have. In the United States, for example, even when military leaders are generally responsive to the President's program, the institutional requirements lend support to the opposition. While the over-all interest of the industrial complex which supports the military establishment may parallel that of the nation, the interest of the firms within it is to increase the scale of their activity. As a consequence, the total operational interest of the complex tends in the direction of a larger military budget. Thus both the military establishment and its industrial complex have a tendency to look with favor on the opposition arguments.

These lines of power become more apparent as new weapons systems proceed through the design and development stage toward production. Moreover, when a system by its very nature can make a claim of "protecting" the country, its chances of ultimate production are increased. Thus in the years immediately ahead, under the guise of "protection" a vast program of active and passive defenses may be undertaken. The installation of such defenses has been referred to as the $50 billion question—indicating a rough order of magnitude of cost. While such defenses hold little promise of preventing immense destruction, they do ensure some protection.

As their design is improved, a President within the terms of the issue, "who can best protect us," must initiate production or permit the opposition to use the issue against the administration in power.

The operation of the profit motive in the United States, and its absence in the Soviet Union, does not in any significant way distinguish the interplay of leadership and opposition in the two states. In the Soviet Union, the military establishment will also tend to favor the argument of an opposition which urges that additional resources are required to protect the country and to take a stronger line in the defense of Communism. In the case of defensive systems the tendency may be reinforced by the historical Russian emphasis on defensive rather than offensive power for the nation's security.

On both sides, allowing the issue to be posed as "who can best protect the country" will result in pressure for increased expenditures for military purposes but possibly little or no more protection in the nuclear age, since the other side will in the longer run take the necessary steps to offset the defense. Moreover, since the security of each remains in the hands of the other, both attain less security as a result of the continual escalation of arms. Since insecurity will be increased, the argument of the opposition will be strengthened and, ultimately, the leadership on one or the other side or both seems likely to be changed.

The only escape from the dilemma of protection is for the leadership to admit that in the nuclear age the country can no longer be protected in the old meaning of the word. A country's boundaries can no longer be made impermeable. On both sides statements to this effect are now made from time to time, but the "inability to protect" has not yet brought forth a major commitment to a new line of policy.

A strategy of interdependence seeks to restate the issue in a broader context. It asks: How can national security be increased? The lines of action recommended are restraint on the use of force and the implementation of programs of common action with the adversary. In the beginning a relatively modest program of preparation is suggested.

The policy of interdependence can, of course, only be maintained by the leadership on one side if there is reinforcing action on the other. Both must be willing to assert with growing emphasis that protection is no longer possible. Both must be willing to initiate or accept a steadily broadening series of common actions.

Once the program of seeking security by interdependence is under way on a substantial scale, the leadership's position *vis-à-vis* its internal opposition seems likely to grow stronger than when seeking protection by increased military expenditures. Each program it initiates for interdependence results in the creation of a new interest group. Each argument of the opposition that not enough is being done can be responded to by further constructive action which will enhance both the security and the welfare of the people. At the same time, if the opposition continues to argue for military expenditures above those necessary for deterrence, this can be met by revealing more and more facts and figures to demonstrate that protection is indeed beyond reach in the nuclear age.

Unfortunately, prospective success cannot serve to overcome initial opposition. In the present context a salient even though modest program would be open to partisan attack as one which involves doing business with the enemy and which would lead to "weakening" the country. Stress on the inability to protect may be precluded because of the possibility that it may be interpreted as weakness by the homefront opposition.

Thus the initiation of the strategy may remain barred unless the opposition, or at least a significant element of it, can be brought to support it. A major opposition-party leader is needed in the 1960s to play the statesman's role that Senator Arthur H. Vandenberg played in an earlier period of national crisis. Before a President seeks to induce his adversary to join in the new undertaking, he must first persuade a significant element of his internal opposition of the validity of the approach. In this dialogue the President will need to dwell not only on the tactical interest of the chosen political leader of the opposition, but on a future which is open to the survival and progress of our way of life, the preparations that must be made and, finally, the opponent's own concern for his place in history.

What is in the interest of the nation's security and welfare? What is possible? These are the questions posed. To answer the first the opposition leader must be taken step by step through the moments of truth which the President has faced as he has come within uncertain days or hours of the climax of a nuclear crisis—a climax which he will have faced fearlessly but certainly not without a sense of horror. He may, for example, dwell at length on the 1962 Cuban crisis when those in command experienced a moment of intense insight. Going on he may describe the uncertainties of this and other crises—the planes off course, garbled messages, strenuous time requirements, the myriad of participants stretched out over the world and their human unpredictability.

Turning to the preparations for war, the President will draw on the entire range of information and intelligence available to him to present a picture of Soviet and American capabilities and limitations in the nuclear age. Khrushchev has said that the Americans have forty thousand nuclear weapons. Are the Soviet leaders likely to be content with fewer, he may ask. Is it beyond our power to imagine a blink that sets the world on the precipitous path to nuclear destruction? As crises reoccur is there not more than a remote possibility that by inadvertence, miscalculation, or chance, rationality will fail and perverse instinctual drives will take hold to push the world over the brink? What then of the argument about who can best protect the nation?

Turning to the future, the President may ask, what is possible? Man, it must be admitted, has not found it easy to transcend his circumstance. The past and future engage in a continuing struggle for the present, yet man's vision of his future may shape the present.

In small matters this is clear. More scientists and engineers are alive today than in all past history. Prior individual and collective investment in their training provides immensely greater potential for the control of nature in the present than was ever available to a previous generation. The investment was made because of a view of the future in which a career in science appeared more profitable, important, necessary, or satisfying than before.

Is a future in which the United States and the Soviet Union move step by step toward interdependence possible? At present both the United States and the Soviet Union look forward to a future in which science and technology play a steadily increasing role. Thus there is a significant commitment to rationality in both societies, but it is a commitment that can hardly be said to be dominant with respect to many aspects of human affairs on the world scene. Should we not begin to expand our investments in a common future?

True, in prudence we must continue to take account of the possible contingency of war. Elimination of all violence cannot be our aim, but sufficient control that it no longer threatens the existence of mankind should be. The aim is a growth of common interests which reinforce the control.

Perception of a gathering consensus with respect to the over-riding importance of controlling violence in the interests of the larger society and the means by which it is to be achieved is a vital ingredient.

Admittedly, some would say inevitably, differences will exist between ourselves and the Soviet Union about what is possible in our time. In the past the United States has developed a kind of enthusiasm for one line of policy, whether expressed as "bring the boys home" or "peace through strength," which suggests a distortion of reality. To abandon force is to neglect the danger from man's instinctual drives. Conversely, an obsessive concentration on control of the environment through reliance on force may be equally dangerous.

The impediments to initiation of programs whose payoffs may be measured in decades when elective officers must defend their achievements before the voters every two, four, or six years are to be noted. Yet our history shows a record of farsighted joint legislative and executive action as splendid as any country in the world. But, for this, bipartisan support is needed. Moreover, it is in the nation's interest since sector by sector there may be an advantage to the state that can take the initiative.

True, the growth of interdependence cannot be predicted in a specific period of years. The inner time sense of both peoples, especially their view of the future, remains uncertain. Yet it is not beyond reason to suggest that, while the growth of viable interdependence may take generations, it could on the other hand begin almost at once and be accomplished in something like a single decade. Success is most promising, however, if the effort is a national, not a partisan one.

Impediments to the initiation of a strategy of interdependence exist, but it is necessary to distinguish the present period from an earlier one in which deterrence was a more relevant and adequate response to the situation. Surely, there are significant differences between the late Stalin era and the present Khrushchev period which, although definitely not calling for the abandonment of deterrence, suggest the need and possibility of other lines of action.

Moreover, it is rational to pursue simultaneous lines of action in any time period and to provide for sufficient investment in each to enable them to have a reasonable chance of affecting the outcome. It is an expression not only of political sophistication but also of internal consistency to engage in programs of deterrence and constructive interdependence simultaneously. The error of relying wholly on the one or the other is pointed up if one considers the obvious inconsistency of relying wholly on interdependent action in the present framework of antagonism. May it not be equally an error to rely overwhelmingly on deterrence and to depend on some fortunate fatalism or determinism for the emergence of a less dangerous world?

Finally, if catastrophe is thinkable because of what may begin as no more than a misinterpretation of a blink, is it not possible that at the very edge of general disaster, perhaps even following the first direct experience of an isolated nuclear explosion, the time of the possible may suddenly collapse into the here and now?

At that moment drawing back may no longer be sufficient unless preparations have been carefully made for moving forward on a broad front toward constructive interdependence. Man, who continually seeks to transform himself, always has the choice of doing it through death or by applying his vital energy to shaping a future with promise.

And what of his own future, the opposition statesman may ask himself. What are his prospects as the potential alternative leader of a center coalition as compared with those of a leader of the opposition? Can the deterrent strength of the nation be preserved? Is it true that the state can no longer protect the society? What of our alliance system? What would be the effect of the new strategy on the economy and on the burden to taxation being borne by the citizen? These are questions the opposition leader would have to answer as he made his decision.

Relationship with Our Allies. A flaw in both the Western alliance system and the Soviet bloc arrangements is that, while within their area of influence they attempt to curtail the chaos of the multistate system, in regard to each other the Soviet Union and the United States have been content for relations to remain largely in a state of nature governed ultimately by force. Thus as soon as an ally has the power, it seeks to reassert its sovereignty in the brutish world of nation-states. France and China are only among the first in this respect. Closer relations between the two great powers might permit them to exercise a more restraining influence on others. Yet, severe limitations would remain. Implementation of certain common objectives, such as no further spread of nuclear weapons, could still require the threat of force and might require its use.

The linking up of the United States and the Soviet Union in common action cannot be done at the expense of their allies but neither can the special position of allies be allowed to prevent it.

If this rule is followed, the internal opposition, while it could from time to time use the complaints of allies to justify criticism of the leadership, would not be provided with a major issue with which to beat it.

In Europe, both East and West, where the major danger of Soviet-American conflict lies, an improvement in relations between the two would appear also to be in the interest of Europe's security. Nevertheless, the new relationship as it develops would reduce the leverage of certain countries on great-power policies. These countries are likely to attempt to counter this reduced influence in whatever ways are open to them. But so long as they are not excluded from major specific areas of common action when they are competent to contribute, the opposition can be kept within manageable bounds.

For the European powers, as for the Soviet Union and the United States, time would be required to accommodate to the changes in the nature of the multistate system as the strategy of interdependence was taking effect. But Europe is much further advanced along this road than either of the two great powers and thus the accommodation may be less difficult. Clearly, a growing recognition of the advantages of interdependence between Europe, East and West, is an essential element in the Soviet-American relationship. Interplay between Europe and the giants, which would contribute in the end to a coherent Greater European Community encompassing all three, is possible. The outcome to be sought is not only the security of all, but a new period of development in which Old Europe plays the equal role to which its talents and resources entitle it. Within the framework of the new Soviet-American relationship—as in probably no other—the German question may be susceptible of settlement. France's requirements for an independent nuclear force are made less plausible, yet her ambitions would be more easily satisfied. Poland's aspirations for a European role are more amenable to recognition. For England the choice of joining Europe or moving still closer to the United States remains open. At the same time the new relationship of the giants can provide a powerful brake against the tendency to autarchy in Europe, which both wish to guard against.

China—because it is isolated, aggressive, and Communist—presents a special problem to any strategy. Ultimately, China must come to terms with the world and the world with China. The main questions are ones of priority and timing. A strategy of interdependence gives first priority to achieving a sense of solidarity in the Greater European Community. During this period China must be contained when necessary. While China's declaratory policy is aggressive, its capabilities are, and will for some time remain, limited in relation to the two great nuclear powers. Ultimately, China must be brought into the community of nations, but this is not a task which can be hurried. While the Chinese may be numerous, the Chinese state is no less vulnerable to nuclear weapons than any other. When that fact is fully appreciated by the Chinese elite, the time will be approaching for the Soviet Union and the United States to consider the mutual problem of China. In the meantime, it is in the interests of both that China's influence, not only in the world at large but in the Communist bloc as well, be kept within bounds.

In the conduct of a strategy of interdependence the motivation of neutrals to remain neutral in relation to the two powers would not change. However, their ability to play an independent role between the two would be somewhat reduced. Their support of interdependence between the two would be useful. Since the neutrals would remain part of the world environment, the great-power interest in shaping that environment would argue for continuance of capital and technical assistance to help meet the emerging nations' requirements for development. In the new setting, economic criteria could be expected to play a relatively larger role than politico-military ones and thus some of the more flagrantly wasteful forms of assistance could be avoided.

Management of the Economy. Who can best direct or guide America's growth and increase its ability to meet our requirements? The present policies lead to a level of Federal expenditures which contributes to employment in the United States. The disadvantage is that a large proportion of these Federal expenditures makes no positive contribution to the well-being of the nation. They are stockpiled in the form of weapons systems which, if they had to be used, would signal widespread disaster.

The alternative policy of disarmament has different limitations from the viewpoint of the United States economy. Cutbacks in military expenditures would reduce the investment in products that cannot contribute to welfare. At the same time hundreds of thousands would have to look for alternative employment not now on the horizon. The general level of economic activity could easily enter a serious decline. It does no good to point to other unmet social needs if the internal political consensus for supporting the expenditures required to meet them is as yet nonexistent.

A strategy of interdependence relies on the motive of national security to achieve a long-run shift in the use of resources from nonproductive to productive purposes. The programs for interdependence will not only enhance national security, but will also serve to satisfy a much wider range of human desires. Moreover, as will be seen in the section on timing (pp. 340ff.), the proposed phasing in of interdependent programs and the subsequent phasing down of military expenditures, should that be possible, provide for a sustained level of demand. Thus, from the point of view of the society, interdependence seems preferable to deterrence since an increasing amount of the Federal expenditures would contribute to national well-being as well as security. Moreover, unlike disarmament proposals, a strategy of interdependence is equally valuable in sustaining a high level of employment and a reasonable rate of growth.

From the Soviet side, a strategy of interdependence may not appear to be quite such an unmixed blessing to their economy. Since they are operating at close to full capacity, the resources for interdependence will have to be directed from other purposes. Among the possible candidates are military expenditures. If they were to divert from military to interdependent action, a comparable shift in United States resource use might be required and, given the present American superiority, could perhaps be accommodated. This question does not arise at the outset because the anticipated level of expenditures is relatively modest in terms of either the GNP or the level of military outgo. Thus, in terms of the Soviet economic problem, straight disarmament may appear to have some advantages over a policy of interdependence. It must be becoming apparent to them, however, that this choice in the present environment is probably not going to be open. Moreover, substantial interdependence holds the promise of being able to open new means of solving some of the more acute Soviet economic problems in agriculture and the consumer industries.

The Promise of the Future. Who can best set forth the goals and show the means whereby the nation may deal with the problems of the present and achieve progress in the future? Surveys of American public opinion suggest that the public is aware of the risks of the present course. The same surveys indicate the public supports, indeed favors, a tough line toward Communism wherever it exists. The American people have learned their lesson well. Strength and courage were necessary to halt the expansionist tendencies of Soviet power. But these valuable attributes are not enough. Security remains precarious in a divided world.

A future which holds only stalemate with the Soviet Union is a future in which the radical right may prosper. The center is in urgent need of a new strategy. The center cannot forever rely simply on military force to protect the nation. The center faces the necessity of preparing to attempt a visible breakout from the present condition of the multistate system toward an international system.

In this undertaking a redefinition of the meaning of security in the nuclear age is essential. An opening of new fronts in the relationship with the Soviet Union is imperative. A program of action is an urgent necessity.

The Soviet Union, no less than the United States, has a vital interest in opening new common pathways to the future. Without a larger element of commonality in strategy, the Soviet Union will be obliged to continue to increase military expenditures, increase controls over the population, and in general move backward toward the dark days of Stalin. The thaw will end and winter return without an intervening summer.

When the path to the future is blocked, those leaders who wish to preserve the present, even though it means returning to the practices of the past, will find a growing opportunity to attain power. Those who seek to get the country moving again, or who set out twenty-year goals worthy of a society, must provide sustenance to the vision or they will be rejected. Whether rejected in polling booth or politbureau, the consequences on both sides will be the same—more military expenditures, less real security.

Stimulation of Program Planning

A strategy of interdependence must be built up of carefully designed and developed program elements. For this purpose an initial investment of possibly a billion dollars may be necessary. If the planning is to be effective and coordinated, a long-run framework must be provided which indicates the scope of the ultimate objectives being sought. Not a ten-year plan but approximate levels of activity will be most useful. Beyond the first stage, detailed planning is not possible because of the uncertainty of the distant future and of the heavy mixture of inconsistent as well as consistent time factors involved. Nevertheless, a brief statement of the longer-run time and timing factors may be helpful in setting the stage for the detailed activities of the preparatory phase which would be carried out both by private groups and by government agencies.

In terms of clock time, of men acting on and reordering the physical world, it is probably reasonable to believe that the United

States and the Soviet Union could arrive at a substantial, perhaps even a decisive, degree of interdependence in a decade or less. In that same period the instruments of aggression and deterrence could easily be reduced to negligible proportions. If this seems remarkable, let us examine why it may be true.

First it is useful to recall that the overwhelming bulk of the physical resources on both sides are already being devoted to ends that are compatible with those of a strategy of interdependence. Consumption in the United States, clearly, and in the Soviet Union, as certainly although in lesser proportion, is already the main objective of production. Thus we are dealing in the main with a fraction of physical output, although a significant one. Deep interdependence might, of course, also modify the relative priorities assigned to various forms of consumption in both societies.

Thus while there is no doubt a significant conversion problem in moving from antagonism to interdependence, it certainly would involve much less than half the total output on both sides and might in the end directly affect no more than ten to fifteen per cent of the GNP at the outside.

Even the lower figure implies important shifts. But compare the requirements of interdependence with the conversion of production of the United States in World War II. In considerably less than five years, the United States shifted forty per cent of its GNP to military purposes. Other countries were less effective but several turned more than one-third of their output to war purposes in a span of five years or less. The physical shift of manpower presents many special and difficult problems but, here again, the experience of the United States in enlarging the armed forces from a few hundred thousand to more than twelve million in the short space of three years must be noted.

But, it will be said, the objectives of war are more exact than those of interdependence can ever be. While this must be true, it is well to recall how unclear the dimensions of the wartime task were to military leaders and others until well after the war was under way. Indeed, to the very end of World War II, a constant series of struggles occurred over the proper allocation of resources. Yet the conversion went on.

The rule of thumb developed, and later applied in Korean War planning, was that the conversion of resources from civilian to military purposes could be achieved along a rising curve in which a threefold annual increment was to be expected. That is, if the base rate was one billion, three billion was a reasonable expectation for the first year, nine for the second, twenty-seven for the third, and so on. The point is that the time required for the physical conversion of resources in an industrial nation is relatively short—to be measured in years not decades.

Since there is very little experience of coordinated redirection of resources by two societies, a rule of two rather than three might provide a better fit. Using a rule of two, once a level of one billion dollars' worth of total resources devoted to interdependence had been achieved, it would take about seven years for the total resources committed to direct common-action objectives to exceed the present mutual expenditures for defense purposes.

Certain physical impediments to the transfer of resources may be noted. If space, for example, should become a field of common action, the need for prior development of new technology or the acquisition of new scientific knowledge might slow the expenditure rate. Scientific breakthroughs seem to be required before large-scale investment in weather control would be found feasible. On the other hand, resource limitations such as a shortage of Americans who speak Russian could be overcome at least as rapidly as the wartime deficiencies in foreign languages, and by improved methods. Existing technology could in many cases be rapidly converted to interdependent purposes. No technological barriers prevent, for example, vastly increased air travel between Moscow-Leningrad and Washington–New York. In other areas reasonably adequate facilities may exist, but new developments might vastly increase the potential. Communication may be such an area. While no serious problem exists in sending messages between Washington and Moscow, swift completion of a world-circling satellite system capable of carrying television programs to the people of many nations could conceivably become a priority objective. Several years might be required to put this in place and provide adequate numbers of receiving sets, as well as to develop mutually acceptable programing standards. Preparatory programs are needed in these areas as well as in many others.

Of Timing and Risk

There are risks in any course, the present one as well as pursuing a strategy of interdependence. In implementation, avoidable inconsistencies in timing between oneself and one's opponent must be guarded against, both with respect to action in the world of clock time and in terms of the world of the possible. Failure to do so may create grave and unnecessary risks, just as the effort to avoid any risks whatsoever may bring on grave dangers.

The advantage of the present course is that it prevents any attempt of the leaders of the Soviet Union to achieve world hegemony by force. Its weakness is that no credible and satisfactory alternative to armed camps has been brought forward. A result of the present interaction may be that, while both sides are deeply desirous of avoiding a nuclear war, nevertheless their actions make that castastrophe more likely. The present course holds little promise of man's transcending his present condition.

There can be no doubt that a strategy of interdependence must for some time rely heavily on military strength to preclude any attempt of the Soviet Union to achieve its goals by violence. At the same time, so long as nuclear weapons systems are maintained, there is a continuing need to do whatever is feasible to reduce the probability of nuclear catastrophe.

Two principal approaches to the problem are open. First, a variety of command and control, deployment, and other measures may be taken to reduce the probability of war by accident or by inadvertence. Second, a series of measures can be taken and a form of behavior adopted which contribute to a strengthening on both sides of a kind of common-law acceptance of restraint of force. During the formative stages of the program of interdependence, restraint on the use of force must come from the will and ability to rebuff, contain, repel, or to defeat efforts to advance by violent means. The aim is to induce restraint by precluding any possible gains through violence. Simultaneously, however, a strategy of interdependence requires a steadily mounting investment in fields which will provide both sides with a means of transcending their present circumstances by constructive action rather than by violence.

We are then, it must be clear, speaking of the conduct of a dual policy—restraint on force and positive interdependence—both prongs of which rest initially in the military power to preclude victory by violence and only ultimately on elimination of weapons. For those who have fallen in love with "peace" and for whom the time of the possible is now, this may be a bitter pill. But their time is not the world's time nor that of the men with weapons ready at hand. For others, disinterested in transcending their present circumstance, proposals for affirmative action will be no more acceptable. Here, again, their time is not the world's time. A new generation is coming on who seek to make their mark. Perhaps if the avenues are open they will determine to do it constructively. In any case they are unlikely to be willing to live forever with the anxiety of recurring nuclear *Augenblicke*.

In the conduct of a strategy of interdependence the correct policy must be determined first by estimates of the physical state of each side, including their military capacity and, second, by the judgment of where each side stands in relation to the other in the realm of the time of the possible.

The Graph (p. 343) illustrates a possible pattern of expenditures in the implementation of a strategy of interdependence and their relationship to military-expenditure levels using a set of approximate numbers—billions of dollars of existing and planned programs. The figures used are intended to indicate rough orders of magnitude, no more. Implementation may reasonably be divided into four periods. Each period has a relatively short and definite physical time requirement for its accomplishment and a longer and indefinite inconsistent time requirement. The former phases are designated by numbered years and solid lines and the

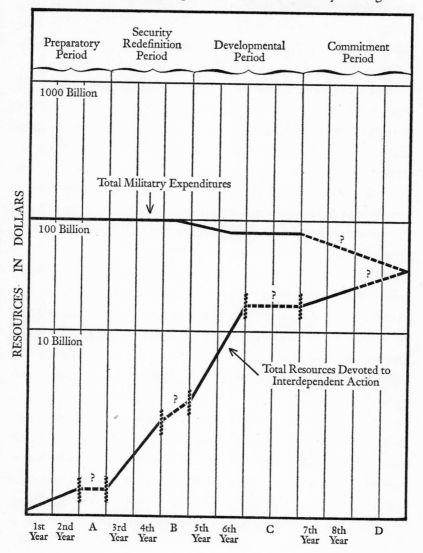

Hypothetical United States and Soviet Union
Investment in Interdependence and in Military Strength

latter by lettered periods and broken lines. Each period has certain characteristics and problems. The four illustrate the changing nature of the gains and risks as one moves up the scale of interdependence. The periods are (1) preparatory,[3] (2) security redefinition, (3) developmental, and (4) commitment.

In each period there may be a number of issues raised which will require review, evaluation, and decision. Should the strategy be accepted and, if accepted, continued? What is the effect of actions taken or contemplated on the power of both sides to maintain strategic stability and restrain or use force in more limited conflict? What are the risks being incurred by overoptimism on one's own side or possible pretense at participation by the adversary? Is the danger inherent in a direct nuclear confrontation being increased or reduced?

In the preparatory period, which may be defined as the time required to increase total resources committed to interdependent action to a level in the neighborhood of a billion dollars, the problems are not physical but political. There can hardly be enduring physical impediments in the less than one-billion-dollar range for two societies whose total output will soon be approaching a trillion.

No change whatsoever in planned military expenditures on either side need be made. Nevertheless, a movement of the suggested magnitude in the direction of interdependence might in the present environment raise great hopes which would have to be deflated. It would also raise deep fears which would have to be

[3] In the previous section (pp. 317–340) the political and policy problems of the preparatory phase were dealt with at length. The following pages discuss the implications of a hypothetical projection of the resources which might be required in the various stages of implementing a strategy of interdependence.

met. In lifting interdependent action to the level of a billion, the risks would be minimal; the gains might also be minimal. Resources devoted by the two sides to military power would remain at one hundred per cent of what they would have been in any case, while resources for interdependence would have arrived at something like one per cent of military expenditures. But since this would be judged, and correctly, to represent a possible first step of a fundamental change in direction, the struggle would be bitter and possibly prolonged. On the Soviet side, it would be no less so—unless, of course, a decision was taken to pretend to participate. But if their actions were a charade, their gains in the preparatory stage would be fleeting. The first serious trial of intentions comes in the following, or security redefinition, period of the strategy.

The security redefinition period, if there was a valid commitment on both sides, might require two or three years. It may be considered as the period in which total expenditures for interdependent action rise from one billion to perhaps four or five billion. Note, however, that again, between this phase and the next, there may be a plateau of indefinite duration while the two societies prepare themselves for the next possible move forward together. As in the preparatory phase there is no physical requirement for upsetting the strategic balance or undermining arrangements to ensure the restraint of force. Yet, in terms of expectations a marginal contribution to avoiding the actual use of force might begin to be discernible as a result of interdependent action. Joint projects would be under way, significant numbers of the citizens of each country might be traveling, studying, or working in the other.

But, at the same time, the possibilities of overoptimism in the

West might have been increased. The Soviet Union, in the security redefinition period, could still be pretending, although as the phase unfolded and more and more of its citizens became involved in common enterprises, this would become increasingly difficult. In these circumstances the United States might still—to the very end of the period—wish to avoid any cutback in its planned military expenditures. If the line were held, the potential power of the nation would be retained.

On the other hand, the time might come for modest reductions in military expenditures. At first this might be no more than proportionate to the modesty increasing expenditures on interdependence. But, even if such reductions in military capability were somewhat greater than proportional to the increase in interdependence, it could hardly affect the strategic balance or markedly reduce the power to restrain the use of force. The possibility of such cutbacks must be considered because, as the end of the interdependence buildup in the security phase is approached, some significant actions may be required to gain momentum for the quantitatively more significant climb in the developmental period.

The developmental period marks the time in which substantial, but not yet decisive, commitment of resources to a strategy of interdependence must be made by both sides. It probably also marks the period in which significant but not vital reductions in military expenditures must occur if the development of a new relationship between the superpowers and others is to be sustained. Unquestionably, it is a period of some risk taken in the expectation of considerable gain. Nevertheless, the conceivable cuts in military outlays, while significant, should and could stop far short of affecting United States retaliatory power.

As the developmental period proceeded, optimism might be running high in the United States. Taxes would be more burdensome as anxiety lifted. The desire to be rid of armaments would grow stronger. Yet even in this period, with sixteen-plus billion going into interdependence, the risks of war remain. The Soviet Union could still be pretending while secretly pushing new technological development, although by now the possibility of this occurring undetected would have been much reduced, as would the possibility of a nuclear catastrophe occurring by miscalculation. Yet the possibility could not be excluded that with a change of leadership on either side or for other reasons the relationship of the Soviet Union and the United States would return to intense worldwide antagonism.

If the developmental period is successful, evidence will have accumulated that interdependence is possible. No disinterested man reviewing the progress at this point is likely to conclude otherwise. The difficulty then, as now, is that many men will feel other interests threatened and many will find their rationality failing as they envisage moving on to the commitment phase. The plateau at the end of the development phase could be a long one.

If the barriers to forward movement are again breached, the movement may be dramatic and far reaching. In a very short span of years more men and resources could be committed to interdependence than are presently engaged in the creation of military strength. As this occurs the weight of interest of leaders and led will shift from conflict to common action. A basis for a stable relationship is put in place. Arms expenditures can fall dramatically, halted only by the concern of the United States and the Soviet Union for their world responsibilities for justice and order.

Within the relationship, internal war will remain the main continuing threat, and sufficient force will need to be retained to deal with it effectively. But this is a long way off, a goal that may never be reached unless the earlier phases are traversed.

The first billion may be the most difficult to obtain. America as the superior power must take the initiative. The strength of a strategy of interdependence is that it seeks to provide the conditions in which men will find it in their interests—visceral as well as rational—to settle their differences short of nuclear conflict.

IO   *Freedom and Common Action*

IN THE modern world the quality and scope of freedom is determined by the way men manage their interdependence. Though men differ on the kinds of freedom they most value, they everywhere share certain broad purposes—survival, well-being, and the enjoyment of life. These purposes are served when they act together. As they act in common their interests become intertwined. When this occurs conflict begins over the specific purposes of action. But gradually as action continues and insight develops, a web of common purposes emerges. A sense of solidarity develops which provides the basis of a broader community. Progress may be slow and halting but, if transactions are unavoidable, the consequence must be violent conflict or adjustment to some common set of purposes however broad or limited. Frequently, in the past, the vote has been for violence. Now, nuclear weapons have raised the cost of violence to the point at which all rational men must choose the search for accommodation; but war cannot yet be precluded.

Interdependence as a strategy can be a positive advantage to both the United States and the Soviet Union. A strategy of interdependence denotes the process by which the two nations create the conditions whereby their citizens, in various roles, engage in common action. In the short run these common undertakings will have a value in themselves. In the longer term, the expectation is that these transactions will lead to a sense of solidarity sufficient to provide a foundation on which the structures for the effective control of conflict in the greater society may ultimately be erected.

Interdependent action opens the door to a safer, more productive relationship between the United States and the Soviet Union. By fostering the shift of resources and attention toward positive constructive purposes, it provides a more stable basis for the relationship between the two. By gradually permitting the reduction of the talents and resources devoted to preparations for bipolar conflict, it places both in a better position to satisfy the needs of their own people and to cope with the needs and rising ambitions of the remaining two-thirds of the globe.

Interdependent behavior will also contribute to reducing the possibility of accidental or inadvertent war. As increasing communication develops between individuals in the two societies, more channels will be open for accurate and effective handling of crises as they may arise. Moreover, the likelihood of parallel perception of events is increased as a result of common experience. Indeed, the physical facilities of communications may themselves be improved sufficiently to make a contribution to crisis management. Common efforts in periods of calm can help to develop that minimum degree of trust which may be crucial to the successful resolution of the inadvertent crisis.

Interdependence as a strategy places highest priority on positive common action for common purposes. What these actions and purposes shall be is something in which all men may have a say. The role of the leadership of both sides is to provide the conditions in which the dialogue may develop and the action occur. A range of purposes and types of action have been suggested. Many of these involve the extension of the role and application of science and technology jointly by the two societies. Others touch on the part to be played by the individual in the developing society—his political role and his enjoyment of life.

The spectrum of possible common action of varying degree and kind encompasses a vast field. In both societies there is a growing commitment to science—to an increased understanding of man's existence, both physical and social. In this realm men are already moved by the universal values flowing from the search for truth. The opportunities for joint endeavor have as yet only begun to be explored and used.

The conquest of space requires a combination of science, technology, and commitment of the society to the exploration of the unknown which help to free action in this dimension from earthbound limits. Not entirely so, of course, since what man does in space must be begun on earth. Yet the costs and challenge of exploring the solar system, understanding our galaxy, and appreciating earth's place in the universe point to the need for common action. A laboratory on the moon has been suggested as a possible place to begin in a substantial way, but the expansion of those significant lines of cooperation already begun should not be neglected.

The extension of man's control over the physical environment of his own planet is by no means completed. The earth, the oceans, and inner space still have many unlocked secrets. Expanded cross-national effort is required for an understanding of the earth's environment and certainly for its control. Weather moves around the earth without regard for national boundaries. The time to lay the basis for its control, as that becomes feasible, is by common action now.

Both the United States and the Soviet Union have been diverted from developing the most rational means of fostering the world-wide spread of technology by their competitive search for power and influence. At the same time it may be said that without the competitive drive, far less might have been done. Competition may be a necessary element in modernization of less-developed areas, but it is not sufficient. Science and technology must be applied to these problems in the same systematic way and on the same scale as they are applied to weapons and space if the task is to be accomplished. The organization of the resources of science and technology for this urgent human task could be a common one even while many specific applications continued to be made for ostensibly competitive reasons. The developing lands have a large stake in the relationship of the United States and the Soviet Union to each other as well as to third areas. Not until the two giants are free of the present aggravated anxiety about each other will they be effectively free to help developing areas solve their own problems on a rational basis in ways that will serve the common interests of mankind.

The United States and the Soviet Union have each in their own way made immense contributions to the extension of political participation throughout the world. The United States, following in the footsteps of the European countries, has stressed the importance of the individual and his right to equal opportunity in shaping the life of society. In this, political action is a most powerful tool. The Soviet Union has fostered, often with considerable success, indigenous organizations to overthrow existing authority. The intentions of the present powers, like the intentions of nations of the past, have been mixed; the consequences of their actions have tended to converge in the direction of more active participation in the life of the society for increased numbers of individuals. There is a growing requirement for a continuing dialogue as to how the conflicts of the increasing numbers of political participants can be handled so as to contribute to constructive rather than destructive development.

Finally, there is the goal of individual enjoyment of life which may be served by interdependent action of the two societies. Relief from the worst of the anxieties of the nuclear age, as well as the satisfaction of basic needs, will make a contribution to this end. Every interdependent action need not be symmetrical; indeed, it cannot be. A broader view of individual interest—of which national interest can be no more than an expression—suggests that the advanced and powerful United States could afford, if it were invited, to help in the solution of some of the remaining problems of Soviet society. As interdependence unfolds, there may well be some other areas in which the Soviet Union will find itself in a position to make a similar asymmetrical contribution. Agriculture is an area in which the United States has an immense comparative advantage and in which the common action for the enjoyment of life might conceivably begin.

A strategy of interdependence thus holds out the opportunity for the two societies to transcend their present circumstances by positive endeavors rather than by violence. At present the prospective violence of arms lies heavy across all lands. Unless the window to the future is opened wide for all to see and take heart, the vital energies of man, magnified a millionfold by nuclear weapons, may be turned against himself. Hands may be lifted to annihilate the present when the future is blocked by fears induced by the evil magic of outworn myths.

There are those among us who would be so unwise as to ask mankind to accept the deadly stasis of the precarious balance of terror. The military balance can serve no purpose other than to block either great power from achieving world hegemony by violence while avoiding destruction. At best it can frustrate ambition. Other means must be found to open the way to a future. The military force required for the balance of terror threatens the survival of both powers, since its tendency is to elevate those who are inclined to transcend themselves by violence—a tendency, it should be noted, which seems at present to be more marked among those who emerge from civilian life than among those professional soldiers whose business is coercion. The threat posed by the balance of terror may be denied by refusing to think of it in the present, but it will continue tomorrow and tomorrow and the day after until the great powers undertake and attain a viable unity by common action.

Ironically, since the balance of terror denies the achievement of victory by violence, it provides the fundamental source of frustration which may be required to turn the two societies to new creative efforts. Thus, premature attempts to uproot and remove this source of frustration should be shunned. A disarmed world without common purpose and great common enterprises might be an even more dangerous one. Nuclear weapons technology will be with us throughout history; though destroyed by agreement, weapons can quickly be rebuilt without agreement.

There is another characteristic of the balance of terror as the starting place of common action. Each side must stand ready to prevent the other from making significant gains by violence. Otherwise, a delusion on one side or the other may gain currency that there is yet another road to the future, which though bloodier is easier than devising common action for common purposes.

At the same time, caution in the containment of violence will be well advised. Conflict within and between great powers as well as among others is likely to continue. In the midst of conflict all violence cannot for a very long time, if ever, be entirely eliminated. Yet an "eye for an eye" is not a prudent rule for the international community. Both sides will be wise if on occasion they stay their hand in the face of violence. Force must serve a purpose. In the nuclear age it should always serve a common purpose—though what is common will prove to be a complicated question not infrequently misjudged.

A strategy of interdependence offers a rational way out of the dilemma of the age of nuclear nationalism. Within the advanced nation-state, conflict is controlled and progress is permitted when force is concentrated but power diffused. In every society a balance must be struck between the needs of the individual and the needs of society. Two methods are used. The first is to devise common purposes of value and processes which will sustain them. The second is the employment of force. Normally, the two methods are used so as to reinforce each other.

When force is concentrated, restraint on its arbitrary use represents a continuing problem. This can be met when power over the affairs of the individual is diffused among different organizations. He thus retains the freedom to associate himself with one or another group. These groups, in turn, represent varying elements of power which must be taken into account in the actions of the state.

On the world scene, in contrast, force is divided and cross-national diffusion of power is inadequate. Thus the ability to control conflict is precarious. Interdependence as a strategy would assign a much higher priority and far more resources to the task of creating a substantial cross-national diffusion of interest and ultimately of power than is presently the case.

The scientific and technological changes of the twentieth century are creating a need and a means for achieving a widened sense of community in the world. The basis of a sense of solidarity which underlies the feeling of community is complex, but two main streams of experience may be seen as contributing to it. These have been termed "traditional" and "instrumental." Traditional solidarity arises as a consequence of attachment to a group. Instrumental solidarity arises, initially, from involvement in a common task. Interdependence seeks to use modern science and technology for the creation of areas of instrumental solidarity in order to prepare the way and to help bridge the gap across the yawning chasm of divided force that at present exists.

A confusion about the nature of the state often stands in the way of achieving order and progress in the greater community. There is a tendency everywhere to view the state as the only association for meeting the needs of the national community rather than as one association among many. The tendency is most marked among the Communist nations.

The search for solidarity is made more difficult by the present outlook of the Soviet Union. On the one hand, it continues to declare that world-wide unity is possible only following the victory of Communism and the working classes. On the other hand, and perhaps more significantly, the Soviet regime remains in an unstable equilibrium caught in powerful centrifugal forces which must be met by efforts to enhance feelings of solidarity. Solidarity can in turn be achieved only at the cost of diffusion of power. For example, nonviolent succession not yet achieved in the Soviet Union requires the increased and ordered participation of the ruling elite. Furthermore, Soviet society can be fully mobilized only by giving the agricultural sector increased participation in economic planning and operations. Influence among other Communist states may be maintained only if there is growing recognition of the need for diversity. Finally, the Soviet Union can attain a secure place in the world only by cultivating an increased sense of common purpose with the rest of the world and by accepting a greater degree of international authority for the control of conflict.

Soviet policy and practice in each of these concentric circles is continually pulled between adaptation to a changing world and long-established Soviet and Russian habits and attitudes toward centralized control and hierarchical authority. The task of the West is so to act as to encourage the diffusion of power while remaining aware that there will be developments within the Soviet Union which may be beyond its power to influence, some of which may be retrogressive.

Two main lines of action are open to the United States. The first requires the steady search for lines of common action in the pursuit of common objectives across the whole interface of the relations of the West with the Soviet people and their government. While diplomacy will play a major part in this effort, the resources of science and enterprise of many kinds will be required if it is to succeed. Attempts at giant steps in one area are likely to prove less fruitful than the steady step-by-step progress across the whole range of contact. It should be obvious that such an approach cannot be successful if it is simply an extra duty of busy operators, though it must be this as well. In addition it will require substantial investment in the design and development of programs which will entice or compel Soviet attention and participation.

Second, efforts to enlarge the area of common action must be reinforced by both symbolic and significant action in the area of arms control and reduction. The frustration induced by the balance of terror, if not relieved from time to time, leads either to disintegrative apathy or to equally futile obsession with perfection of military security. Timely measures of arms control and reduction can help to sustain a belief in a constructive future. They can help to provide the setting in which constructive action can proceed. Moreover, their direct contribution to the avoidance of accidental or inadvertent war should not be underestimated. Restraint on the use of force will remain a problem for a long time. Whatever can be done either to reduce symmetrically the reliance on the use of force for security or to inhibit its use in the pursuit of national objectives is likely to prove advantageous to the individual and to his society.

Interdependence as a way of controlling conflict is not a new idea. That it has not yet become the dominant strategy of any great power is due to the strenuous nature of the commitment to action required of both individuals and society.

Individuals who engage effectively in common action require

great courage and great balance in their view of life. Courage is required because the initial undertakings are likely to be hazardous, difficult, and lonely. Balance is needed because of the need to keep in mind the interests of their own society, the requirements for common action, and the limitations and differing objectives of both their foreign partner and his society. The risks to the individual may be considerable and the rewards forthcoming only if his efforts become part of a movement forward on a vast front. In short, conscious interdependence requires the commitment of the bravest of the free men who, while acknowledging that no man's action will be decisive, know that the actions of each individual count.

The commitment required of society as a whole is, of course, no less than that of its talented members. But it is something more. If the future is to be shaped, resources must be committed in the present. Interdependence is not a matter of words but of deeds. For deeds to be timely, pointed, and effective—planning, training, research, development, and testing are essential requirements in the modern world. These all demand resources—money—in significant amounts. Adequate resources are by no means the entire answer, but without resources opportunities will be lost, progress will be halting, and the entire effort can come to a sickening stop. The modern world is being built on a grand scale and the creation of its interdependent parts cannot be less so. It may be unnecessary to add that in this realm, as in all others, government need not and should not be the sole source of resources.

Because of the strenuous nature of the commitment, it is essential to emphasize the importance of the criteria of sufficient action discussed in the beginning. They apply to the total range of interaction of the two societies. Briefly they are: (1) experience must contribute to the convergence of values in the two societies; (2) experience must be germane to the present stage of development or interrelationship of the two sides; (3) experience must be material to the control of conflict, that is, it must contribute to the restraint of force or to the cross-national diffusion of interest and power; (4) resources for the conduct of positive programs must be both adequate and substantial; and (5) the experience must be cumulative—it must gain a momentum of its own.

The time required for a strategy of interdependence to become a decisive factor in the relations of the United States and the Soviet Union presents a picture of uncertainty. This is not because of insuperable problems in directing large resources to new ends. Quite the contrary. If past experience in converting from peace to war and back again is any guide, the physical problem of shifting a hundred billion or more to common-action programs could be accomplished in scarcely more than a half dozen years.

Rather, the uncertainty arises from the inconsistent and erratic ability of men to shift from one set of means and purposes to another. In times of crisis or great events such shifts may appear to occur almost instantaneously. But in most times, changes in outlook and structure have taken decades and even generations. Since the rate of change may depend on the degree of integration of the society, great mobility and good means of communication may speed the process.

But the uncertainty runs deeper. Modern science and technology are providing powerful tools to transform the world. Clearly, the means are already abundantly at hand to crush it catastrophically by violence. There is no uncertainty about achieving world-wide destruction in little more than minutes, should this path be chosen. When it could happen is open to conjecture. Similarly, though much less obviously, the knowledge is available to create the physical conditions for a good life for all. When it will be achieved is also open to a wide range of opinion. What is true of war and of development is also true of an interdependent relationship between the United States and the Soviet Union. The means are readily at hand or can swiftly be devised; what is uncertain is when and at what rate men will put them to use.

All these uncertainties arise from the unclocklike and inconsistent time frame within which man acts. "Time drags" and "time flies" are common expressions of this inconsistency. What is involved is the pace and direction in which man moves to transcend his present situation. Our uncertainty arises from lack of knowledge of the regularities, if they exist, which govern the pace at which man transcends himself. It is an uncertainty that seems likely to persist for some time—inconsistent time.

This form of uncertainty creates many hazards for a strategy of interdependence. Perhaps the most important arises from the possibility that the Soviet and American tables of inconsistent time are radically different. We may be ready to broaden our primary allegiance in a fortnight while they may be yet a generation away from the same point. Such hazards must be met by fixing our judgment of the pace of Soviet change by the scope and steadfastness of their commitments to common action. In uncertain times men must be judged by their actions, just as when one is in a foreign land and knowledge of the inhabitants is insufficient.

For more than a half century, since the old order crumbled, men have been engaged in a vast quest for new sources of solidarity. Both class and sovereign nation-state appear insufficient as a foundation for the emerging international system. As man's horizons have been broadened by science and technology, a set of universal values has begun to gain acceptance; science contributing by a persistent search for truths which will be true everywhere; technology by providing the means of communication and mobility which permit the truths to be swiftly carried to the most distant lands. But progress is not unimpeded; old myths which served well in their time are raised again and again to veil the future and cloud the present. Men who lean on the past rightly warn of premature abandonment of hard-won gains. The future which is ours cannot be won by wishing for it or even by deeply believing in it—though belief in the form of a profound commitment to action is an essential beginning.

The future must be won by work—intelligent, persistent, purposeful work. Since the future must be shared with all who will live in it, working with others to shape it is essential. While accepting the need to work together, some would stop at the borders of the family, or the tribe, or the state, or class. But the material conditions of our world make all these lines of demarcation insufficient as the ultimate boundary of common action. Today, the world requires an immense array of transactions which lace all mankind together while acknowledging a decent and prudent respect for the lesser circles inherited from earlier times in which man has found a sense of community.

The ultimate sense of unity which mankind seeks cannot be imposed from above. Unity will emerge from the work of committed men, who without regard to class, nation, or clan of origin strive to shape the future. Common purposes must be found to point the way. The entire effort must be permeated by a willingness of each to project himself into the place of every other—a feeling of love because the others are human. Then and only then will unity arise, almost unnoticed, in the midst of common action.

EPILOGUE[1]

IN THE last few months of his life President Kennedy and his advisors were deeply engaged in charting a new course for the nation. In a series of speeches and actions beginning in June, 1963, he sought, while taking note of old problems, to open a more promising path to the future.

Of the nature of the task he said, "We live in an age of interdependence as well as independence—an age of internationalism as well as nationalism. . . . Today there are no exclusively German problems, American problems, or even European problems. There are world problems." [2]

In June at American University in Washington, D.C., President Kennedy set forth what, in retrospect, may be seen as the first public statement of a conception of a strategy of interdependence. The widening breach between the Communist parties of the Soviet Union and China was about to culminate in a full-scale rupture. The deadly lesson of Cuba still provided an impetus to new efforts to strengthen the peace. The time was well chosen.

The President saw the need for the Soviet leaders to take a more

[1] Drafts of *A Strategy of Interdependence* were circulated in Washington in the spring of 1963. The final version was completed in the summer. This epilogue takes note of some of the public developments since that time.

[2] "Address of President J. F. Kennedy at the Paulskirche, Frankfort," June 25, 1963, *The Department of State Bulletin*, Vol. XLIX, No. 1256 (July 22, 1963), p. 119.

enlightened view of world affairs and asserted that the United States could help them to achieve it. But to do this, he said, "We must re-examine our own attitudes—as individuals and as a nation—for our attitudes are as essential as theirs." [3] New ways of thinking about peace, about the Soviet Union and about the cold war are required, he emphasized.

With respect to the cold war, he said, "a new context for discussion is necessary." [4] Increased understanding between the Soviets and ourselves is needed. This will require increased contact and communication. We must conduct our affairs so that it is in the interest of the Communists to agree on a genuine peace; while defending our interests, we must avert confrontations which force a choice between humiliating retreat and nuclear war. We must exercise restraint and avoid needless hostility. We must strengthen the United Nations and help it to keep the peace inside the non-Communist world.

In midsummer the President spoke to the nation in support of the nuclear Test Ban Treaty which had just been initialed in Moscow. He stressed that the achievement was not a victory for one side, but for all mankind. It was the first step toward peace. Quoting an ancient Chinese proverb, "A journey of a thousand miles must begin with a single step," he urged Americans to take the first step. After full discussion, the Senate of the United States ratified the treaty. The journey was begun.

In September, before the United Nations General Assembly, President Kennedy took another step. He proposed, in terms more

[3] "Toward a Strategy of Peace," Address by President J. F. Kennedy, American University, Washington, D.C., June 10, 1963, *The Department of State Bulletin*, Vol. XLIX, No. 1253 (July 1, 1963), pp. 2–6.
[4] *Ibid.*

direct than ever before, a substantial expansion of cooperation in space between the United States and the Soviet Union. He said, "There is room for new cooperation, for further joint efforts in the regulation and exploration of space. I include among these possibilities a joint expedition to the moon. . . . Surely we should explore whether the scientists and astronauts of our two countries—indeed, of all the world—cannot work together in the conquest of space, sending some day in this decade to the moon not the representatives of a single nation but the representatives of all of our countries."[5] He also lent support to a number of other world-wide actions including a global communication satellite system and a world-wide program of farm productivity and food distribution.

In October President Kennedy, in a special announcement, gave his support to the sale of American grain to the Soviet bloc as being in the United States interest. If not a new policy, it was a powerful precedent for enlarged trade in other fields. Under President Johnson's leadership, Congress ultimately backed the decision.

At the 100th Convocation of the National Academy of Sciences President Kennedy expanded on other aspects of the strategy saying, "Recent scientific advances have not only made international cooperation desirable but they have made it essential. The ocean, the atmosphere, outer space, belong not to one nation or one ideology but to all mankind, and as science carries out its tasks in the years ahead, it must enlist all its own disciplines, all nations

[5] "New Opportunities in the Search for Peace," Address by President J. F. Kennedy, September 20, 1963, *The Department of State Bulletin*, Vol. XLIX, No. 1267 (October 7, 1963), p. 532.

prepared for the scientific quest, and all men capable of sympathizing with the scientific impulse." [6]

Before the Protestant Council of the City of New York, President Kennedy dealt with the problems of limited conflict in the new context saying, "The United States and the Soviet Union, each fully aware of their mutually destructive powers and their worldwide responsibilities and obligations, have on occasion sought to introduce a greater note of caution in their approach to areas of conflict. . . . little wars are dangerous in this nuclear world." [7]

During these last months, the President sought to explain the necessity and nature of the dual strategy he was pursuing toward the Soviet Union. He said,

> In times such as these, therefore, there is nothing inconsistent with signing an atmospheric nuclear test ban, on the one hand, and testing underground on the other; about being willing to sell to the Soviets our surplus wheat while refusing to sell strategic items; about probing their interest in a joint lunar landing while making a major effort to master this new environment; or about exploring the possibility of disarmament while maintaining our stockpile of arms.
>
> For all of these moves, and all of these elements of American policy and allied policy towards the Soviet Union, are directed at a single, comprehensive goal—namely, convincing the Soviet leaders that it is dangerous for them to engage in direct or indirect aggression, futile for them to attempt to

[6] "Science and International Cooperation," Remarks by President Kennedy, October 22, 1963, *The Department of State Bulletin*, Vol. XLIX, No. 1273 (November 18, 1963), p. 779.

[7] "Our Obligation to the Family of Man," Remarks by President Kennedy, November 8, 1963, *The Department of State Bulletin*, Vol. XLIX, No. 1274 (November 25, 1963), p. 807.

impose their will and their system on other unwilling peoples, and beneficial to them, as well as to the world, to join in the achievement of a genuine and enforceable peace.[8]

In the last months of 1963, progress was made in a number of areas of East-West relations. The test ban agreement was followed by tripartite discussions (United States, Soviet Union, and United Kingdom) which laid the ground work for a nuclear weapons free area in space. Khrushchev proposed that observation posts be established on both sides of the Iron Curtain. Apparently, he had in mind combining this measure with the thinning out of forces in Germany and the establishment of a nuclear free zone. The Soviet Union also voted in favor of extending safeguards to large reactors at the General Conference of the International Atomic Energy Agency. Agreement was reached on a draft declaration of legal principles for outer space. There was also agreement on the allocation of radio frequencies in outer space. Discussion opened on the mutual establishment of consular offices. Technical talks on the implementation of the Civil Air Transport Agreement made progress. During this period, as well, the Soviet Union appeared to be stepping up its purchase of capital equipment from the West. Meanwhile, manifestations of the Sino-Soviet split continued. In the West the feeling grew that the Soviet Union was seriously seeking a *détente*.

On taking office President Johnson affirmed the continuation of the Kennedy policies. He also asserted his intention to seek to strengthen and to extend the foundations of peace. As a result of the action of the past few months, hope for a more secure world

[8] "Transcript of Kennedy Address at University of Maine on Relations with Soviet," October 19, 1963, *The New York Times* (October 20, 1963), p. 38, col. 5.

mingles with the lingering sadness at the loss of a world leader. The United States must act with justice and restraint. But peace is more than the action of states. It is a way of living for all. An abiding respect for the dignity and worth of each human life is essential as is the intelligent pursuit of common goals. Each of us has some power over others. Each must have a sufficient sense of his own worth to permit him to give to, rather than take from, his fellow man.

APPENDIX
Human Behavior and the Control of Conflict

"Who has ever come across a solitary man?"
DE JOUVENEL

THE DRAMA of the Titans is not the whole story. In the collision of the Two Worlds, the conflict, whatever the banner under which it is waged, is carried on by men who interact with other men. Thus, though there may be no compromise possible between "Communism" and "capitalism" or between "freedom" and "totalitarianism," there can be compromise between men. If control of conflict is to be viable and meaningful, it must rest on those characteristics which all human action involving others has in common, thereby fostering the creation of common modes of behavior leading to restraint. The alternative is to view the conflict as being not only between opposing systems but between opposing types of men—Homo Sovieticus versus Homo Americanus—who differ so fundamentally in behavior that no common pattern is possible and therefore no permanent hope for peace.

In our view, all human action which involves others has certain characteristics in common. This similarity arises from the nature of the individual—the way he perceives and acts in a social environment.

Thus we now turn to make explicit the view of man which we hold and from which our prescriptions for action flow. What follows may be obvious to some and obscure to others. While recognizing that it is not customary today to articulate the premises that are held with respect to the nature of man, we have judged it useful to do so. Moreover, in the confidence that all social acts have certain characteristics in common, we believe that man's behavior in small groups may provide useful leads and insights—provided they are used with care—for the great trans-oceanic confrontation with which in the end we must deal.

Hobbes gave currency to the belief, now widely held, that the actions of men are best controlled by fear of punishment. Force, he said, is the cement of society. To what extent actions which are tacitly based on his view will result in the resolution or avoidance of a clash between two nuclear sovereigns is problematical. But perhaps Hobbes would have considered such a clash inevitable.

Adam Smith, and those who followed him in the development of economics, found a number of predictable regularities in the relations of men and resources which have proved of great utility in certain kinds of analyses.

Finally, Freud, concentrating on the individual, found man governed by a wild and Rabelaisian assortment of obscure and hidden motives. Examining man close at hand, he was impressed with the complexity of his needs and their early origins. Freud's successors, while differing with many of his specific conclusions, may safely be said to view man as a complex web of needs and relationships, about which simple generalizations cannot be made.

In the following paragraphs we shall not try to probe either the brute nature or the psyche of man. Nor will we concern ourselves with the relations of men and resources as such. Our attention will center on the relationships of men in groups and the interaction of groups. Our assumptions are two: that man is complex, and that he has the capacity to learn. The ideas we develop are best viewed as hypotheses or propositions which find support in psychology and the other social sciences. If these ideas seem to have promise, despite the fragmentary nature of the supporting studies, one can only regret the failure of many men of affairs to incorporate them into their analytical thinking.[1]

One of the major impediments to introducing a program to control conflict is the role played by abstractions, words, or symbols in modern society. When a course of action which has served a useful purpose is given a name or label, it is less likely to change than if it had been left merely as a method of operation. Thus when conflict is aroused, an individual may cling to a phrase quite unsuited to the new source of conflict. In this way "capitalist" in the Communist lexicon continues to be evil even though the performance of capitalists has changed radically.

The needs of an integrated personality and the desire to see some pattern in the mass of information being received can give rise to what Ralph Waldo Emerson, and social scientists after him, have dubbed "the foolish consistency . . . of little minds." [2] Morton Deutsch emphasizes the feelings of the individual which lead to excessive striving for consistency.[3] Charles E. Osgood, on the other hand, points to the reaction of the individual to inconsistent information:

> The proof is overwhelming that when a leader or an average citizen is faced with inconsistent information, a remarkable degree of psychological stress toward consistency is produced within

[1] In this Appendix we consider the insights from social science which may be relevant to the control of conflict. As might be expected, we have found no significant body of research of an empirical nature that provides a simple formula for the solution of the problem, but we have found a substantial body of knowledge which opens new vistas of the possibilities present in the modern world to secure its survival and progress. Moreover, in the time available our search was necessarily incomplete, and it is quite possible that certain relevant work may have been overlooked. Out of our review, a concept of action which may be applicable has emerged. While we believe it is well founded, its decisive testing on the international scene will require a great investment of men and material.

[2] Ralph W. Emerson, *On Self-Reliance*.

[3] Morton Deutsch, "Psychological Alternatives to War," unpublished paper, p. 16. Presidential Address before the Society for the Psychological Study of Social Issues, The American Psychological Association, New York City, Sept. 4, 1961.

the individual. This stress resolves itself in a variety of ways such as denying the truth of one of the assertions or of the new event. In short, human beings generally react to events which do not fit their expectations, to propositions which are inconsistent with their existing attitudes, with mental adjustments designed to preserve as simple and stable a world view as possible.[4]

He has given to this mode of thinking the name "psycho-logic." "Psycho-logic," he continues, "is of immense importance in helping people to simplify the world in which they live. For many purposes, it may be harmless and even increase mankind's total sum of happiness." In a two-party system, for example, it helps the voter in making his choice and probably contributes to stability of the society. Thus, if the voter likes the President and the President happens to praise a Congressman of whom little is known, the Congressman may be raised in the voter's estimation. Unfortunately, in international affairs, psycho-logic may have peculiarly harmful and even dangerous consequences. Its dangers arise from the lack of opportunity to employ effectively the normal corrective processes of reality-testing before it is too late to avoid the consequences of oversimplification. It also, for example, supports the mirror image that many a United States citizen has of the Soviet Union and many a Soviet citizen has of the United States.[5]

[4] Charles E. Osgood, "Graduated Reciprocation in Tension Reduction: A Key to Initiative in Foreign Policy" (The University of Illinois, Urbana: The Institute of Communications Research, Dec., 1960), unpublished paper, p. 31.

[5] Thus, in a speech entitled "Misconceptions in Soviet and American Images," delivered before the American Psychological Association in Aug., 1961, Dr. Ralph K. White of USIA described the effects of the tendencies of both the United States and the Soviet Union to oversimplify the image of the other. Basing his observations on an analysis of several thousand pieces of material emanating from the Soviet Union and the United States, he found considerable support for the idea of a mirror-image relationship between Soviet and American thinking. The validity of his analysis was accepted by many of the psychologists, whose intensive study of the nature of man's behavior and learning had prepared them to accept cultural differentials in the judgments of men. It is of interest that a member of

The need to place an action in a context in order to understand it is another way of viewing the need for consistency. In order for us to understand a Soviet action, we must place it in a setting shaped by past experience. They must do the same with respect to our actions. Since the other's act normally emerges from a unique background, this is a demanding task never perfectly performed.[6]

---

the United States Senate, in criticizing Dr. White's speech, accepted almost in its entirety the validity of his statement of the American image of the Soviet Union, while rejecting the reality in the Soviet image of the United States. The Senator's comments were balanced by the reaction of a leading Soviet theoretician who accepted the truth of the Soviet image of the United States but rejected almost *in toto* the reality of the American image of the Soviet Union. It is important to recognize that Dr. White was not arguing that the two systems were identical, only that they had very similar simplified images of each other.

[6] Deutsch (*op. cit.,* pp. 10–11) describes what he interprets to be a working-out of this rule in the field of disarmament: "Mutual distortions arise because of an inadequate understanding of the other's context. Take, for instance, the Soviet Union's reluctance to conclude any disarmament agreement which contains adequate provisions for international inspection and control. We view this as a device to prevent an agreement or to subvert any agreement on disarmament which might be worked out. However, as Joseph Nogee has pointed out in his monograph on 'The Diplomacy of Disarmament' [*International Conciliation* (New York: Carnegie Endowment for International Peace), January, 1960, No. 526, p. 275]: 'Under present circumstances, any international control group reflecting the realities of political power would inevitably include a majority of non-Communist nations. Decisions involving actual and potential interests vital to the USSR would have to be made continuously by a control board the majority of whose members would represent social and economic systems the USSR considers inherently hostile. Any conflicts would ultimately have to be resolved by representatives of governments, and it is assumed that on all major decisions the capitalist nations would vote as a bloc. . . . Thus, for the Soviet Union, representation on a control board along the lines proposed by the West would be inherently inequitable. . . .'

"I may assert that one can subjectively test the creditability of the Soviet position by imagining our own reactions if the Soviet bloc could consistently out-vote us at the UN or on an international disarmament control board. Under such conditions, in the present world situation, would we conclude an agreement which did not give us the security of a veto? I doubt it. Similarly, one can test the creditability of the American position by imagining that the Soviet Union had experienced a Pearl Harbor in a recent war and that it had no open access to

As the above discussion of the role of symbols or abstractions has indicated, there is no easy road to the control of conflict. Conflicts exist in every situation in life, creating the problem of control and pointing up the need for the introduction of sufficient restraint to enable society to function effectively. Optimism about success at the international level is certainly unwarranted at the present time, but the achievement of restraint sufficient to permit the preservation and growth of a world community is not precluded by anything we have found. While much remains to be understood about the control of conflict at this level, such control may be within reach, provided that an intent to do so can be nurtured, and provided that sufficient resources are devoted to the effort—resources, it must be added, which will continue to be required as long as man exists on earth. It is, of course, in this longer perspective that institutionalization of international restraint may be of particular importance.

Fundamental to our view of the control of conflict are three propositions:

1. *The control of conflict is a learned social process.*

2. *The process involves the exercise of restraint, which is often accompanied by a sense of frustration that may lead either to aggression or to more adaptive behavior.*

3. *In the control of conflict between two groups their purposeful interaction with each other is the most significant factor to be taken into account.*

Control of Conflict Is a Learned Social Process

Government leaders are men, and they must apply what they learn to policy-making. The challenge to human cerebration is the same in

information concerning the military preparations of the United States. Under such circumstances, in the present world situation, would it be less concerned about inspection and control than we are? I doubt it."

many contexts. How, then, does man learn? The evidence is not complete, but those explanations which treat man as a single system seem to provide the most reasonable basis for understanding. Essentially he learns by acting in a particular environment. Thus he learns a social process by acting in or with a group or organization. Finally, when two or more groups (or nations) exist together they learn restraint from interaction.

What is meant by viewing man as a single system? It means taking into account his past, present, and future, together with the environment in which he moves; his expectations and capacity for innovation; his limitations arising from past experience as well as his present condition. In each man the past and future struggle eternally for the present. In viewing the totality it is worth remembering that, while the present is immediate and the past remote, the latter is long and the former fleeting. Yet the future is the time from which most of men's motivations seem to flow.

Hadley Cantril puts it as follows:

> Each transaction of living involves numerous capacities and aspects of man's nature which operate together. Each occasion of life can occur only through an environment, is imbued with some purpose, requires action of some kind and the registration of the consequences of action. Every action is based on some awareness or perception which in turn is determined by the assumptions brought to the occasion. These assumptions are in turn determined by past experience. All these processes are interdependent.[7]

In learning a new social process both purpose and the relationship between assumptions and action are of peculiar interest. We now turn to a brief consideration of these elements of the total process. They will be followed by selected examples from the growing body of experimental studies on how man learns or, to use a more general term, adapts.

[7] Hadley Cantril, *The "Why" of Man's Experience* (New York: The Macmillan Company, 1950), p. 59.

Purpose is central in organizing and sustaining man's action. Purposeful action is that intended to achieve something of value to an individual, group, or nation. The importance of purpose in orienting and sustaining human activity arises from the inclination of the individual to attach a value attribute to all his activity. As Cantril put it, "An outstanding characteristic of man is his capacity to sense the value in the quality of his experience. . . . All human wants, urges, desires, and aspirations are permeated with some value attribute." [8] Thus the ability to influence the actions of others depends in large undertakings on the ability to devise and to communicate a sense of values that will be shared by others.

Man brings to each new situation a set of assumptions and mixture of purposes which affect his perception both of the events in the situation and of the alternatives open to him. Many would agree that these assumptions flow from the individual's past experience. Few would be willing to accept wholly the "probabilistic" nature of the assumptions they use in confronting each new situation. Indeed, to act effectively the individual momentarily looks upon both himself and his environment as constant—if not absolutely fixed.[9] Out of the need for constancy and the requirement for changing one's assumptions to fit changing conditions many of the dilemmas of human existence arise.

Action and perception are inseparably related. Thus, the most significant aspect of learning is understanding the relationships of oneself to one's environment. These relationships are best learned through action. Only in action does one find an operational understanding of the relationship of things with reference to a particular space and time framework.

It is generally agreed that the environment is undergoing constant

[8] *Ibid.*, pp. 22–23.

[9] F. P. Kilpatrick and Hadley Cantril, "The Constancies in Social Perception," in Franklin P. Kilpatrick (ed.), *Explorations in Transactional Psychology* (New York: New York University Press, 1961), pp. 354–367.

change. What is not so widely perceived or understood is that the actor or learner himself operates within this process of change, and his very perceiving and acting constitute a part of the change in relation to the environment. Perceiving, then, constitutes gaining an understanding of the probable significance of the changes within the environment. Based on his understanding of these probable significances, the individual develops a set or pattern of unconscious assumptions. They serve as probability calculations, as value systems, or as concepts for dealing with the objective world, which has been constructed through active participation in it.

In summary, the individual seeks to create and maintain a world which deviates as little as possible from the world he has experienced in the past, which is the only world he knows, and which offers him the best possible chance of acting effectively and continuing to experience the particular set of satisfactions he seeks. At the same time his vision of the future, if it is to be achieved, requires action which may differ from past behavior. Learning is, then, the process of modifying one's view of the world so that it permits more effective and satisfying action. This requires not only action within the world, but a modification of purposes and assumptions about it to permit more effective action in the future.

A continuing problem is that the fundamental nature of the connection of the individual and his environment always escapes him. One may agree intellectually that what one sees in a new situation depends on the assumptions one brings to it as the result of past action. But immediately there will arise a situation which is so value-laden that an exception will be made.[10] These attributes of man are common not only to the public at large but to their leaders as well.

[10] This holds true even in extremely simple situations. For example, size is generally judged to be a function of the distance of a known object from our eye. Two balloons that appear the same size are judged to be the same distance from us; if one is larger, it is generally nearer. Our past experience with similar objects

We have seen earlier that there is a widespread assumption of a prolonged and inevitable conflict between the United States and the Soviet Union. This is an assumption built up by past action which is not seen as maladaptive by either side. But to find an alternative relationship requires questioning of past assumptions and actions—not wholly devoid of risk—to test and explore other courses. In doing so it may be possible to modify certain assumptions on both sides.

What people see in a situation depends upon their past experience.[11] That you may judge a man by his actions is generally accepted. That a man learns to judge his own actions is sometimes overlooked. Through actions man builds suppositions for use in the future and tests those which have proved useful in the past. Action as used here includes not only bodily activity in the usual sense but the more abstract acts such as intellectual analysis and the formation of value judgments.[12]

---

leads us to believe that this is true. It is a constant fact on which we may rely. Thus, when one balloon is then inflated slightly and the other reduced in size, the common judgment of nearly all observers is that the larger balloon is moving closer and the smaller receding. The point is *not* that what we see is an illusion, but that what we see is the result of past action *and* present perception. Our common experience in the physical world is that, of two apparently similar objects, the larger is nearer.

[11] In an experiment where different scenes were presented simultaneously to each eye, one a scene of violence and the other a peaceful scene, reports of what was seen were different for different groups. Among police officers there was a pronounced tendency to report seeing the violent scene as contrasted with other groups which were more evenly divided. Other observers have found that the impassive face of a man in a picket line looks "threatening" to a representative of management, but "determined" to a representative of labor; their experience and their attitudes toward him differ, and thus their perceptions. Many observers have pointed out that one of the most constant sources of difference in recommendations for action arises between those who assume people are "things" and those who assume they are people. This general difference in the assumptive world was illustrated in a civil defense television program in which one speaker indicated that the loss of half the population was bearable, and his critic stressed that a family which lost half its members was hardly a family.

[12] Between nations, it has been suggested, action may be best understood in

The meaning of an action changes not only with the object of the action but with its purpose and with the environment in which it is taken. The taste of food may be determined by eating it. The dimensions of physical space may be determined by moving about within it; the nature of matter by manipulating it. The capabilities of a weapons system are discovered by measuring its performance and estimating its reliability but more surely by using it. When man acts on matter he is somehow always engaged in solving a puzzle. He searches for elements of constancy in the behavior of the physical world or shapes elements of that world into tools and weapons which can be used repeatedly with accuracy and dependability. Once shaped to his purposes he can count on the tools remaining the same except for normal wear and tear or "unusual conditions." Of course, in complex instruments these conditions may require a whole program of action in themselves.

When man seeks to act on or with his fellow men the consequences are more complex because, unlike inanimate matter, they change significantly as he acts. To the extent that others are aware of his action they may in some degree participate in it. If his actions seem intended to serve a competitive or conflicting purpose, their actions will be designed to offset his advantage. If they seem to serve a complementary or common purpose, others may act to help achieve it. In any event, man must act, and in order to do so he must assume a certain constancy in himself and others. In a social setting, whether cooperative or competitive, what does this involve?

First, it requires that we take action in terms of what "will be" at the point when we expect our act to take effect. As in catching a ball we act in terms of where the ball will be at a future moment, so, far more, do we act in terms of what the future holds in a social situation. If we

---

terms of the total flow of information beween them. See Stephen Withey, "A Theory of International Threat and Tensions" (University of Michigan, Institute for Social Research), unpublished paper.

view the future as filled inevitably with conflict, then our actions along the path toward it must be in terms of conflict.

Second, action also requires the assumption of a certain constancy about oneself. In a social situation this is often referred to as role-playing. Thus, an officer must be brave and authoritative, a negotiator conciliatory and clever, a scientist objective, and so on.

Action requires, then, both generalized assumptions or probability judgments about the other and oneself, and a relationship between the two projected forward in time. What makes social problems infinitely more complex than those involving simply the physical world is that this same process involving the selection of probabilities about self and other and their relationship is going on in the other person at the same time. In a sense it may be said that in any transaction between two people there are four entities involved—one's image of self and other, and the other's image of self and other—all of which are but probabilities representing a kind of running average of past experience projected into the future.[13]

Thus, in an environment in which conflict is widespread, the most difficult steps to take will be the first ones, since these will require a significant shift in the view of the future which is widely held. One approach is simply to seek to induce the assumption of restraint in the conduct of the conflict. But since the assumption of conflict is essentially a probability judgment built up in past experience, it will require many actions, some of substantial significance, not only to change the assumption but to begin to modify the purposes of the other side. Risks will be involved, but these can be controllable risks, hardly of the dimensions

[13] It should be noted that in dealings between two different cultures the problem of effective action is compounded not only by the differences in background of two individuals but by the subgroup and deviant individuals within a culture who may have contributed to the building of national assumptions of how a man from the other culture will act.

posed by the assumption that conflict by any and all means is the probable course of the future.

A change in assumption involves a learning process which cannot succeed overnight. The main points to keep in mind about this process are:

1. Man has goals and purposes in life which arise from his tendency to attach value attributes to all aspects of his experience. Empirical science seems as yet to have very little light to throw on this process but testifies to its existence.

2. Man learns by acting in a situation, in his environment. He brings to a situation certain assumptions. He tests and modifies these assumptions by acting. As he acts he receives the results of his actions and validates or modifies his assumptions.

3. In making his assumptions he treats both his environment and himself as constant, in the sense of a probability calculation based on past experience and future expectations.

4. The need to assume a certain constancy in oneself and another may lead to maladaptive behavior when either has changed or when either is located in the wrong context. It may also lead to error when assumptions flowing from the need for constancy are not subject to verification by action. Moreover, assumptions based on long experience are essentially probability calculations, and not easily or significantly modified either by random actions or by a limited number of contradictory events.

5. In a social transaction one's behavior changes or validates not only one's own assumptions about self and other but the other's assumptions about himself and his opponent. Thus any action involving another person has at least four discernible elements.

Frustration May Lead Either to Aggression or to Adaptive Behavior

The control of conflict involves the exercise of restraint, which may be accompanied by a sense of frustration that may lead either to aggression (or other unproductive behavior) or to more adaptive behavior.[14]

Restraint, if it is to induce restraint in one's adversary, must be for reasons, and provide opportunity for actions, that not only seem good to one's own side but also appeal to the other as well. The complexity of man and the state make this a difficult criterion to meet. Control of conflict cannot be successfully achieved simply by satisfying one particular need. In human affairs the meeting of the needs of one side always impinges on the needs of another. Thus the requirement is for the opening of acceptable avenues of action within an unavoidable framework of restraint.

One of the most universal methods of channeling conflict in all societies is the projection outward to some more remote and "outside" entity. In past periods this has served to remove conflicts from the lower, more intimate, perhaps more vital level of social organization to one which was or seemed less significant in the life of man. The progress of civilization is in one sense the history of the development of restraints and acceptable channels for action at a higher level for the conflicts created at a lower level.

If states had not become so powerful, and if conflict could be easily confined, the projection of conflict into the international sphere might be accepted as it was in times past. Unfortunately, nuclear powers have become just that, and conflict tends to spread to new situations and encompass an ever expanding sphere of an individual's or a group's

[14] Frustration in the case of a nation appears to arise either from external restraint or from its own internal dynamics; e.g., the tensions and frustrations within the Soviet Union by no means all arise outside its borders.

life, unless the frustrated needs are rechanneled and directed to compatible purposes.

The degree of frustration may vary with its intensity and duration and the extent to which the victim sees ways of relieving his conflict. Whatever its origins and however it is described, frustration produces a response, of which aggressive action is one category. The problem of the control of conflict is essentially one not of attempting to eliminate all frustration or all possibility of aggression but of providing a social framework and alternative courses of action permitting the frustration to be worked out within restraints that preserve the fabric of society. This is true whether we are dealing at the level of the family, the small group, the corporation, or the nation, or at the level of relationships between nations.[15]

The environment plays a significant role in shaping the way in which adaptation to the need to restrain or rechannel aggression occurs. Society is a most important element in this adaptation as it sets up a system of penalties and rewards which are issued to those who display certain kinds of behavior and become certain kinds of persons. Failure to fit into these prescriptions is punished by the deprivation of the things most desired.[16] Normal persons seem to cope adequately with frustra-

[15] Just as frustration cannot in practice be regularly satisfied by meeting the particular need that gave rise to it, so it cannot be overcome merely by providing an occasion for its release. Many social engineers have advocated culturally planned means for the discharge of frustrations or the discharge of aggression rising from frustration. Indeed, many of the arguments made for the common games which characterize all societies suggest that they provide a means of catharsis for the release of the daily accumulation of minor frustrations. Such evidence as is available raises questions about the adequacy of games for this purpose.

[16] Parents reward certain kinds of behavior and punish others, and in this way restrain the child and lead him to conform to certain norms of society. Even when a child is not likely to be caught, internalized standards which he has developed as a result of the training of his parents may cause sufficient anxiety so that he will have to turn to other ways of releasing his tension. The result of this process is not only that the child must behave but that he must examine his impulses to find those with which he can live without excessive anxiety.

tions and forbidden impulses and only fight against them when no other alternative remains. The extent to which individuals and societies can cope with their anxieties seems to vary greatly from one time to another and from one society to another. The two main ways of dealing with a hostile situation which involves conscious problem-solving and the working out of a new relationship with the person or group toward whom hostility is felt or from whom hostility is received, are: (1) to change the perception of the hostile situation, or (2) to change the situation itself.

Individuals and groups use a variety of mechanisms for eliminating their hostility in ways acceptable to their own group. These include repression, projection, displacement, and sublimation. Repression involves very simply making the unthinkable truly unthinkable. Projection is a sophisticated way of gaining relief from anxiety by simply attributing one's own thoughts and feelings to other persons; this may account for many aspects of the mirror image found in the United States view of the Soviet Union and the Soviet view of the United States. To the extent that projection provides the basis for such views there may be grounds for even more anxiety on both sides than is felt today.

Displacement involves finding a new object of hostility when the original object is so close or sacred that one cannot accept the idea of making it the object of hostility. There are many who feel that displacement accounts for numerous problems of conflict on the international level as well as on other levels of social life. One by-product of displacement is the development of stereotypes of one's "opponent" or "enemy," which may be viewed as group norms or standardized forms used in expressing hostility. All groups must cope with the problem of intra-group hostility and the threat this poses to internal order. To contribute to the solution of this problem, it seems to have long been more or less legitimate to develop and hold stereotypic views about one or more neighboring groups.

In essence, all nations' stereotypes of their opponents describe them in the following terms: They care more for themselves than they care for us. They are self-centered. They believe themselves to be the chosen people. They are clannish. They use different standards in dealing with us from those used in dealing among themselves. They are willing to cheat us and steal from us, and use force against us. They are aggressive and expansionist. They wish to prosper even at our expense. They are happy when they beat us. Deep inside, they hate us. They feel us to be a hostile people or at least a hostile system.

It is important to notice that stereotypes do not necessarily depend on significant differences between the two groups for their development. Among any two nations there will always be differences. However small these may be, they may be used to provide a basis for the development of antagonistic stereotypes. To put it another way, all stereotypes may have a grain of truth, but even a grain can provide a basis for their continuing vitality.

We thus return to the facts that aggression and hostility occur at all levels of society; that displacement or projection of this hostility to an external target has frequently been found useful in the past; and that the development of stereotypes is a regular consequence of these phenomena. Societies, then, tend to act in terms of the stereotypes which they hold of others. In addition, they may also act in terms of the stereotypes which others hold of them. Both these patterns help to reinforce the stereotypes and make them "true."

In times past, societies have developed intricate systems of positive and negative restraints for controlling hostility and aggression within the society. Laws and norms have been developed for judging when the manifestation of hostility is excessive and subject to social censure or restraint. Most significantly, new purposes and new forms of social action have been developed which enable people to work together in ways that foster the redirection of behavior laden with hostility and guilt into socially acceptable channels. Sublimation is the term given to the substitution for primitive or hostile action of behavior of a higher form that is harmonious to the individual and acceptable to society.

Today, great national conglomerations pursuing historic interests are charged with hostility for each other. A new structure for the international environment seems called for—one which will both reduce the power of nations to act without restraint and channel action in directions which do not jeopardize the continuity of the individuals and groups making up the nation-states.

The Target of Control Is the Relationship between Two Groups

The analysis thus far leaves unanswered the question where to begin in the control of conflict between two nation-states. Are there any leads from science? Slender as they are, they suggest that the functional relationship between two groups is the most significant factor to be taken into account in seeking to control conflict, induce restraint, or ensure stability. At present, functional interdependence between the United States and the Soviet Union is distorted and does not play an adequate role in encouraging restraint. The task ahead, therefore, is to increase the scope of interdependence which contributes to restraint and a sense of solidarity. Neither third persons nor nations, neither internal power elites nor the demands of the internal economy, are as important as the interaction of the two parties involved in conflict or restraint. This does not imply that other factors on occasion may not be of great significance, but that their importance must be judged in terms of their effect on the functional relationship between the two—in this case, the United States and the Soviet Union.

The critical components of this relationship in the case of two great states are complex and not well understood. Here we will be concerned with three general categories: (1) purpose, (2) action and the perceived result or payoff, and (3) the structure of the environment in which purpose is sought in action.

These elements have been examined by game theorists and by experimental psychologists like Morton Deutsch in simplified two-person situations. In laboratory experiments over the past several years, Deutsch has been exploring the role of intention or purpose in bargaining situations.[17]

In one of his more important experiments he worked with three different motivations. These were: (1) *cooperative,* in which the participant was led to feel that the welfare of the other person was of concern to him and that the other person felt the same way; (2) *individualistic,* in which the participant was led to believe that his only interest was in doing well for himself without regard for the other person and that the other person felt the same way; and (3) *competitive,* in which the participant was led to feel that he wanted to do as well as he could for himself and that he also wanted to defeat the other person and that the other person felt the same way.

In the experimental situation he found that a cooperative purpose led primarily to a cooperative choice resulting in mutual gain, whereas a competitive orientation led the individuals to make noncooperative choices even though the result was mutual loss. With the individualistic orientation, the action of the individuals—to cooperate or not—was very much a function of other variables of the experiment. In both the competitive and individualistic orientations there was a persistent tendency for each participant to expect more cooperation than he was willing to offer. The point of interest here is that, even when cooperation would be mutually beneficial, agreement in the absence of shared purposes is made difficult, and interaction may become antagonistic.

Competitive purpose may indeed lead to conflict. But competition

[17] See, for example, Morton Deutsch, "The Effects of Motivation Orientation upon Trust and Suspicion," *Human Relations,* Vol. XIII, No. 2 (1960), pp. 126–128.

may exist without generating unalterable hostility, as hundreds of athletic contests between schools testify each Saturday. These are instances of "friendly" competition which are structured so as to restrain the conflict. Nearly all such examples of competition without unlimited conflict have other characteristics, the most important being that a win for one side does not preclude a win by the other side at some other time and in some other circumstance.

Conversely, successful cooperative arrangements must be continuously adapted to changing circumstances if the interaction is to remain cooperative. In the political arena, in which multiple motives are at work and which permits opportunities for shifts in group alignment, generalized cooperation is frequently altered to conform to specific situations involving multiple goals and several groups, as the party organizations in many states illustrate.

Experiments suggesting the importance of purpose and common action in the functional relationships between two groups as the key determinant of conflict, restraint, or cooperation have been conducted during the past decade at the University of Oklahoma.[18] A group of normal boys was taken to live at an isolated camp. At first all the boys were permitted to play and work with each other. They were then divided into two groups so that friendships which had developed were split. There followed a period in which each of the two groups lived, worked, and played separately. By the end of this first phase, two group structures with a leader and a hierarchy had developed. Group norms had also arisen which controlled the behavior of the members of the group.

The two groups were then brought together in situations which were competitive and led to mutual frustration as a consequence of the interrelations between the two groups. The result was a strengthening in each group of solidarity, of democratic action, and of friendships. On

[18] Muzafer Sherif, *et al., Intergroup Conflict and Cooperation: The Robbers Cave Experiment* (Norman, Okla.: University of Oklahoma Press, 1961).

the other hand, out-group hostility, name-calling, and fights between the two groups developed.

Next, the two groups were brought together to enjoy mutually pleasant experiences. These experiences, it was found, did not in themselves produce a marked decrease in the existing state of conflict between the two groups. It was not until the two groups were brought together under conditions which required common action for the achievement of overriding purposes that intergroup conflict was gradually reduced.

The experiments cited stress that the result of functional interaction can, therefore, be either to agitate or to mitigate conflict. Obviously, one cannot apply the results of small-group research directly to the international system. Yet, is there any good reason why the same principles do not hold? Should we not seek, as interaction between the United States and the Soviet Union occurs, so to design it as to contribute to the mitigation rather than the aggravation of conflict? The added complexity of the interaction must, of course, be taken into account. For example, a large portion of the American-Soviet conflict is indirect, carried on through others or through various communications systems. These forms of interaction require further investigation in their own right. Thus, while even an experiment with a simplified social system such as that above may suggest insights into the operation of the international system, more complex simulation involving a larger number of groups and more complicated systems is needed.

Nevertheless, the work in the social sciences to date does at least two things. First, it provides valuable leads which may be tested and verified at the international level as well as by further research on a lower level. Second, it sets a standard of operational diagnosis and use which other explanations must meet if they are to warrant serious consideration.

The line of reasoning we have examined holds open the possibility of modest but continuing successes resulting from a constant effort to develop common goals and to open the opportunity for continuing interaction in seeking to attain them. In the course of this interaction norms of acceptable behavior will develop which lawyers, jurists, and philosophers can enlarge upon, codify, and erect into laws and moral codes for further limiting those actions which are found to be excessively conflict-creating. Moreover, the task is such that government officials and policy-makers are equipped to make their contribution. They share with many others the essential skills needed to devise situations structured to encourage interaction in the development of complementary and common purposes.

As we have seen earlier, the socialization of man at any level involves the imposition of restraints on some of his goals. These restraints may imply some individual and group frustration. In the face of such frustration, the group may resort to aggressive action. Or, if the situation so demands, the group will find ways of modifying aggressive impulses in constructive and acceptable directions. This is not to imply that more forceful means for repulsing and confining aggression may be quickly laid aside. Acting with restraint so that it becomes an internalized norm, not only within oneself but within the other fellow as well, is a complicated learning process which can occur only over time and by interaction with the other man or the other group. At every level there are failures of restraint from time to time and a continuing need to have force available. This will hold at the international level, especially since up to now it is the last frontier within the world community into which hostility, generated from individual and group interaction, may still be projected with relative freedom from guilt.[19]

In sum, we find nothing in social science which suggests that the control of conflict through the introduction of interdependence at the international level is precluded. The task is complex and the effort must

[19] It is suggested not that families and nations, or small groups and the international community, behave in identical fashion, but that they can all be viewed as behaving as systems made up of men. Thus what is known about the behavior of individuals and groups may be applicable to the behavior of nations, not because their behavior is the same but because of this common factor. As dynamic social systems, they seek to control themselves in an environment and are in turn influenced by it. See Stephen Withey, *op. cit., passim.*

be sustained and general, but there is no evidence precluding reasonable success. Man applies his learning power to many difficult situations in life and learns to modify them, cope with them, or to adapt to them. There is no *a priori* reason to exclude the problem of peace. What is needed is the opportunity to learn through acting in the environment. Since there are two sides on which the outcome depends, opportunity for common action seems essential. Moreover, while action within a formal organization such as the United Nations can at times be useful, at other times far less formal organizations may be more suitable to the particular stage and area of learning. Success would seem more likely since all those who possess nuclear weapons begin by sharing a common purpose to avoid their use. The nature of the opportunity may be of critical importance. The urgency stems from the fact that the purpose of avoiding nuclear war, standing alone, is subject to many kinds of erosion—technological, psychological, and social.

From our search thus far, one general hypothesis emerges. It is that *effective control of conflict seems to require the opportunity for some form of common action or interaction in the pursuit of common purposes of overriding value in the particular setting or situation.* The importance of common action flows from the fact that men check and change their assumptions mainly by action. Acting together, while a necessary condition, is not sufficient: there must be something in the nature of a shared purpose. While it is clear that the case in which one side seeks total victory does not meet this test, the myriad situations short of this need to be studied extensively to determine those kinds of common purpose that can be developed on the international scene. Clearly, both sides share the desire to survive. The problem is one of devising methods of common action to ensure mutual survival, along with action to ensure that the multitude of other purposes which continue to be pursued does not overwhelm or undermine the paramount purpose. The implication is that these purposes must undergo certain changes which will require common action.

INDEX